Walking the Rift

Walking the Rift

Idealism and Imperialism in East Africa,
Alfred Robert Tucker (1890–1911)

BY
JOAN PLUBELL MATTIA

☙PICKWICK *Publications* • Eugene, Oregon

WALKING THE RIFT
Idealism and Imperialism in East Africa, Alfred Robert Tucker (1890–1911)

Copyright © 2017 Joan Plubell Mattia. All rights reserved. Except for brief quotations in critical publications or reviews, no part of this book may be reproduced in any manner without prior written permission from the publisher. Write: Permissions, Wipf and Stock Publishers, 199 W. 8th Ave., Suite 3, Eugene, OR 97401.

Pickwick Publications
An Imprint of Wipf and Stock Publishers
199 W. 8th Ave., Suite 3
Eugene, OR 97401

www.wipfandstock.com

PAPERBACK ISBN: 978-1-5326-0074-6
HARDCOVER ISBN: 978-1-5326-0076-0
EBOOK ISBN: 978-1-5326-0075-3

Cataloguing-in-Publication data:

Names: Mattia, Joan Plubell.

Title: Walking the rift : idealism and imperialism in East Africa, Alfred Robert Tucker (1890–1911) / by Joan Plubell Mattia.

Description: Eugene, OR : Pickwick Publications, 2017 | Includes bibliographical references.

Identifiers: ISBN 978-1-5326-0074-6 (paperback) | ISBN 978 1-5326-0076-0 (hardcover) | ISBN 978-1-5326-0075-3 (ebook)

Subjects: LCSH: Tucker, Alfred, 1849–1914. | Church of England—Missions—Africa, East. | Missions—Africa, East. | Imperialism.

Classification: BV2121.N7 M28 2017 (paperback) | BV2121.N7 M28 (ebook)

Manufactured in the U.S.A.   05/22/17

Tucker sketches have been reproduced by permission of the parish of Durham, St Nicholas and Durham County Record Office and by the Church Mission Society.

To all scholars and future students of African
and British Colonial studies.

Contents

Illustrations | ix
Acknowledgments | xi
Abbreviations | xiii
Introduction | xv

Chapter One
The Great Rift: Empire and Ideals | 1

Chapter Two
The Marriage Question | 15

Chapter Three
Art as The Handmaiden of Empire | 36

Chapter Four
Karibu Complexity: The Unwelcome Slavery Dilemma | 62

Chapter Five
Mission and Church: Struggle Within | 83

Chapter Six
The Mission and The Fort | 114

Chapter Seven
"Dusky Brethren": Consultation with The Africans | 140

Chapter Eight
Conclusion | 174

Appendix 1: Colonial Personalities: In Order of Appearance | 193
Appendix 2: Abolition Time Line—East Africa | 198

Bibliography | 201

Illustrations

Figure 1—Bar Chart Showing Number of Pictures by Subject Matter | 42

Figure 2—A Headwind: Victoria Nyanza (Feb. 9, 1891) | 44

Figure 3—Dan Kiongozi (Feb. 27, 1891) | 45

Figure 4—Mt. Meru from Mochi Mission Station (Feb. 13, 1892) | 47

Figure 5—The National "Shauri" Tree, Taveta (Feb. 10, 1892) | 48

Figure 6—Rope Bridge at Taveta (Feb. 10, 1892) | 48

Figure 7—"Threshing Beans:" A Village of the Bakonja Ruwenzori (Aug. 1898) | 49

Figure 8—Kwa Sakwa's Village, Kavirondo (Dec. 7, 1892) | 50

Figure 9—The Camp Taveta (Jan. 29, 1892) | 50

Figure 10—The Rev. T. R. Buckley and the Katikiro of Toro (July 7, 1898) | 51

Figure 11—View from My Room—Baganda (March 10, 1893) | 53

Figure 12—Taveta Mission (March 1895) | 53

Figure 13—Mission Station, Toro (Aug. 1898) | 54

Figure 14—A Storm: Bethlehem (Mission Station), Toro (Aug. 1898) | 55

Figure 15—Nzoi (October 20, 1892) | 56

Figure 16—Example of Camp Scenes—In the Camp at Unyanguira (Sept. 9, 1890) | 57

Figure 17—Example of African Buildings—The Kings' House (Jan. 1880) | 58

Figure 18—Example of Mission Station—Rabai (Jan. 26, 1892) | 58

ILLUSTRATIONS

Figure 19—Example of Landscape Camp Scenes—In Ugogo (Aug. 29, 1890) | 59

Figure 20—Example of Landscape—Saadani (July 18, 1890) | 59

Figure 21—Example of African Towns—Zanzibar | 60

Figure 22—Example of IBEA Station—Fort Smith, Kikuyu (Nov. 12, 1892) | 60

Figure 23—Example of People—Taveta (Feb. 8, 1892) | 61

Acknowledgments

LINGERING OVER A FINE dinner in Florida, my friend and owner of the local book store asked: "If you could do anything in the world without thought of money or time what would it be?" My answer (go to Africa and teach) was the beginning of this project. Within a year my answer had become reality and in due course, while lingering over another fine dinner, this one in Dar es Salaam while the candidates for "Miss Tanzania" glided through the dining room, another friend, Headmaster of the Mvumi Girls School, asked another question in regard to post graduate work: "What's stopping you?" These two questions, and the two people who asked them, have played a significant role in the initiation of this work, and I thank them both.

As the lightning flashes from east to west so is the mind of Werner Ustorf, Professor Emeritus from the University of Birmingham. I thank him for his insightful, sometimes brilliant and occasionally startling comments which helped give me direction in this research without dampening my own initiative and ideas. When confusion arose from multiple options, Professor Hugh McLeod, also from Birmingham, could be counted on as a calming presence, making time in a busy schedule to read paragraphs or pages, answer questions about English social systems while sitting in his office high in the rafters of the Arts Building.

I thank the cadre of international students who attended the post graduate research seminars during my time at Birmingham who were always willing to interact with ideas, discuss, or offer suggestions. I am especially grateful to the students from the Congo who had personal knowledge of Byaruhanga's research, which was published in the U.S. and so not so well known in Britain.

While researching day after day in the Special Collections at the Birmingham Orchard Learning Resources Centre, the staff became familiar faces. I came to appreciate their readiness to assist me to solve a puzzle or retrieve a record. In fact, such was the case in all the various British libraries that I visited in regards to this project. Although their records were less abundant, the staff at the various African institutions were gracious and as helpful as they were able to be; most especially Mr. Patrick Rimba Tsuma, the records keeper at Mombasa Memorial Cathedral who allowed me to examine the fragile records like a father handing me his only child.

Tudor Griffiths was very generous to share, not only experience of research trips, copies of records and his dissertation; but also he and his wife opened their lovely home in Wales for a week-end of hospitality and conversation of Tucker. I would also like to thank Sue Davy and Frankie Stahlhut for their kind and enthusiastic offer to proof-read which took a big weight off my mind and helped my pocket-book as well.

But most of all I wish to thank my generous and unselfish husband, Lou, who has provided the lion's share of my support and encouragement. Without him my life would be dull and this work would have remained only a dream.

Abbreviations

ACKA Anglican Church of Kenya Archives
BGCA Billy Graham Center Archives
CMS   Church Missionary Society
CMSA Church Missionary Society Archives
DCL   Durham Cathedral Library
IBEA Imperial British East Africa Company
KNA   Kenya National Archives
LPA   Lambeth Palace Archives
MUA   Makerere University Archives
NLS   National Library of Scotland
PRO   Public Records Office
RH   Rhodes House Archives
UCUA Uganda Christian University Archives
UNA   Uganda National Archives

Introduction

HEADING NORTH OUT OF Nairobi in our vintage 1984 Toyota Land Cruiser, it was not long before the road sloped upward out of the city and into the lush African countryside spotted with small settlements, roadside shops and countless people walking in the red dirt along the side of the road, with their plastic bags full of colorful fresh produce from local markets. The road curved up and up until we crested a large hill and found ourselves on top of a great plateau which opened up on a vast horizon. We pulled off at a roadside overlook next to a little tea shop and stepped out of the car. What we saw was stunning beyond words. Here, perched high on a mountain overlook there lay before us a view of the world as we had never imagined. It was as if the ground had disappeared below our feet and hundreds of miles north and south there lay a great plain as far as the eye could see. Then directly west, beyond the vastness of the African plain, rose another escarpment, thousands of feet high, shrouded in mist and clouds. This was The Great Rift Valley that stretches all the way from Lebanon in the Middle East down through the Eastern edge of Africa and south to Mozambique some 4000 miles. The view is staggering and immense. Astronauts orbiting the earth in space have often commented that the Great Rift is the most visible and impressive geological formation on the planet.

The Great Rift is the product of millions of years of enormous crust movement as two gigantic plates, the African (Nubian) Plate and the Somali Plate have pulled apart leaving the land in between to settle deeper and deeper forming a broad vast plain surrounded by giant ridges on each side. Besides this incredible geologic structure, it is also believed that humans began their long migration process from the fertile richness of forests and lakes which produced an explosion of plant and animal life. The forces which created all this magnificence continue to this day with formation of new lakes, hot water vents, volcanoes and upheavals.

Introduction

It was in this land that the earliest peoples developed tribal societies and spread outward; establishing civilizations, thriving cultures, rituals, religions, and the means to survive in the diverse environments from desert to rainforest. The East Coast of Africa was first explored by Europeans in the Age of Discovery in the Fifteenth Century but they would not reach the interior until the Nineteenth Century. In 1840 David Livingston would travel the interior from north to south and east to west and would be followed by countless other explorers and adventurers as well as by traders. In the mid 1800's missionaries would be expanding all along the African coastline as the continent became a focus of a growing evangelical fervor. In particular, Zanzibar and Mombasa became centers in East Africa for missionary activity. British imperial interests were also beginning to make their presence known by the later 1800's with the arrival of representatives of the Imperial British East African Company. Others would soon follow to guard and protect British commercial interests: these would be soldiers, administrators, engineers, along with settlers who all combined would complete the vanguard of Imperial expansion.

It is in this mix of assorted people that encountered each other in East Africa that this story will unfold. Missionaries, traders, colonial administrators, Arabs, and the various peoples of African society will meet each other and the world will change for all of them. That this initial encounter was not easy is an understatement. This book will uncover a snapshot of the tensions that grew between the various actors, and their own internal struggles as well. Like the immense, pulling and scraping ever present on the Great Rift, we will explore the tensions of that early colonial period. You will meet slave girls, pompous royal administrators, ambitious trading companies, Sultans, and an assortment of unknown missionaries full of zeal and diverse motives. All of this will be seen through the perspective of Alfred Robert Tucker, the third bishop of Eastern Equatorial Africa from 1890–1897 (and Bishop of Uganda until 1911) whose territory included all of Kenya, Tanzania, and Uganda. At the heart of this story are the original letters which paint a picture quite different from commonly accepted portrayals of missionaries as agents of the State and imperialists in a different form. Based on deep research into the original archives a different, more subtle view emerges. Rather than a cursory and one dimensional rendering of these Colonial and Victorian missionaries, a more complex interplay between all the parties is involved. It is an invitation to notice the fault lines

INTRODUCTION

between African, Missionary and Colonial Administrator as they struggle to influence the human endeavor in the Great East African Rift.

This book is a fresh approach to examine the interaction of cultures in a colonial setting; an approach which gives voice to the archives, acknowledges the involvement of western agents and the resourcefulness of non-western participants.

CHAPTER ONE

The Great Rift
Empire and Ideals

MISSIONARIES ARE MYSTERIOUS CREATURES. They have been a constant presence for the last two millennia in every part of the globe, from the steaming jungles of Central America to the open bushlands of the African savannahs to the frozen north slopes of Alaska and to the infinite islands of the South Pacific. Some have been bullies. Some have endured great hardships; sickness, poverty, and death in solitary outposts. Some have been heralded as heroes, brave and compassionate souls sacrificing all, and have returned to their homelands to banner headlines or have been elevated to sainthood. Yet what do we really know of these men and women? So little is actually known about most of them that some call them invisible, the ghosts of empire past.[1] They also seem to possess the ability to be the "shape-shifters" of empire history; sometimes noble, sometimes not, or both simultaneously. Whether the missionaries were from the Global North or the Global South, the picture is equally dark.

In a popular undergraduate textbook for African Studies at universities in the United States the motivations and attitudes for a complex panoply of missionaries spanning several decades are generalized into a few pages containing un-detailed remarks such as the following:

> Few Christian missionaries were directly active agents of European imperialism. But they were an essential ingredient of the

1. Christensen and Hutchinson, *Missionary Ideologies in the Imperialist Era*, 5.

increasingly assertive European presence which was a forerunner of imperial control. In a number of cases Christian missionaries played a significant role in promoting and shaping the advent of European colonialism.[2]

If "few" were agents of imperialism and only "a number" promoted colonialism, then what attitude would categorize the remaining majority? Admittedly, it is impossible to categorize individuals in great detail in a survey intended to present the macro-picture; still at least some recognition of differences and groups could be attempted. With the exception of Ajayi Crowther and David Livingstone, who are specifically named, there is no attempt made to draw attention to pivotal figures, complexity, differences in opinion or approaches to indigenous cultures. *The Oxford Illustrated History of Christianity* does acknowledge the diversity, as does noted historian Adrian Hastings, but very few specific examples are employed.[3] In spite of thousands of small popular missionary publications, hagiographies, pious stories, and martyrologies, invisibility still haunts the missionary figures of the nineteenth century.[4]

The missions themselves contributed to this invisibility by the production of mission fund raising propaganda. By glossing over some facts and presenting others over optimistically, the eighteenth and nineteenth century missionaries created an extremely durable mythology; the image of the heroic, self-sacrificing missionary bringing light to darkest Africa. This image was later uncritically adopted in the 1960's by post-colonial scholarship, but with the values reversed, the missionaries became the uninformed bad actors and the indigenous people the innocent victims.[5] Such incomplete rendering leads to a dubious view of missionaries, enduring stereotypes and caricatures which are widely held and taught.

2. Shillington, *History of Africa*, 292.

3. McManners, *Oxford Illustrated History of Christianity* and Hastings, *The Church in Africa, 1450–1950*.

4. The Yale Divinity School Library has more than 100,000 mission publications, 2800 linear feet of archival and manuscript material, 300 linear feet of pamphlets and "extensive holdings" on microfilm according to their June 2003 web site. There are currently 1,583 publications on Christian mission published per month and if the areas of missiology, mission history, missionaries, and mission organization are combined there have been 193,063 titles published in total from statistics found in the *International Bulletin of Missionary Research*. And these statistics do not even include the Vatican holdings on mission which, according to the *World Christian Encyclopedia, 2002*, are the largest in the world.

5. Peterson and Allman, "New Directions," 1.

Despite the stereotyping, this mythology has lately begun to show signs of wear when scrutinized by some historians including Andrew Walls and Lamin Sanneh. Both give an alternative interpretation by placing emphasis on the transmission and translation of the message itself, and less on the agents who handed it on—including their cultural packaging. Other scholars also question the past understanding of missionaries calling for a re-examination of the missionary enterprise in Africa. One fresh examination was initiated at the University of Minnesota which places more emphasis on mutuality, calling the colonial encounter "the long and mutually informing debate out of which missionaries were as much changed as were their African adherents."[6]

The study of missionary narratives is a research area with great potential, but the reluctance of many in the academic community to engage the mission literature may continue to sustain invisibility. Calls for engagement appear and some studies are accomplished but the knowledge of the existence of mission documents, outside of a small circle of missiologists with the willingness to engage them, is only just beginning to come into frame.

Jean and John Comaroff, noted African Studies specialists, have added their own observations,

> We persist in treating the evangelists not as individuals possessed of socially conditioned biographies that make a difference but as a taken for granted, faceless presence on the colonial stage.[7]

Lack of knowledge sometimes leads to popular presentations of missionary work, such as those contained in *The Cottonwood Bible* or *The Color Purple*, that are rather lacking in documentation. There is a negative attitude toward missionaries in general which hinders a comprehensive portrayal. This is not a new attitude. Gerald Portal, the first Special Commissioner to Uganda arriving in Zanzibar in 1889 observed about the missionaries: "They are energetic, it is true, —theirs is the energy of fanaticism."[8]

The hurdle that contributes overwhelmingly to the invisibility goes far beyond negativity or bias. The most difficult obstruction to a complete portrayal of Victorian empire personnel is the master narrative used by scholars as a backdrop to studies in this area. The master narrative is simply the big story which makes smaller stories intelligible.[9] The prominent

---

6. Ibid., 4.
7. Comaroff, *Of Revelation*, 54.
8. Portal to Lady Portal, May 29, 1889, Rhodes House Archives, Mss. Africa, S 112/73.
9. Cox, *Imperial Fault Lines*, 1–19.

master narrative is western expansion and indigenous surrender; and the constantly repeated refrain within this master narrative, one that has become stale to the point of meaninglessness, is European initiative and indigenous response.

Jeffrey Cox, Professor of History at the University of Iowa, breaks the western expansion master narrative into four sub-categories. The first category, the celebratory master narrative, portrays the missionaries (both African and European) in a very positive light. Into this category are mission history scholars of the 1940's and 1950's such as Kenneth Scott Latourette or C. P. Groves. Certainly many of the articles sent home for publication by the Victorian missionaries themselves would fall into this group. For example, news of Mr. J. C. Price, one of the pioneer missionaries to Mpwapwa, Tanzania:

> The world has heard little of J.C. Price, but a truer hero never lived. At the time of Bushiri's troubles he refused to listen to the suggestion of the Consular authorities, that he should leave his post and seek the safety that was offered to him in Zanzibar. He preferred to share the fate of his people ... only eight or nine weeks later he was struck down with black water fever, and in a few short hours passed to his rest and his reward.[10]

Other celebratory writers include Eugene Stock, Jocelyn Murphy, and Stephen Neil.

The second category is called the nationalist approach. Ironically, nationalist history writers continued the celebratory theme, except those being celebrated were the indigenous heroes responding to imperial aggression. The nationalists approach is a derivative of the celebratory style which was being rejected, but with the roles of missionary and indigenous hearer reversed.[11] Despite its attempt at balancing the scales, there is a weakness to this approach:

> Christianity, in this account, was either about "cultural imperialism" (the nationalist account) or about "modernization" (the liberal/functionalist account). Neither account took African religious or political initiatives seriously: Africans seemed to be sealed within a comprehensive but brittle cultural system which allowed them little creativity in the face of powerful European cultural brokers.[12]

10. Tucker, *Eighteen Years*, 151.
11. Chatterjee, *Nationalist Thought,* but Peterson and Allman also articulate this shift.
12. Peterson and Allman, "New Directions," 2.

In this view Africans either accepted the European worldview, rejected it altogether in favor of a traditional African worldview or adopted a dual practice.[13] The deficiency in this view is that the fluid, adaptive and durable cultural system of Africa is not acknowledged, neither is the extremely important place held by the missionaries in the African communities which hosted them. Vestiges of their importance still linger in the names of places or institutions; such as Binns Primary School (Mombasa), McKay House (Dodoma, Tanzania), Willis Road (Kampala), or Bishop Tucker Theological College (Mukono).

Overlapping somewhat with the nationalist's point of view is a third category called the Saidian point of view, named after Edward Said, an Arab Protestant scholar, for many years at Columbia University in New York. The Comaroffs as well would be included in this category. In this narrative, studies seek to unmask the missionaries as complicit with the imperial agenda. It is assumed that missionaries were an arm of the imperial efforts of Britain and were simply imperialists in a different form.[14] It is very easy to arrive at this viewpoint by perusing through the archives; the quotes that back-up imperial attitudes voiced by the missionaries are many. At the same time there are many who do not fall into this category, and neither group is explained within the context of Victorian culture. Missionaries who were imperialists were not alone; the attitude was prevalent among leading clergy, politicians, and scientists.[15] At the same time the unmasking narrative ignores the diversity and the subtly of Victorian missionary opinion.

The fourth category of master narrative is the providentialist point of view. Missionaries are presented in a more sympathetic manner and is often a position held by historians in the field of mission studies. This approach insists that a higher power is present and involved in moving history forward to create a multiracial community (the Kingdom of God). Given this approach it is not surprising that their scholarship remains almost invisible in the fields of imperial history, nationalist history, and western

---

13. Fast, "In At One Ear," 147–74. Duel practice was caused by the inability of the missionaries to address key issues in African culture.

14. Beidelman, *Colonial Evangelism*, 5–6. "Christian missions represent the most naïve and ethnocentric . . . facet of colonial life . . . Missionaries aimed at overall changes in the beliefs and actions of native peoples, a colonization of the heart and mind as well as body . . . demonstrating a more radical and morally intense commitment to rule than political administrators or businessmen."

15. Bonk, "All Things," 291.

post-colonial studies despite "high standards of fairness, documentation, scholarly distance . . . and a sustained attempt to promote history from a non-western point of view."[16] The critique of the providentialist school is that it fails to face completely the accusations of Said. The most subtle defense asserts that the missionary motives for involvement in the imperial enterprise were different from colonial administrators; the least effective defense asserts that the majority of missionaries were never in favor of colonialism.[17] A distinction in motives between colonial administrators and missionaries may be correct, but the integration of ideas and personnel between these two groups makes such distinctions hard to maintain.

Within the category of providentialist is Lamin Sanneh, professor of Missions and World Christianity at Yale Divinity School, whose work has become well known in Mission Studies. Sanneh argues that Christianity is very transferable into other cultures, more than any other of the major world religions. This is due to the mutable and much translated character of its sacred text. As the ideas of the Bible were translated into African societies, a distinct form of Christianity was created. Missionaries were involved in the introduction but they were only a small part of a much larger expansion of Christianity that was powered by indigenous and non-western agents. The old and worn out model of missionary initiative and non-western response is checked on the shores of Africa when the missionaries encounter African languages. At this point the missionaries were only part of a much larger process of religious change that in many cases was beyond their control, or even their knowledge.[18]

Sanneh chooses to emphasize the African agents. At times the Europeans are portrayed as outside carriers of westernized ideas which were then integrated by the Africans, other times they are co-workers ("stimulators" and revitalizers") and partners with the African translators.[19] Since Christianity does not become authentic until it is made African by the Africans, the missionaries' part is secondary and there is a tendency to discount the first generation of converts until the second generation makes the change legitimate.[20] Sanneh's insights regarding the reciprocity between

---

16. Cox, *Imperial Fault Lines*, 11. Andrew Walls, Brian Stanley, and Lamin Sanneh would be included in this category.

17. Stanley, *Bible and Flag*, and Frykenberg, *India*, 183.

18. See Musisi, "Morality," 51–74.

19. Sanneh, *Translating*, 160, 167, and 173.

20. Cox, *Imperial Fault Lines*, 13.

Europeans and Africans does not extend outside the language translation project. Since language translation involved a small number, the remainder continue in shadow, still caught in the old paradigm of European initiative and African response.

There is a need to expand the concept of reciprocity put forward by Sanneh. Recent scholarship proposes a master narrative which recognizes the imperial involvement of the missionaries but at the same time gives voice to the multiple stories contained in the archives detailing how missionaries, administrators and indigenous peoples were engaged in a joint endeavor[21] There was mutual respect, admiration, and frustration, but there was also an essential contradiction between the realities of western imperialism and the aspiration to create a multiracial community. The missionaries were straddling two opposing forces: the concept of universal values, such as brotherhood and equality, and the imperial context of those values in which one group was subjugated to another.[22] Concepts such as hybridity and transculturation attempt to move beyond polarities but there remains within these explanations a dominant group and a subordinate group, without the partnership and mutuality which the archive reveals.[23] Many Europeans were as much changed by the encounter as the Africans.

> The history of the British Empire should not be seen as resulting in either the spread of western "civilization" and enlightenment on the one hand, or the imposition of alien customs to the wholesale detriment of indigenous cultures on the other. It involves both these processes. Imperialists and colonized were each capable of openness and insularity, of giving and taking.[24]

Without dodging the racist, imperialist, and ethnocentric tendencies of the pioneer missionaries, at the same time the record is full of expressions of respect, friendship, partnership and the recognition of wisdom. For example, in the discussions regarding the constitution for the Ugandan

---

21. Ibid., 15.

22. Marshall, *Cambridge*, 206. "The fundamental egalitarianism of much in the Christian message was no more lost in colonial African or India than it had been a century before when West Indian slave owners did everything they could to restrict missionary activity."

23. Ustorf, "Missionarsreligion," 63–84. Presents the ambiguity of Spieth, the Director of the Bremen Mission in Togo//Ghana, by distinguishing between secular religion and mission religion opening new attempts to revisit the encounter between Europeans and Africans.

24. Marshall, *Cambridge*, 186.

church Mr. Rowling, one of the British missionaries, "wanted to know what special arrangements would be made for safeguarding the positions and rights of the 'superior race.'"[25] On the other hand, J.C. Price, the pioneer missionary in Ugogo, Tanzania writes: "The Chief of Mpwapwa said, 'If God wants to take you [that is, if you are to be killed] let Him come and find you here!' Not a very heathenish suggestion, after all, thought I."[26] Or as Pilkington, the primary language specialist for East Africa noted: "I wish I could send you in full Henry's [Duta's] sermons; logical, forcible, interesting, scriptural explanations of the work of Christ for sinners. He is a very able man; he would be above the average in Europe. I doubt that he has his equal in Africa . . . his sermons are compositions, not rambling discourse and are delivered admirably."[27] Along with appreciation there is also the curious juxtaposition of egalitarian belief and subtle dominance — sometimes in the same letter. For example, Miss Harvey, the head of the girl's school in Freretown writes of the daughter of the African pastor at Freretown: "my dear friend, who is perfectly competent to take charge of the school *in my absence*, [emphasis mine] one to whom I can turn for advice and help."[28] As one of the leading scholars in this field observes: "Many of the missionaries managed to be racist and anti-racist simultaneously."[29]

This book takes seriously the views regarding master narratives as summarized above, but also the observation that there are many untold micro-narratives which, if revealed, gradually propel us toward an alternative master narrative. The extensive Church Missionary Society Archive, housed at the University of Birmingham in Britain, contains many of these smaller stories.

The focus of this research is on a representative missionary in one of the most important missionary societies in East Africa as he struggled with the conflict between universal Christian values and the imperial context of his efforts. It is not intended to be a broad presentation of the history of missionary work in East Africa, or even of one person's life. It will explore one micro-narrative topically and attempt to test an alternative master narrative: that the missionaries operated in the tension between two opposing ideas, one with a premium on equality and one which subjugated one group

---

25. Tucker to Baylis, January 7, 1907 (sic) 1908, CMSA, G3 A7 O / 70.
26. J. C. Price in CMS Annual Report, 1890, CMSA, 52.
27. Pilkington to CMS, Annual Report, 1892.
28. Harvey to CMS, Annual Report, 1891, 47-48.
29. Cox, *Imperial Fault Lines*, 15.

of people to another. It will look into the invisible ranks of the nineteenth century missionaries and focus on major tensions encountered by the Church Missionary Society project in East Africa using the prism of one of the leading figures of that effort—Alfred Robert Tucker (1849—1914).

Travelling extensively and holding simultaneously the position of Director of the Mission and Bishop of an indigenous church allowed a view point which encompassed a broader breadth of information than a single missionary stationed in one location. As the third Bishop of Eastern Equatorial Africa for seven years (1890—1897) until the diocese was divided, he was the primary overseer for a large area covering present day Uganda, Tanzania and Kenya, interacting with numerous missionaries and colonial administrators. After the division he then remained the Bishop of Uganda until 1911. In effect he was the initiator of long-term episcopal ministry in the diocese as the first bishop, James Hannington, was killed in route to the interior and the second, Henry P. Parker, died of fever on the southern shores of Lake Victorian Nyanza—both after only one year in residence. Because Tucker maintained a "vigorous episcopate of twenty-one years" his long tenure affords a broad swath of insight into the imperial period stretching from 1890 to 1914.[30]

The Bishop's imperial leanings are evidenced by his very successful fund-raising for the continuing administration of the Imperial British East Africa Company in Uganda. At the same time, later in his career, he was critical of the colonial administration especially on the policy of forced labor on the cotton plantations in Uganda, seeing it as a hindrance to the development of an indigenous economy. Tucker ordained forty-seven African clergy and wrote a constitution for the Ugandan Church integrating the European missionaries equally with their African counterparts, yet at the same time was very instrumental in lobbying for the Uganda protectorate, making him a figure of paradox.

Tucker was one of only a small number of missionaries (only 17%) with a university degree—his from Oxford.[31] Before his ordination at the age of thirty-three, he was a professional artist, the son of two itinerant landscape artists who settled in the Lake District in Britain. Immersed in the evangelical wing of the church while at Oxford (1880 -1882), he had a passion for the conversion of souls and for the underprivileged. He pos-

---

30. Davis and Weaver, *Dictionary*.

31. This percentage has been calculated from the listing of missionaries in the East African field in the year of Tucker's arrival from the *Register of Missionaries and Native Clergy: 1804-1904*, Part 1, CMSA.

sessed an iron will and a cast-iron constitution all wrapped up in the velvet glove of an artistic temperament. After serving two parishes in England as a curate he volunteered with the Church Missionary Society and was immediately nominated to become Bishop in East Africa. He departed for Africa on the day of his consecration, leaving his wife and small son behind in England for the duration of his twenty-one-year episcopate. He itinerated over his vast diocese, travelling over 22,000 miles and so became known as "The Uganda Express" or "The Squire." His letters and autobiography from East Africa contain countless observations from the period of initial encounters. Beginning with a small following of Christians clustered on the coast, in Uganda, and along the caravan trail in Tanzania; his tenure concluded with over 100,000 Christian adherents in Uganda alone. Using the roughly 4,500 Tucker letters, it is possible to follow the progression of British influence from a scattering of advisory personnel to a full blown Protectorate in Uganda and Kenya. The letters and reports are also intriguing in their record of the technology of communication and travel; from runners along the caravan trails to railroads, telegraphs, bicycles, steamers and the first cars.

Tucker was an artist turned missionary and did not completely give up being an artist but used his gift continuously for documentation, fundraising, and personal income throughout his career. Artists are creators of images and have the capacity to create worlds; whether on canvas, on stage, or through words. Tucker certainly had the power to create with both paintings and words. His letters and writings had great force to bring about realities and he was appreciated as a gifted platform speaker.[32] Tucker the artist was, through his decisions, creating a world in East Africa that was passing away in England, with landed gentry, squires, village vicars, and aristocratic Bishops. Simultaneously, he was also creating a different type of reality, one tailored for an African setting, but engineered none the less. Possibly his present faded image is the just reward for one who imposed an image on others. Or perhaps the broad brush strokes of others have painted over an original.

Teddy Roosevelt, who visited in 1909, called Tucker and his missionaries, "one of the most interesting chapters in all recent missionary

---

32. There are innumerable invitations and references in the CMS Archives to his many preaching/speaking engagements, comments throughout on the numbers he attracted, great applause and appreciation recorded in the Lambeth speeches, and descriptions in most of the writings of co-workers.

history."[33] But in the present day Tucker is not well known. Although he wrote an autobiography in 1911, shadows and ambiguities remain due to his highly stylized writing style. At the time of publication many of the figures included were still active in public ministry possibly leading to a reluctance of revelation. Even if deceased, some had living relatives still producing powerful images, such as Sir Gerald Portal. Yet comparisons of Tucker's autobiography with private letters reveal his unguarded opinions.[34]

Tucker's candid image of himself was somewhat that of a patriarch, going forth to an unknown land, part of God's overriding plan of salvation for the chosen African people touched by his administration. He was older than most of his European colleagues, and he did not shrink from a strong paternal approach, as seen in a letter to Semler, the African pastor at Freretown, "as you appeal to me as a father I desire to advise you as one."[35] A similar approach is found toward the European clergy. To Leakey he writes, "And now let me give you a little fatherly advice. When next you write to your Bishop, do not charge him with 'unjust and unfair treatment.' It is unbecoming, unseemly and unworthy of you. I may be obliged to receive such letters but there is no obligation resting upon me to reply to them."[36] He was quite defensive of his episcopal authority and leadership role. He wrote to W. A. Crabtree, a CMS missionary and priest, "As a matter of fact, I have a *RIGHT to require that no adult be baptized without a reference to me* . . . [emphasis his]. In this diocese I am the interpreter of church laws in this matter."[37] But this strong imperial flavor also had an opposite side. Dr. John Howard Cook writes, "His touch was tender as that of a woman on such occasions [of trouble], as all could testify—whether European or native—who experienced it."[38] While acknowledging that the members of the diocese may have been developmentally behind Europe, he reasoned that this was due only to a lack of knowledge of the transforming work of the Christian Gospel. In his view, civilization followed Christian belief and not the other way around; and the development manifested in Africa as a result may not look exactly like what the Gospel had produced in Europe.

---

33. CMS Annual Report, 1911, 63.
34. Billy Graham Center Archives, Box 135/1 and Box 135/2.
35. Tucker to Semler, September 25, 1898, CMSA, G3/A5/O/191.
36. Tucker to Leakey, November 25, 1904, CMSA, G3/A7/O/249.
37. Tucker to Crabtree, May 29, 1899, CMSA, Acc. 27/ F1/2.
38. Cook, "Tucker," 167.

If the missionaries were caught between opposing ideals, Tucker's fellow workers were definitely caught between opposing impressions of the Bishop. In his journal Nickisson, who travelled to the interior with Tucker, expresses appreciation, "The Bishop gave us a grand Bible reading from Ephesians 2:18—24."[39] Another positive impression comes from A. B. Fisher, an ordained CMS missionary: "He was of commanding appearance, with long mustache, heavy eye brows, abundant dark hair, determination, common sense, patience, and a great sense of humour."[40] But Mr. Nickisson also gives a slightly exasperated account.

> We saw a large herd of zebras at some distance but the Bishop would not allow me to go after them lest I should overtire myself! ... I told the escari (sic) to save me the skin and to give the meat to the men, a portion to our boys. When I got back I found the Bishop had already given the carcass in my name to Mr. Heath with the same injunctions practically. ... The Bishop went ahead as usual.[41]

And finally: "The Bishop had several shots at various animals but without success. Fisher said to me that he had never known anyone so fond of shooting such a bad shot."[42] Although the well-known tension between the evangelical, reformed theology of the CMS and the seemingly unreformed concept of Anglican bishops may have been a factor in such interactions, there is an element of respect as well as resentment, tinged with ridicule.

There were differences also between Uganda and Mombasa. Mombasa missionaries were unresponsive to Tucker's leadership and due to these differences he did not find the work on the coast to be satisfactory. When the diocese was divided, the CMS was surprised that he chose Uganda as his see; possibly due to the fact that he had already invested four years in Mombasa and environs. But Uganda had a very high profile in England and to be the Bishop of this area certainly boosted his personal profile. Tucker did not seem to find this aspect a burden.

The African response to Tucker contains similar contrasts. Immense crowds greeted him warmly in trips around the diocese. Baskerville, CMS missionary and priest, recollects: "The natives adored him. He was, they said, their best friend, their father. No one was too small or too humble

---

39. Nickisson, "From Mombasa to Mengo," CMSA, Acc. 109, p. 27.
40. Fisher, "A. B. Fisher of Uganda," CMSA, Acc. 84, Book I, 1890–1892, p. 134.
41. Nickisson, "From Mombasa to Mengo," 51 and 54.
42. Ibid., 64.

to be received by him and he would take infinite pains to understand the words of each one then to help them as far as he was able."[43] At the same time Baskerville recalls: "He had an imperial mind and his grasp of native politics was marked."[44] The contrast between open humility and political astuteness may account for the variety of reactions Tucker received. At various times the African teachers in the coastal part of the mission did not hesitate to threaten resignation when they felt their pay was too low; as did the teachers in the Uganda mission.[45]

The colonial government had its own views of Tucker. These were not always complimentary, as Tucker was often combative towards colonial objectives; such as forced labor, land distribution, taxes, marriage laws, and immigration policies. This pattern of criticizing the colonial administration was to change with the tenure of the next Bishop of Uganda, John Willis.

The missionary movement of the nineteenth century, following hard on the imperialist urge of the same period and embedded in the social mind-sets of the time, was not a steam-roller flattening all individuality before it.[46] At the same time, the individual missionaries were not solitary figures painted on a stark canvas without reference to structures, events and ideas around them. An interaction between these two options exists. The missionaries were ground between two opposing ideas: firstly, a mutual egalitarian vision and secondly, an imperial context. We will examine the micro-narrative of one of the leading figures in the Victorian East African encounter to re-examine and reframe an inadequate understanding of the dynamics involved in the initial phases of interaction.

The nineteenth century missionaries are invisible because they are either "sainted" or "villain-ized," leaving obscured and unexplored a more realistic, if ambiguous picture. But pictures which contain shades of grey actually present a clearer understanding. To examine the various color tones, the ambiguities and contradictions, in the micro-narrative of Tucker would enable us to see him in a more realistic way and therefore to re-think the all-pervasive nineteenth century missionary stereotype.

---

43. Baskerville recollections, Billy Graham Center Archives, 135, Box 1 folder 5.
44. Ibid.
45. Tucker to Fox, May 29, 1905, CMSA, G3/A7/O/137.
46. Comaroff, *Of Revelation*, 9. ". . .attention has not been paid in southern Africa to the consciousness and intentionality of those identified as 'agents of domination.' Quite the reverse: their actions continue to be seen largely as a reflex of political and economic processes.

There is no doubt that a legacy has been left by the colonial period in East Africa. Human, political, philosophical, and institutional factors involved have caused this legacy to be a mixed blessing for all concerned. Even after one hundred and fifty years, a mixed response to overseas personnel is still noticeable and sometimes baffling. Co-workers from the North and South may find it difficult to interact without unravelling or at least understanding the dynamics that continue to produce repercussions.

But a new approach is needed as Sanneh writes: "The old categories of antagonism and alienation by which we have assessed the missionary impact are insufficient."[47] By addressing and exploring the concept of the invisibility of pioneer personalities using fresh concepts and categories, *Walking the Rift* should help to expand the ongoing discourse in the area of imperial history and intercultural encounters and make a helpful contribution.

---

47. Sanneh, *Translating*, 173.

CHAPTER TWO

The Marriage Question

ARRIVING IN MOMBASA HARBOR on May 14, 1890, sick and weak from unsanitary food preparation on board the "Ethiopian," Alfred Tucker, third bishop of the immense territory comprising the Diocese of Eastern Equatorial Africa (1890–1899), was greeted with the words, "Cotter dead" by Mr. Bailey, the missionary assigned to meet him. Tucker's immediate response to this news of the loss of one of the Mombasa missionaries was to acknowledge "the intense anguish of my mind when with such tidings ringing in my ears and feeling physically weak and ill I set foot for the first time on the shores of Africa."[1] It would be far from the last death among the Church Missionary Society personnel in his twenty-one year episcopacy in East Africa but, with the history of death in the East African endeavor and the uncertainty of his own well-being so close at hand, the gravity of the greeting elicited the anxiety laden response recorded above.[2]

Yet death would not be the only major issue to face Tucker as he began his ministry on the African mainland. In the environs just on the northern edge of Mombasa, a substantial missionary village had grown up over the previous twenty years. Freretown, a community of freed slaves established by the Church Missionary Society (CMS) in 1873 was now under the direction of an English CMS missionary, Harry Kerr Binns (Islington, 1875).

---

1. Tucker to Wigram, May 16, 1890, CMSA, G3/A5/O/133.

2. The first two bishops of the Diocese of Eastern Equatorial Africa died shortly after arrival; James Hannington after only one year and four months and Dr. HP Parker after a tenure of exactly the same length.

Bishop Tucker's letters give no indication to foreshadow the clash he would experience between his imperial tendencies to bring order and law where he found nothing familiar and the need to exercise spiritual nurture as part of the emerging African church.

With time being short and arrangements pressing for his initial inward trek to visit the twelve mission stations in the interior of the diocese spanning present day Kenya, Tanzania, and Uganda, Tucker lost no time looking around the Mombasa base camp named Freretown, and was cautiously impressed with what he saw.

> Here is the girl's school, here's the boys and there the church. Hark, what sound is this? It is the evening hymn being sung with a depth of feeling, a precision and beauty of resonance, that would do honour to any school in England . . . God grant that I may not be disappointed as I penetrate (as I mean to do) beneath the surface.[3]

But disappointed he eventually became. After only five months in residence in Mombasa interspersed with trips to Uganda, England, Jilore and Chagga, Tucker produced a report for CMS headquarters as to his impression of conditions in Freretown.

Much of the report dealt with his assessment of the moral state, lack of vision, and career success of the inhabitants of Freretown which, Tucker felt, emanated from the dormitory system with its lack of night supervision, communal sleeping platforms, and shabby buildings. Tucker's phrase for the state of affairs at Freretown was "living beneath their privileges."[4] However, in addition, two pages of the report dealt with what became known and referred to in subsequent letters as "the marriage question."

Freretown serves as a microcosm illustrating the clashing of the missionary vision of a shared faith with spiritual equality, and the imperial environment into which this faith was implanted. It was a unique collection of missionary challenges which ranged over a whole series of civil matters; including law, courts, marriage, divorce, personal disputes, education, etc. The matter of marriage is one that surfaces to the greatest extent in the archived letters and so offers greatest detail.

It is within the institutions adopted or established in the mission field that the rubbing of the two tectonic plates of universal values and the imperial context of those values is the most easily recognizable.[5] Since marriage

---

3. Tucker to Wigram, May 16, 1890, CMSA, G3/A5/O/133.
4. Tucker to Wigram, June 3, 1892, CMSA, G3A5/O/238.
5. Cox, *Imperial Fault Lines*, 8 and 18.

is one of the most basic institutions of any society it is not surprising that the tension would be articulated in the "marriage question." It would be a matter of great importance to the missionaries in the field, the administrators at CMS headquarters, and the initial personnel of the Imperial British East Africa Company, as they all sought to interact with the collected community of Freretown and with the newly established formal Muslim government of Mombasa.

THE MISSION VILLAGE

The mission villages in Africa began around 1816 with the visit of Edward Bickersteth of the CMS to the makeshift settlements developing around Freetown in Sierra Leone.[6] Bickersteth, a former solicitor turned priest, was quick to see the potential of the gathered masses for the ranks of the church, partnering with the government who provided schools and churches while the CMS paid for and recruited teachers. The concept of a missionary controlled African community spread to other locations.[7] Freretown, on the East African coast, was one among many; others include Kuruman, Bethelsdorp, Theopolis, and Genadendal. Although the inhabitants of mission villages were not forced to live there, in the areas where the villages thrived the alternatives were often tenuous; sometimes involving tribal warfare, or social dislocation due to slavery or the blending of multiple cultures. When African power was strong, such as in Uganda, mission villages were small or non-existent. But where African authority was weak, the villages grew and where African leaders were non-existent the leaders of the mission villages became civil authorities.[8] Such was the case at Bagamoyo, the White Father's enterprise on the Tanzanian coast, Robert Moffat's village of Kuruman in southern Africa, and at Freretown, only nominally under the auspices of the Sultan of Zanzibar.

Although the freed slave villages could be seen as a type of reservation, a place to put dislocated slaves, the missionaries saw them as a place to evangelize, educate, and demonstrate an alternative civilization. This civilization was sometimes equated with English culture but at other times it drew, perhaps unconsciously, upon a concept which can be recognized in the monastic traditions of England's history: the colony of heaven. The

---

6. Yates, *Venn*, 113.
7. Hastings, *Church*, 209. Also Strayer, *Mission Communities*.
8. Hastings, *Church*, 211.

colony concept was strong in the Moravian/Pietistic communities having a hallmark of withdrawal from the world, as in the Basel Missions on the Gold Coast. But for missionaries with a state church background such as the Anglicans, even those with a pietistic spirituality, withdrawal from the world was not a well-worn path. They were much more comfortable stepping into the role of civil authority.[9]

The missionaries saw the operation of mission villages as "a practical way to begin the Christianization of Africa, as some sort of natural extension to their own household and domestic life-style,"[10] a phrase which again calls to mind the alternative domestic life-style of the pioneer monastic communities from Ireland to England, such as Lindisfarne. The mission villages obtained a similar function, becoming a bridge between cultures. But, it was a bridge that would become a cul-de-sac.

In the absence of shared traditions and customs the villages were sometimes hard to manage, with violent elements not interested in conversion but still needing care. Stepping into the civil authority position, the missionaries discovered, could hinder effectiveness, eat up time and engender resentment. Tucker complained about the amount of time the Secretary at Freretown spent in secular work.[11] When strong civil power developed, African or European, the civil authority held by the missionaries evaporated, as will be seen in the case of Freretown. Eventually the CMS moved away from the mission village concept but while it was operational the relative stability of the mission village, due to unstable social conditions, caused many inhabitants to accept unfamiliar rules (such as monogamy) in exchange for the protection and patronage of the mission estates, whose leaders were viewed by the surrounding people as village headmen. For example, there is no record in the Tucker archive of overt resistance to monogamy as in the study of the role of Hermann Yoyo and West African mission Christianity.[12] Nevertheless passive resistance can be discerned from the review of the marriage registers of Freretown and their documentation of multiple unions. One thing common to all mission villages, despite the diversity, was that the European mind, rather than

---

9. Hastings, *Church*, 210.

10. Ibid.

11. Tucker to Baylis, August 31, 1893, G3/A5/O/242.

12. Ustorf, *Bremen Missionaries,* 375, and Binns to Lang, September 13, 1892, CMSA, 112/P/260.

African custom, controlled the details of life.[13] However, this was only partially the case, as shall be seen in the unfolding of "the marriage question" at Freretown.

Initial Procedures

Tucker's initial assessment of the arrangements for marriage in the Freretown settlement was a negative one springing primarily from the practice which he described as "office marriage."[14] In looking through the marriage registers for the village the Bishop discovered that the native pastor, Ishmael Semler, under the direction and with the full knowledge of the European missionary, Mr. Binns, was recording unions which did not meet with Tucker's definition of Christian marriage. Marriages between Christian men and Christian women were not the problem. These were performed in the church at Freretown and duly recorded in the register. The problem for Tucker was the recording in the same register non-church marriages of baptized Christians to non-baptized persons; and the recording, also in the same register, unions where both parties were non-baptized members of the community; and also, the recording of second marriages (without the pronouncement of a divorce) when a spouse had been deserted by his or her partner—in essence, the unintentional practice of Christian polygamy. However, the idea that such a form of Christian polygamy was taking place did not seem to be recognized by Tucker. In his correspondence, despite the debate taking place elsewhere such as in the Bremen Mission in the Gold Coast, the Moravians in Tanganyika or the Lambeth Conference of 1888, the word polygamy is never used and the pros and cons of the narrow concept are never enumerated or discussed.[15]

All the above mentioned unions were initiated using what Tucker referred to as an "irregular semi-religious service" held in the office of the Secretary—the title given to the chief executive officer of a designated geographical division of the CMS effort in East Africa.[16] The service consisted

---

13. Hastings, *Church*, 214.

14. Tucker to Wigram, June 3, 1892, CMSA, G3/A5/O/238.

15. Ustorf, *Bremen Missionaries*, 375–83. Moravian Traugott Bachmann established a policy of acceptance in Tanzania; Hastings, Ibid., 319. Despite Bishop John Colenso's support in his Letter to the Archbishop of Canterbury leading to the Lambeth debate, polygamy was officially rejected in the Anglican expression of Christianity.

16. Tucker to Wigram, June 3, 1892, CMSA, G3/A5/O/237.

of several prayers along with the writing of the names in the church register. Tucker strongly objected to this ceremony which prompted him to write a memorandum recording his opinion of the situation and circulating this opinion to the missionaries in Mombasa and to CMS headquarters in London.

The memo outlines four points of recommendation: 1) The registration of the "native marriages" of non-baptized Africans cannot be seen as a Christian action and was done solely because the civil government of the village was in the hands of the mission.[17] 2) The registration of unions between baptized and non-baptized individuals cannot be confused as a Christian ceremony by the Africans and therefore also should not be done by the mission personnel. 3) The remarriage of a baptized person after desertion by a partner cannot be allowed to occur. Tucker's main concern seemed to be only for the baptized as no mention is made of what might be done for the unions of non-baptized individuals after desertion by a partner. 4) The church can pronounce a formal separation to baptized persons who have been deserted by a partner but without the possibility of remarriage.

Binns, as the missionary in charge of Freretown and the Secretary of the Mombasa area, was quick to add an additional explanation to Tucker's report; this being sent to CMS headquarters three months later. He acknowledged the accuracy of the Bishop's numbers—twenty-six office marriages were indeed performed—and then proceeded to offer mitigating circumstances which, in his mind, made exception to the normal operating procedure practiced in England. In three of the entries both parties were baptized Christians but had been deserted by their original partners. "All three of the women had been deserted by their husbands, two of these husbands we had no means of ascertaining whether they were alive or dead . . . the third . . . was living in Mombasa with a Swahili wife."[18] Two of the men in this set of entries had also been deserted by their first wives who had subsequently disappeared; only one man had been single at the time of this registration. Binns also went on to inform the Committee that, whereas seven of the office marriages were between baptized and non-baptized persons,

---

17. At this point in time Freretown operated quite independently as the 1887 treaty between the Sultan of Zanzibar and IBEA did not make provision for a civil government outside that of the Sultan's which did not concern itself with the marriage of Christians. In addition the British Consul-General, Col. Euan Smith was operating only in an advisory capacity to the Sultan.

18. Binns to Lang, September 13, 1892, CMSA, 112/P/260.

The Marriage Question

the un-baptized were under instruction for baptism and subsequently not practicing traditional religions. Sixteen of the office marriages were solely registrations of traditional unions. Binns explained that women deserted by their husbands were in danger of starvation or entering into prostitution to support themselves; whereas single men had difficulty working and simultaneously accomplishing the rigorous chores of domestic duty such as gathering wood, water, and cooking; therefore, out of compassion Binns felt a different set of operating procedures had to be in operation. Change was not always European pressing upon African.

Upon receiving the Freretown Report from Tucker and the letter of explanation from Binns, the CMS Committee did two things: First, they wrote to Binns reinforcing the first two points of Tucker's memo.[19] Writing on behalf of the Church Missionary Society, Fredrick Wigram, the Honourable Secretary to the General Committee from 1880–1895, suggested that civil marriages (i.e., marriages between any other than two baptized church members) could now be registered by the newly established authority of the Imperial British East Africa Company (IBEA) and that until such time as this could become practice they should be registered by a lay person of the mission in a separate book other than the church marriage register. If the church in Freretown wished to discipline those members who had contracted a union with a non-baptized person, that was up to the Bishop and the local church authorities to decide.

Secondly, on the third point of Tucker's memo, the CMS sought to gather more information and advice from the Archbishop of Canterbury, Edward White Benson. What especially concerned the Committee was the idealistic hardline taken by Tucker prohibiting the remarriage of the innocent party after desertion or adultery. Wigram writes: "This is clearly drawing the restrictive wall tightly in a church just emerging from barbarism than is practically done in England."[20] But the CMS had limited power to interfere with the decisions of a seated bishop, even one they had created; hence the appeal to the Archbishop of Canterbury. Having been instrumental in the birth of a diocese and in the installation of a bishop in East Africa, they were now subject to his decisions in matters of church policy; a fact that caused much confusion.

There is no record of any direct response to Bishop Tucker from Archbishop Benson on this subject. However, the Archbishop's response to

19. Wigram to Benson, Nov. 18, 1892, LPA, Benson 112.254–57.
20. Ibid.

CMS was informative rather than directive. Archbishop Benson referenced a similar problem experienced by Bishop Blyth in Haifa, who decided to withhold Confirmation as a discipline to those who contracted mixed marriages or serial marriages.[21] He also made it clear that his diocese could not officially release members to remarry after desertion in the life-time of the other partner. However, in England, the Bishops in Convocation of 1885 decided that if the member chose to remarry after a civil divorce the ceremony could be performed in a church by a clergyperson whose conscience allowed such a step. The Archbishop saw no reason why a similar track could not be taken in the mission field and conveniently side-stepped the problem which CMS was experiencing in its pioneer missions; the lack of an official mechanism for the pronouncement of divorce, hence the inadvertent polygamy taking place in the Mombasa mission.[22]

Unable to let the matter rest, Wigram made one last effort to receive some direction or clarifying instruction from Archbishop Benson. Referring to the action of the Bishop of Sierra Leone, who in essence set up a divorce court, and to the similar difficulties experienced by the Bishop of Lahore; he pleads: "Your Grace does not indicate any way out of the difficulty, nor assert that a solution is impossible. Perhaps it is one of those matters in which pioneers in the mission field must be left to their own discretion. But without any definite guidance, one fears that through lack of knowledge some might err seriously in their solution of the difficulty."[23]

Tucker was then indeed left to his own discretion as there was no further response from the Archbishop. His discretion was to follow along in his previously chosen path expressed in his original memo. He writes to Frederick Baylis, the Corresponding Secretary of the CMS from 1892–1912: "It may be convenient for you to know that I look upon that correspondence [between Wigram and the Archbishop] and the circular of the Bishops in Convocation as endorsing my action entirely."[24] However, one small problem remained—the clause which made provision for a clergy person to perform the marriage of a previously married person, if his conscience did not object. Tucker may have initially assumed that all of the clergy under

---

21. Wigram to Benson, Dec. 9, 1892, LPA, Benson 112.263-64.

22. Benson to Wigram, Dec. 27, 1892, CMSA, G3/A5/L6/445.

23. Wigram to Benson, Dec. 29, 1892, CMSA, G3/A5/L6/444. and Wigram to Tucker, Dec. 30, 1892, CMSA, G3/A5/L6/440.

24. Tucker to Baylis, Aug. 31, 1893, CMSA, G3/A5/O/242.

his jurisdiction would have been unable to do so with a free conscience. But this does not seem to be the case.

A year later in a follow-up report of a sub-committee of the Mombasa Finance Committee about the state of Freretown, Tucker speaks about the production of the report itself and about the question of church discipline if a church member chose to contract a mixed marriage or re-marriage. About the report itself, Tucker wished the Committee to understand that he had "absolutely nothing whatever to do with its preparation . . . I should have retired from the chairmanship of the Finance Committee during its discussion."[25] And secondly, he lamented the fact that the administration of Freretown needed to be in the hands of someone who had higher expectations of the moral capabilities of the Africans and who upheld only one standard, the Word of God, in the exercise of church discipline. Based on this comment it is arguable that Tucker's memo about remarriage of divorced persons was not being totally adhered to and that possibly the practice of the blessing of mixed unions might well have continued in Freretown under the direction of Binns.

Tucker was consistent in his beliefs; he did not require anything of Africans that he did not believe was required of Europeans. Even if England itself decided to allow the remarriage of divorced persons, he did not agree and refused to alter his opinion. He did not believe in remarriage regardless of where one lived. With respect to Matthew chapter nineteen and verse nine, which some members of the CMS Committee believed seemed to sanction remarriage for the innocent party of adultery or desertion; despite repeatedly drawing his attention to it, Tucker had no comment.[26] Tenacity (some would say bull-headed) was one of his strongest traits and part of the reason for his longevity in Africa. Scripture or no scripture, his mind was made up. And that was the end of it.

IMPERIAL FRERETOWN / IDEALISTIC FRERETOWN

Bearing in mind that imperialism subjugates one group of people to another, the establishment and operation of the Freretown mission village as a separate and independent unit of social organization, completely set apart with its own civil government and not subject to the sultan of

---

25. Tucker to Baylis, Sept. 26,1893, CMSA, G3/A5/O/263.

26. "And I say to you: whoever divorces his wife, except for unchastity, and marries another, commits adultery" (Matt 19:9 RSV).

Zanzibar's authority, is a clear illustration of the blend of imperialistic impulses and high ideals of the pioneer missionaries. Sir Bartle Frere, after whom the village was named, was sent to Zanzibar January 12, 1873 by Lord Granville in the Foreign Office to negotiate with Seyyid Barghash, the Sultan of Zanzibar, an end to the slave trade in his dominions.[27] After several months of unsuccessful talks Frere informed the Sultan that a naval blockade would be put in place to forcibly deny the flow of goods to and from the markets in Zanzibar until such time as the Sultan gave in to his demand. Not surprisingly, very shortly after this announcement the Sultan signed a treaty with the British government on June 5, 1873 which closed the slave market in Zanzibar (but did not abolish the institution of slavery). It was in the context of this classic example of gunboat diplomacy and luminescent imperialism that Freretown was established; an illustration of the "fusion of missionary and political effort" that was part of the ethos of the Victorian empire.[28] Almost as a symbol of this fusion, it was well known that a government gun was mounted to the top of the mission buildings in Freretown.[29] Although Britain had a Consul-General in Zanzibar beginning in 1850, he was careful to cultivate the appearance of holding an advisory position. The charter for IBEA was granted in 1887 and a fledging administrator, MacKenzie, arrived and was replaced by a full-time one, de Winton, in 1890—simultaneous to the arrival of Tucker. Up until this time the civil authority of the freed-slave colony rested in the hands of the mission as no other authority existed with which the leaders of Freretown felt comfortable regardless of the presence of the Sultan of Zanzibar, whom Tucker called "a puppet leader," and who had become a formal governing presence fifty years prior.[30]

At the same time, Freretown was also an illustration of the ideals of universal Christian religious values even if wrapped in the trappings of empire—a situation which was endemic in the actions of the missionaries. They envisioned a community of equality and order governed by their own distillation of Biblical principles—a city set on a hill that would be a "show and tell" of what Christianity, Commerce, and Civilization could

27. Biographies of Sir Bartle Frere can be found at britishempire.co.uk/biography/frerebartle.htm, June 20 2016.

28. Moorhouse, *The Missionaries*, 88.

29. CMS Annual Report, 1897, 113.

30. Said bin Sultan conquered Mombasa in 1837 and moved the capital there in 1840. Tucker to Fox, July 31, 1894, BGCA, 135 /1 /1.

offer the Africans; Mission villages were part of the attempt on the part of the missionaries to create what some call a "pious fantasy in the African wilderness."[31] Modelled after the settlement of the White Fathers at Bagamoyo, Freretown was a 1,200 acre estate seeking to establish a cash crop, become self-supporting, and provide the Africans an economy that might become an alternative to the slave trade.[32] To right the wrong of slavery was perceived as a duty, a moral obligation, and part of the ethos of the time that propelled the mission forward.

> To arrest the destruction of mankind, to throw a blessing upon a continent now in ruins, to give civilization and to spread the mild truths of the Gospel over a region...was a higher and nobler road, and his [Buxton of the CMS] desire and prayer was that Her Majesty [i.e., England] might tread it, and that, crowned with every other blessing, she might 'shine, the leader of applauding nations, to scatter happiness and peace around her, to bid the prostrate captive rise and live, to see new cities tower at her command, and blasted nations flourish in her smile.'[33]

Or as Eugene Stock writes,

> The British nation is now, and has long been, most deeply criminal. We desire, therefore, while we pray and labour for the removal of this evil, [slavery] to make...Africa the best remuneration in our power for its' manifold wrongs.[34]

The Church Missionary Society and its missionaries at Freretown were reaching for egalitarian ideals in their goals of a parallel system to slavery, but also in other ways. Not only did they provide vocational training, along with both secular and religious education, but they also endeavored to add to their ranks a small cadre of African teachers who would, with time, lead the African Christian community. Ishmael Semler, the African priest at Freretown, was one of this number as was William Henry Jones the priest at Rabai (both ordained to the priesthood by Tucker), and James Deimler the headmaster of the boys school in Freretown; plus a handful of others mostly known only by their first names: Daniel the boys dormitory superintendent, Octavia the girls dormitory matron, Jeremiah the

---

31. Comaroff, "Through the Looking-glass," 6.
32. It was pointed out by Hardinge, the Gov. of Zanzibar, that this was an imperial idea. Why not accept slavery as a legitimate institution of the indigenous people.
33. Moorhouse, *The Missionaries*, 27.
34. Stock, *History of CMS*, 91.

native catechist at Taita, and Mr. Tofiki at Mamboia—just to mention those named in the reports of Tucker's first year of service. Some were listed only as "the native catechist at Kamlikeni or "native Bible woman."[35] The schools and dormitories were meant to be a resource for recognizing these future leaders to be sent on for higher training; and the recognition was not done only by the Europeans, as hundreds of references to consultations with Africans, dispersed throughout the archives give evidence.[36] Freretown was to be an example of an alternative society that both the European and African Christians believed would bring a needed change to the existing order.

Freretown was a mix of universal ideals and cultural imperialism. With an attempt to establish "freedom" and "education" in Freretown it was evolutionary that other civil matters should be brought to some modification as well. Marriage, perceived by the Victorians as being a critical feature of an ongoing and healthy society, was high on the list of institutions to be brought under regulation by authority. If no other strong authority existed to regulate, it was merely a matter of propriety to create one. Thus both imperial and church ideals could be satisfied.

Both cultures interacting in the initial encounters of the Victorian era, held to sexual standards as a means of discipline and control. Both groups believed sexual unions were powerful forces in society needing protection and regulation lest harm transpire. However, these standards were quite different for each group. In the west an emphasis was placed on chastity and monogamy. Regardless of a huge variation of sexual norms, East Africans were not without standards or morality; in fact, they were preoccupied with morality, with the belief that such a powerful force was sacred, having the power to renew society or to harm it.[37] African morality tended to revolve around respect; with rules or taboos involving positions, overt verbalization, nakedness, touching, in-laws and public displays of affection. The number of partners was generally not an issue as long as the rules were respected. Some missionaries, such as Binns, made an attempt to understand these differences. Even Tucker showed that he was aware, even accommodating of certain African customs and rules. For example, he explained to government officials that the disarming of Her Majesty's soldiers by the Kiama after they were caught stealing was in keeping with identification

---

35. CMS Annual Report, 1889–90. CMSA.

36 J. C. Price, CMS Annual Report, 1890, 52; Walker, CMS Annual Report, 1891, 61; Pilkington, CMS Annual Report, 1892.

37. Heald, *Manhood and Morality*, 492.

requirements in tribal law.[38] But his strong belief in a prescribed set of marriage standards set forth in scripture prevented any accommodation for baptized Christians, whether African or European. In this his imperial tendency to enforce his rules and require complete obedience seems to have been unenforceable, not only for the African but for the European as well, as several references to missionary improprieties attest.

IMPERIAL TUCKER/ EGALITARIAN TUCKER

Bishop Tucker had the ability, not unlike other missionaries in CMS service, to embody simultaneously idealistic goals such as spiritual brotherhood together with imperial attitudes of superiority. He maintained a dual responsibility during his twenty-one years in East Africa being both the Director of the East African mission for the CMS and also the Bishop of the indigenous church. Holding these two responsibilities at the same time caused a great deal of confusion. On the one hand Tucker was a part of a Western hierarchical organization with its center of decision-making in London. His nationality and educational training reinforced his loyalties to that organization. At the same time, he was the bishop of the African church and had a commitment to foster an independent indigenous organization; self-supporting, self-governing, and self-propagating. This dilemma could never be fully resolved and served to reinforce the tension between the two grinding forces found in Tuckers' thought and actions.

In Freretown, on the one hand, Bishop Tucker never questioned the fact that the civil government of the mission station was in the hands of western missionaries. His letters to CMS describe the practice as a necessary situation, explaining the arrangement repeatedly, and almost apologetically, to the headquarters in London. "Registration of native marriage . . . is allowed for the sake of law and order on the ground of the civil government of the settlement being in the hands of the mission."[39] and again just seven lines later "Ought that registration (permitted for the sake of law and order at Rabai and Freretown) . . . be permitted?" [of mixed couples][40]

He never suggested that the civil government and the maintenance of law and order should have been in the hands of the Sultan who granted the

---

38. *Kiama*, governing council of elders. Tucker to Baylis, August 31, 1893, CMSA, G3/A5/O/242.

39. Tucker to Wigram, CMSA, G3/A5/O/238.

40. Ibid.

land for Freretown to be built. He writes in some detail of the operation of that civil authority,

> Every Monday morning those who have been charged with offences against the laws of the settlement are brought before the secretary for trial. Assaults, thefts, and such like charges are now, I am thankful to say, referred to the Company's representative in Mombasa for settlement.[41]

Assaults, thefts and the like could have, from the beginning of Freretown, been referred to the law courts of the Sultan of Zanzibar, but they were not. Tucker accepts the status quo and is happy to refer such cases to the European civil authority, the IBEA administrator, recently assigned to Mombasa.

On the other hand, when Tucker's Episcopal duties took him to other parts of the diocese, Kampala for example, he operated under the administration of the African kings or tribal leaders. Frequent visits to and consultation with the Kabaka (the King), the Katikiro (the Prime Minister), the indigenous leaders of the church and "chiefs of various degrees" were the order of the day.[42] Despite the presence of missionaries in Mengo and on their estates on Namirembe Hill the civil government remained in the hands of the Ugandan king. Bishop Tucker confirms this as he writes,

> It is usual at these barazas [gathering of officials] for the king to hear cases involving a breach of the law. . . . Sentence had been given by the king to this effect, "that so many cattle and sheep were to be paid by the offender as a fine, together with two women." The Christian chief interposed, "But Christians do not give men or women; they give cattle and goats, not human beings." The result was that the king altered the sentence to the effect that no women were to be given, only cattle and goats.[43]

Tucker did not seek to interfere with this civil authority in Uganda beyond giving advice even when the subject involved slavery to which he was intensely opposed. It is possible to ascertain from these different approaches to African leaders and civil governing practice that Bishop Tucker had a contradictory position, operating at times above indigenous leaders and sometimes in concert with them. Although he would have explained

---

41. Ibid.
42. Tucker to Wigram, Dec. 30th, 1890, CMSA, G3/A5/O/124.
43. Tucker, "From Mengo," 684.

The Marriage Question

the difference as resulting from being totally focused on the establishment of the gospel regardless of who was in power, it cannot be ignored that African power was stronger in Uganda and weaker on the coast.

Bishop Tucker can be seen to display both imperialistic tendencies and a high idealism when the marriage question is examined closely. First, he endorsed or initiated practices regarding the marriage question which show an imperial orientation in the new setting in which the missionaries were operating. For example, the practice of keeping a marriage register at Freretown for the entire community. This was a carry-over from a state church environment in England in which clergy were in essence representatives of the civil authorities and every person in a defined geographical area (the parish) was a member of the state church. This practice was automatically, and without question, transposed into the new community although exactly which civil authority they felt they were representing is unclear. Tucker and the Mombasa missionaries were unable to think outside their cultural patterns on this particular issue. The registration of the Christian marriages at the church at Freretown was understandable, as these were the internal records of a voluntary organization. But the registration of African Non-Christian marriages, as if the missionaries were agents of a civil authority and in imitation of procedures in England, was an unnecessary imposition on the non-Christian residents of the mission village. Rather than acceptance of the indigenous customs and acknowledgement that these must run parallel to the Christian mission, the Mombasa missionaries, Tucker included, created and accepted a system which was familiar to them, but unnecessary, which subjugated the African style of contracting a marriage to the English style. According to Mr. Binns and Bishop Tucker, the registration was used as a teaching mechanism in order to hold up what they believed to be the superior nature of Christian marriage and to encourage the Africans to "seek His blessing on their union."[44] But the examples of the married African Christian leaders living among the community at Freretown might have accomplished their goal without imposing a formal system from the outside. Bishop Tucker writes about what he considers the positive influence of the African Christian leaders in Freretown,

> I may say in starting, and I say it with deep thankfulness, that the life of no agent of the Society at work in Freetown can from a moral point of view be described as 'unsatisfactory.' . . .I do not know one with a spot or suspicion on his or her moral character. . .none

---

44. Binns to Lang, Sept. 13, 1892, CMSA, 112/P/260.

of whose moral character I am suspicious. And so far I thank God with all my heart.[45]

But the imperial impulse was strong and the formal establishment of a procedure to register the marriages of all residents of Freretown, Christian or non-Christian, was accomplished.

It must be acknowledged that Freretown was an artificial community, not one which grew organically on English Point, as the area came to be called. It was created from many people groups rescued from slave ships and gathered together from various locations and therefore, it did not have a central organizing factor or tribal custom. On the contrary, it had many. When two residents chose to marry, which custom could they use; the custom of the husband's people, the custom of the wife's people, the custom of the coastal people, or the custom of the missionaries? And again, which tribal leader would preside at the ceremony; these leaders were now far away as Freretown residents had been forcibly taken to the coast each from their various inland villages. Therefore, it may have seemed quite practical to look to the missionaries to give some kind of formal sanction to their union. With the gift of land from the Sultan to establish a village the missionaries had in essence become tribal chiefs of a new mixed community. However, their desire to evangelize this group reinforced imperial tendencies causing them not to refer some matters to the Sultan of Zanzibar which rightfully might have fallen under his authority.

Another way in which Tucker displayed a type of imperialism was in his practice of informing headquarters back in London of his decisions regarding marriage registration. Tucker did not consult the CMS before writing his official memo on marriage. He wrote of his independent decision: "In view of this state of things I have felt myself obliged to issue the following memorandum on the marriage question. These pressing questions seem to require a statement of opinion from the Bishop."[46] However, once written, he did feel compelled to send them a copy and appeal to the London headquarters to take action. "In my opinion it [the dormitory system at Freretown affecting the moral climate and resulting in a breakdown of marriage] has been such a failure that a very solemn responsibility rests upon the Committee to take immediate steps for a through reformation."[47] The Parent Committee received the report which included the marriage

---

45. Tucker to Wigram, June 3, 1892, CMSA, G3/A5/O/124.
46. Ibid.
47. Ibid.

memo, used it to create ideas, combined it with information from other sources, and eventually took action and gave directives. This illustrates how Tucker, being the CMS director of the mission in Mombasa, was part of an organization with imperialistic structures and modes of operation. The decisions affecting the living conditions of the residents of Freretown were made in London at the center of empire after information was sent from the field. This power flow was also instrumental in reverse, from the center to the periphery. The report which Tucker wrote to describe and assess the conditions at Freretown was a fulfilment of a directive given to Tucker by the central headquarters.

> Two years and a half ago I received a letter from Mr. Binns in which he stated that the Dormitory system was such an utter failure that the girl's dormitory was. . .a feeder to the ranks of prostitution. . .he begged that the system might be abolished. I placed his letter before the [Mombasa] Finance Committee and the opinion of that body coincided with that of the Secretary [Binns]; and the [Parent] Committee was asked to send out a special Commissioner to investigate the facts. This request I placed before the Parent Committee personally. It was considered that I was the proper person to make the inquiry and accordingly was suggested to undertake it.[48]

Tracking the marriage memo and the initial report on the conditions of Freretown through the archives it is possible to see the inner workings of the CMS administration, based on an imperialistic model. It was a model into which Bishop Tucker was tightly interlaced and never able to entirely extricate himself.

The final illustration of the imperialistic attitudes present in Tucker's thought is found as he records his judgment on the "moral laxity" of Freretown. But in them we also find an intertwining of an opposite emotion. "The inclination to love and violence, service and domination, is part of the historical structure of the occidental missionary mindset."[49] Tucker's letters revolving around the marriage question and the spiritual state of Freretown are no exception to this observation. He muses: "Of course we must bear in mind the antecedents of these poor people. They come to us in all the wretchedness, moral, physical, and spiritual of the most degraded of mankind. There is all the force of hereditary habit to be overcome; all the

48. Tucker to Baylis, Aug. 31, 1893.
49. Ustorf, "What If," 151.

tendencies of ages of heathenism to combat. What wonder then that rules are flaunted?"[50] Observations such as these illustrate the intrinsic sense of cultural superiority that seems to go hand in hand with empire.

Yet in the very same letter the Bishop points out with a touch of recrimination the innate, superior intelligence he finds at Freretown: "I must not forget to acknowledge the fact that there are bright earnest Christian boys and girls to be found in the dormitories . . . for whom I thank God. They are there not as the fruit of our arrangements but rather in spite of them."[51] Also again recapping his points he says: "The native agents of the Society engaged in the work at Freretown are morally, so far as I can find out, without reproach . . . there are some, the Semler family for instance, for whom I thank God."[52] He is not alone in this assessment. It is echoed in the words of Ms. Harvey, who headed the girl's school in Freretown who writes "in high terms of the native women teachers."[53]

It might be said that the Evangelical emphasis on the doctrine of regeneration tended to emphasize the two opposing viewpoints of universal egalitarian ideals and imperial presence. After a tirade about the sub-standard morality of the residents of Freretown, Bishop Tucker concludes, "Still one must not forget that holiness of life is possible even to those who in times past have been most degraded. We must not limit the power of the Grace of God. We must keep before the eyes of the people the highest possible standard, the standard of the Word of God."[54] Despite a persistent cultural superiority toward the Africans, Tucker also consistently believed that Africans were capable of high standards of behavior, education, and theological thought; of spiritual equality with the missionary—possibly even spiritual superiority over some segments of the English church. This is evident in the marriage question by the fact that Bishop Tucker refused to budge from his initial position regarding the re-marriage of separated Christians. He continued to hold the African church to a higher standard then what was the practice in England.

---

50. Tucker to Wigram, June 3, 1892, CMSA, G3/A5/O/124.
51. Ibid.
52. Ibid.
53. CMS Annual Report, 1891, 47.
54. Ibid.

The Marriage Question

THE FINAL NEGOTIATION

Although the marriage question had reached a conclusion with the Ecclesiastical parties there was yet still one further negotiation to be undertaken and that was with the fledgling colonial administrators in Zanzibar. It had come to the attention of the Bishop that two African Christian couples had been granted a divorce by Mr. Jenner, the IBEA magistrate in Zanzibar operating under the authority of the Sultan and using the Sharia law. In response to detailed questioning by the bishop, Hardinge, the Consul-General of Zanzibar, drafted a thorough summary of his knowledge of Muslim law in regards to Christian marriage which he sent to Mr. Pugott, the acting administrator in Mombasa, to the Foreign Office, and to Bishop Tucker.[55]

Hardinge maintained that under "Mohammedan" law Christian marriage between Christians was considered valid. The *Wali* (or Muslim judge) had no power to dissolve it; this could be done only by an Ecclesiastical authority. Unfortunately, no such court existed in the dominions of Zanzibar and to form one, according to Hardinge expressed opinion, would not be considered expedient as canon law would jostle with the Sultan's authority. He proposed that divorces between African Christians could be litigated under English law before Mr. Pugott in Mombasa with appeals to the Sultan's IBEA magistrate in Zanzibar. It was clear to him that African Christians were subject to the Sultan and to *Sharia* law and since that law considered Christian marriage indissoluble (even if both husband and wife later became Muslim) he saw no conflict.

Hardinge speculated that Mr. Jenner's action of granting divorce may have occurred because the parties were not professing to be Christian or because one of the parties had become Muslim, in which case the marriage was considered void under the laws of Zanzibar. If it had been found during the hearing that the parties were Christian, the case would have been deferred; or if found subsequently the pronouncement would be without effect.

The letters to and from Hardinge and Tucker regarding the marriage issue are quite illuminating in regards to the dilemma in which the missionaries found themselves. Before the arrival of the first colonial administrators the tension between imperial goals and religious values was fought out within the conscience (possibly sub-conscious) of individual missionaries, or even among the missionaries themselves with their various opinions; as in the conflict between Tucker and Binns. It was more of an internal

---

55. Hardinge to Pugott, August 29, 1894, PRO, FO 881.

affair. But once the administration of the country began to progress in earnest, with English personnel in place who began to take action and formal rules began to be developed, obligations were required of the missionaries leaving them with less ability to practice creative solutions.[56] Hardinge's response to Tucker's complaints was to begin to enforce the *Sharia* law and to begin to develop a formal avenue for the hearing of African Christian divorce cases. He writes: "Native Christians subject to the jurisdiction of the Sultan of Zanzibar would be governed by the law of Zanzibar, that is to say. . .the Sheria or Sacred Law of Islam as interpreted by local usage and tradition."[57] And again in the same letter: "The IBEA Company exercise authority derived from the Sultan, and administers his law, i.e. the Sheria, to such of the inhabitants of the territory leased to them by His Highness as are not by treaty under a foreign jurisdiction."[58] Therefore the dilemma of straddling the two opposing world views became more overt. Tucker and the leaders of Freretown were no longer free to ignore the laws of Zanzibar as they had in the past; hearing cases of civil disobedience, harboring runaway slaves, and deciding rules for dissolving marriages.

In continuing to insist that separated Christians were not permitted to re-marry, Tucker was clinging to his very idealistic interpretation of a universal Christian religious value and also simultaneously, in an imperial way, seeking to impose that interpretation on an existing system. Here we see two tectonic plates chaffing within an individual missionary. At the same time a more formalized expression of imperialism began to press against his position as Hardinge began to develop a procedure for African Christians to dissolve a marriage, using English law as a basis—an appeal once again to the imperial center for a solution to a local problem.

One other complication to the dilemma of the missionaries in the marriage question involved the independence of the individual African. Adults in the Freretown community were mobile; freely moving to Mombasa if they wished or returning inland and thus removing themselves from the rules and structure of the mission village. They also had the freedom to convert and un-convert to the various religions available. Therefore, both options, an idealized, egalitarian Christian commonwealth or an imperial

---

56. CMS Annual Report, 1898. Major MacDonald writes: "All British subjects must stand together whatever their profession. I have no hesitation asking them to assist." During the Sudanese uprising in 1897 all male missionaries were summoned to Kampala to take part in disarming the garrison by translating orders.

57. Hardinge to Pugott, Aug. 29, 1894, PRO, FO 881.

58. Ibid.

outpost, were set aside for a third—one in which Africans played both sides to their own advantage.

CONCLUSION

January 1894 was the last letter from Tucker to Baylis regarding the marriage question. Lord Kimberly had upheld Hardinge's interpretation of Sheria law; the Wali had no ability to dissolve a Christian marriage, this must be settled by Christians themselves. Tucker, whose whole point was the non-dissolvable nature of Christian marriage, declares the "conclusion of the whole matter is entirely satisfactory."[59] If Christians continued to seek divorces they were to be handled as a matter of church discipline. Another letter about marriage does not occur until 1902, when a new marriage ordinance was written to formalize the way unions were registered.

The Freretown report containing the memo on marriage and the resulting letter trail, provides an excellent opportunity to observe the tension that developed between the missionary aspiration to create a multi-racial community governed by universal Christian religious values and the imperial setting in which this was endeavored. Freretown had imperial beginnings and at the same time egalitarian goals. As Tucker entered this milieu his own dilemma of being both the director of a CMS mission with an imperial structure and the bishop of an indigenous church moving toward independence became apparent. The marriage question gives a glimpse into the internal tensions of the Victorian missionary. Operating within an emerging imperial structure, intact with documentation of cultural superiority, at the same time they sought to acknowledge the mutuality of the abilities and spiritual position of the resident Africans. Due to the political weakness and lack of interest of the Sultan in Zanzibar and resistance against the Muslim faith, Tucker accepted the independent, missionary-led civil authority carried on at Freretown. As formal British administration increased the dilemma of the missionaries became more acute. Even if they had wished to continue to operate independently regarding the marriage question, they were not free to ignore the colonial authorities who began to hold the missionaries accountable to local law and, where necessary, to English law. Even so, Tucker continued to hold African Christians to an even higher standard than was used at home, evidence of his faith in their regenerated abilities.

59. Tucker to Baylis, January 8, 1894, CMSA, G3/A5/O/44.

CHAPTER THREE

Art as the Handmaiden of Empire

PROFESSIONAL ARTISTS WERE QUITE frequently essential personnel during the early Victorian voyages of discovery in East Africa. David Livingstone's 1857 Zambezi expedition included a professional artist, Mr. Thomas Baines, to record ethnographic studies, geographical features, and botanical specimens of interest. Painters, unlike photographers, had the ability to recreate fast moving events. For example, "Elephant in the Shallows of the Shire River, the Steam Launch Firing" by Thomas Baines, 1859, depicting an elephant charge was painted at a later date from a description given by George Rae. The artist himself was not present at the event. Mr. Baines showed his belief in the superiority of paint to photography by painting himself in the bottom left of one of his pictures as if asking the question; "Can a photographer do this?"[1] The emphasis that Victorians placed on popular science and the beliefs and teaching of John Ruskin, that art should reflect accurate and informative geographical and anthropological records, helped to carry artists into unknown places. Victorians had a compelling curiosity for foreign, unknown and exotic scenes. Some artists, such as Turner, Lear, Lewis, and Phillip, travelled widely painting such scenes to satisfy the domestic Victorian appetite.[2] The recording of the unknown was not limited to professionals by any means, and the diaries and journals of government officials, explorers, businessmen, and tourists often included maps and sketches; as documentation, to remind the traveler of

---

1. Jeal, *David Livingstone*, 41 and 185.
2. Wilcox and Newall, *Victorian Landscape* 58. Also Treuherz, *Victorian Painting*, 65.

the adventure, or to show those at home the destination—much as photographs would be used today.

Missionaries, as well, included sketches in their diaries, journals, and letters home. Some of these tracings, such as landscape scenes in the diary of Nickisson of the Church Missionary Society in Nassa, were private and untrained in nature, while others, such as those of Archdeacon Walker in Uganda, showed more ability. Those sent to the Church Missionary Society from Mr. Burt, the missionary in Jilore, had a map like quality and were sent home to the mission oversight committee to illustrate building plans or mission station lay-outs.[3]

Art was used for a number of purposes, with professional artists, such as Baines, often producing works for public exhibition, and private individuals and missionaries, such as Nickisson, producing illustrations for private uses. However, in the person of Alfred Robert Tucker (who also painted under the name of Alfred Maile) there is a rare opportunity to examine the collection of a missionary and a professional artist whose art was used for both private and public purposes. Alfred Tucker came from a family of artists; his father, mother, and four brothers all practiced the same profession. As there is no record that he attended any formal schooling it is likely that he was educated at home, as were many middle and upper class children.[4]

Tucker was trained in art at an early age by his father, who felt that, of all his sons, Alfred had the most potential to be a successful artist.[5] Selling his first painting at the age of fourteen, his career as an itinerate landscape artist was a full-time occupation from 1863 until 1880 when he entered Oxford as an undergraduate. While studying, and during his early career as a curate (at St. Andrew's, Clifton, 1882—1885 and St. Nicholas, Durham, 1885—1890), he continued to paint, exhibiting nine paintings in all at the Royal Academy and two at the Grosvenor. Tucker speaks of John Ruskin as "my old teacher."[6] Both were at Oxford in the same time period and both lived in family homes in the Lake District; Tucker at Woodlands in Langdale, Ambleside and Ruskin at Brantwood on Coniston Water. Following his 8 years in the two curacies he was appointed Bishop of Eastern Equatorial Africa in 1890.

3. Enclosure in Tucker to Lang, April 11, 1892, CMSA, G3/A5/O/1892/163.

4. Ford and Harrison, *A Hundred Years Ago*, 22. "In 1868 about a tenth of Oxford and Cambridge entrants had been tutored privately, and about the same proportion thirty years later."

5. Shepherd, *Tucker of Uganda*, Preface.

6. *Uganda Notes*, May 1909, Vol. X, No. 5, CMSA, G3/A7/O/193.

Tucker's body of work is documented in catalogs and letters. There are nine Royal Academy paintings: "Homeless" (1874), "Christchurch, Oxford" (1885), "The Cathedral, Bayeux" (1888), "The Interior of St. Maclou, Rouen" (1888), "Dinan, A Showery Day" (1889), "The Victoria Nyanza" (1894), "Goldinesdachl, Innsbrook" (1907), "A Wet Night, Nismes" (1913), "Monreale Cathedral, Sicily" (1914). Two watercolors were exhibited at the Grosvenor Gallery on New Bond Street: "September—Melbrake, Cumberland" (1881) and "The Church of St. Laurent, Rouen" (1881).[7] One-hundred-and-thirty-one sketches are deposited at the Durham County Record Office illustrating Tucker's confirmation journeys and episcopal visitations during his twenty-one years in Africa. Some of these have been reprinted in Church Missionary Society newsletters. A few sketches and watercolors were given to individuals: "Raymond Portal's Grave" was given to his mother, "Ripon Falls" is now hanging at Uganda Christian University, and "Galilee Chapel" was given to Durham Cathedral.[8] References to his artwork are found in the diaries of contemporaries, in newsletters and newspapers.[9] Bishop Tucker's autobiography also contains original illustrations.

Through the titles and dates of the works it is possible to trace Tucker's painting itineraries in France and Italy. In the Durham deposit the subject matter and the number of times each subject is sketched give a clear indication of what Tucker considered important to record while in Africa, but also an indication of the tension between the ideals of empire and those of the Christian missionary enterprise are clearly seen. Sometimes it is possible even to see this tension within the same sketch.

The sketches of Bishop Tucker were part of a process which helped to shift power from the periphery of empire in Africa to the center in London. Drawings, maps, or reports could carry information from the peripheries to the center "where a particular kind of power, crucial to colonialism was consolidated, a power of possessing the ability 'to act at a distance on unfamiliar events, places, and people.' "[10] Landscapes, botanical drawings, or

---

7. Graves, *The Royal Academy*. And "Goldinesdachl" in Tucker to Carus Wilson, June 5, 1907, BGCA, 135 /1/3.

8. "Portal's Grave" is mentioned in Portal, *The British Mission,* 241; "Ripon Falls" at Uganda Christian University by the writer, Aug. 2004; and "Galilee Chapel" at Durham Cathedral Library on a list of gifts given by the family, but is currently missing.

9. For example, the diary of H. H. Hensen, Dean of Durham Cathedral during Tucker's tenure as sixth Canon and also H. E. Fox in *The Record,* 19 June 1914, and *Intelligencer*, January 1903.

10. Tobin, *Picturing*, 25; Latour, *Science in Action,* 243 and 220.

ethnographic drawings were carriers of the images of distant places which were gradually accumulated and became familiar to Europeans who gained knowledge of places they had never seen.[11] Tucker's art was sent home, and combined with descriptions of situations, people, or events to enable the Church Missionary Society and others to give directions affecting people they had never met and places they had never visited. Each piece of information was accumulated and recombined with additional information to mobilize further action that eventually reversed the balance of power.[12]

For example, Tucker's sketch of the dormitories at Freretown and a report about the living conditions were sent back to the CMS Corresponding Secretary. The Corresponding Secretary attended a meeting of the General Committee and presented the sketch and the report. The committee analyzed and extracted details from Tucker's offerings and created lists, minutes, and agendas. They then combined the information with the reports of other missionaries and government officials. Using all this information the Committee was able to discuss problems, devise solutions, and send instructions, all without ever seeing Freretown. The collection and accumulation of information allowed those at the center to represent the world "in its absence," to localize distant places and take action.[13] This elevated the committee from a local authority to a universal authority. They had the ability to re-arrange relationships, which resulted in the power to relegate the local knowledge found in the peripheries to local influence only.

A further example of the impact of his art would be his sketches of the mission stations allowing the committee to see for themselves the type of housing in which the missionaries lived and worked. As the pioneer period moved into a more permanent situation, the missionaries requested sturdier, more durable, European style houses, believing that living in the reed and mud house style of the indigenous people was a source of ill-health. After reviewing the problem using all the information available to them –from medical sources, letters, reports, suggested house plans from missionaries in the field, and Tucker's sketches—the General Committee of the CMS decided to send funds for European style houses. The European style

11. Tobin, *Picturing*, 213–14. Wilson, *The Victorians*, 557. The artists' selection of subject matter illustrates the ability of the artist to filter information for the audience and create a world.

12. Tobin, *Picturing*. Also Matthew, *Nineteenth Century*, 151, briefly acknowledges the concept of cycles of accumulation and the corresponding control that it made possible.

13. Latour, *Science in Action*, 246–47.

house became a mark of status, taking precedence over the local building style. Yet Tucker himself continued to live in an indigenous style house, built for him by the Ugandans, until his retirement in 1911. Such renditions of him living in indigenous style accommodations is more than art, it is a picture of a man comfortable with surroundings, and no higher than his African flock.

Although Tucker was involved in this empire building activity, at the same time he was also influenced, and his opinion mitigated, by his idealism. Henry Elliott Fox, Tucker's rector at Durham, his commissary and later General Secretary of the CMS, writes of these idealistic motivating factors which led Tucker to take a position in East Africa:

> Twenty five years ago a young artist was engaged in painting a picture, which he hoped would find a place in the Academy. It was the figure of a lonely woman struggling up a street in a wild, stormy night, the sleet driven by the wind into her face, a little baby at her bosom. And doors and windows were shut in her face. The picture was called 'Homeless.' As the man painted it and the artist's imagination filled his soul, it seemed to come to him as a living reality, and he put his brush down and said, 'God help me! Why don't I go to lost people themselves instead of painting pictures of them? . . . I want to go to that part of the world where men seem to be most lost. I have come to the conclusion that East Africa is the place where I am most wanted.[14]

Fueled by the abolitionists and aided by Livingstone's call to replace the slave trade with legitimate trade and industry, missionary candidates flooded to East Africa from the 1850's to the beginning of the twentieth century. What they hoped to offer Africa was the much repeated phrase, "Christianity, Commerce and Civilization." Embedded in this idealism shared by government and church alike was a range of belief–that the European way of life, culture, and government was, at the most, somewhat superior to that of the Africans and at the least, somewhat necessary. There is nothing in the teachings of Christianity that prohibits commerce; these two ideas can co-habit. Western civilization and commerce also partner well. But Christianity and western civilization are sometimes at odds. Like a cell with two nuclei, the slogan was destined to split into two parts.

---

14. Fox, *The Gleaner*, January 1903, 14. The picture was donated to Lambeth Cathedral but may have been destroyed by an incendiary device during WW2.

The first nucleus is that of empire with the perceived destiny of Britain to liberate and tutor the world. The second nucleus of Christian idealism derives its force from the teachings of Paul: "There is neither Jew nor Greek, there is neither slave nor free, there is neither male nor female; for you are all one in Christ Jesus."[15] All of those who became Christians were perceived to be on equal footing, brothers and sisters in Christ. Samwili Mukasa of Mulengo reflects this mind-set in a letter to Tucker in which he writes: "And we beg you very much to consent to come in here to the house on Mulengo, of your brother, your kinsman, for there is no difference because Christ has made us all kinsman in His blood, which thus joins us."[16]

Although the exclusive claims of Christianity folded in nicely with those who felt that England was uniquely gifted to bring the world forward into the light of Western civilization, the second nucleus of equality and brotherhood was ever present eventually growing into a competing world view and a pulling apart into separateness. The tension caused by this pulling apart, can be seen clearly in Tucker's letter to the CMS Corresponding Secretary, Mr. Lang, as they debate the wisdom of building one of the hallmarks of western civilization, an expensive church building:

> The objects at which we aim (or rather ought to aim) is so to carry on our work so that gradually one European missionary after another, as the native church becomes stronger, may be withdrawn until at last she stands alone, strong in the Lord and in the power of his might. Is that granted by the Committee of the CMS? If not, I can go no further. We part company here. For this is my ideal if not that of the Committee . . . How are these people (when left to themselves as we long and hope and pray they may by God's grace be some day) how I ask are they to maintain such a fabric?[17]

The decision of building the church was being made at CMS headquarters in London, in the mindset of empire, yet it directly affected the indigenous Christians in Mombasa. At the same time, Tucker's deep belief in the eventual independence of the African church is evident. His letters, like his artwork, reflect the peculiar position in which the missionaries found themselves.

The most prevalent region depicted by Tucker is the interior of what is now Kenya—thirty of his sketches found at Durham are of a trip from

---

15. Gal 3:28 RSV.
16. Samwili Mukasa to Tucker, CMS Annual Report, 1896, 95.
17. Tucker to Lang, April 5, 1892, CMSA, G3/A5/O/161.

Mombasa to Mochi [now spelled Moshi], just over the border of what is now Tanzania; and thirty-two are scenes along the northern caravan route to Uganda, which is the present day railroad line in Kenya. The next most sketched region was the Kenyan coast: Mombasa, Zanzibar, and Sadaani [now spelled Sadani] having nineteen contributions. This is followed by the southern caravan route to Uganda through present day central Tanzania which has fifteen. Uganda, in and around Mengo, has only eight in this collection and five are taken from the southern shore of Lake Victoria, Usambiro. The smallest number is from the Lake itself, having only four. A bar chart gives a visual picture of the subject matter produced by Tucker during his African journeys:

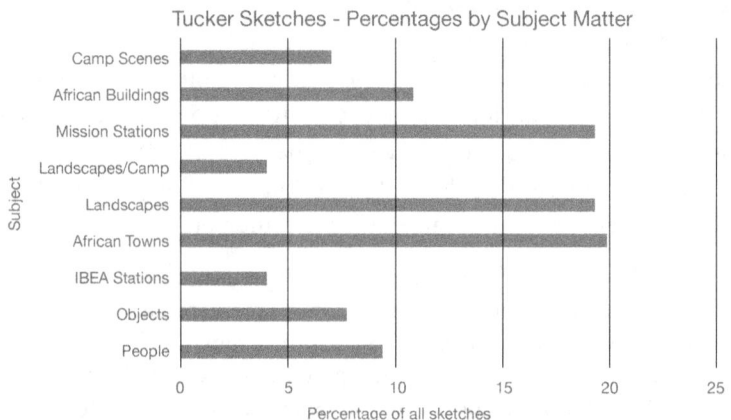

Figure 1—Bar Chart Showing Number of Pictures by Subject Matter

Tucker is best known as a "landscape and architectural painter" so perhaps it is not surprising that the landscape sketches and the architectural together are an overwhelming 76.1% of Tucker's work in this particular collection. The sketches are referred to as "watercolor sketches" and "sketches in water colors" and two of the sketches have been worked up into watercolor studies in black and white.[18]

William Pyne, a nineteenth-century writer and landscape painter, referred to watercolor painting as "a new art, originating with the English, and perfected within the age whence it began—that English school, as it now stands recorded, the admiration of all nations."[19]

18. "A List of CMS Missionary Books, 1882–1932." UCUA, 02BP/230/29 and *Uganda Notes*, July 1909, Vol. 10, No. 7, G3/A7/O/252.

19. Wilcox and Newall, p. 13.

A strange nationalistic flavor clings to this thought and dovetails with the empire building mind-set found throughout the nineteenth century. To be a landscape painter or a watercolor artist was to be English, an admired designation. A particularly English form of painting was the country house portrait in watercolor.

Tucker's watercolor style of art, his art training, his association with the Royal Academy and his experience as an itinerate landscape painter placed him firmly into an essentially English mind-set and genre. His words to CMS leader Eugene Stock are an illustration of this outlook, "I am now not very far away from Kilimanjaro, in the midst of those who of God's creations seem to be the farther removed from light and liberty. And yet only a few weeks ago I was in London in all the turmoil and rush of civilization's great center. The contrast is almost indescribable."[20] Yet the sense of his civilized superiority captured in this quote is in tension with two things. Firstly, Tucker's obvious admiration of the African landscape, architecture, and people, as seen in his sketches such as "A Headwind: Victoria Nyanza" (see Fig. 2) which later became the subject of an 1894 Academy painting. Secondly, both are in contrast to Tucker's thoughts found consistently recorded in his letters and sermons which will be explored in following chapters.

20. Tucker to Stock, Feb. 3, 1892, CMSA, G3/A5/O/94.

Figure 2—A Headwind: Victoria Nyanza (Feb. 9, 1891)

THE TENSION IN TUCKER'S ART

Looking closely and individually at Tucker's sketches the interaction of empire thinking and egalitarian ideals seems captured and frozen for all time on each page, an illustration of an internal and possibly unconscious tension. For example, in a sketch of an African porter (see Fig. 3) the subject is named, "Dan Kiongosi" (leader in Swahili) and is not presented as a nameless specimen or an unknown bearer of burdens. He sits upon a load that would be carried by two porters at each end of the pole; but he is not one of these. In his hand is the drum which, as a leader, he uses to beat the pace for the caravan—the mark of his position. Caravan porters and leaders were not slaves or serfs, but employees with wages regulated by supply and demand and reinforced by the Imperial British East Africa Company and later by the Colonial government. Dan Kiongozi wears his traditional clothing. Bishop Tucker felt that Africans should not be forced to wear Western clothing in order to avoid alienating them from their families and clans.²¹ Yet Kiongozi has a Christian first name, his tribal first name has been unwritten and replaced with a Westernized or Christian one. Thus, in this one small rendering the tension between the ever pressing Empire mind-set and Christian idealism can be seen overlapping in the simple everyday life of an African man.

Figure 3—Dan Kiongozi (Feb. 27, 1891)

If sketches revealed this ongoing tension, then so did his words. Tucker's sermon at the division of the diocese illustrates quite clearly the opposing ideals balancing the empire mind-set.

> I come now to the question of control. Naturally the European missionary thinks that he can do things much better than any Native. He therefore attempts to do everything himself. In this (in my opinion) he commits a grievous blunder, and unless turned from his purpose will mar the development of any Native Church with which he may have to do. The fact is, the Native can do many things much better than the European, and should be used from the very beginning. The missionary should do nothing that the Native can do.²²

21. Tucker to Baylis, March 4, 1895, CMSA, G3/A5/O/102.

22. Tucker. "A Charge," KNA, Pam. 62, 266.02341067 Tuc. Reprinted in *Intelligencer*, February 1898, 89.

The fact that Tucker was a landscape watercolor artist, with all the accompanying associations, illustrates the influence of imperial thought patterns in Tucker's life. Yet his words and sketches also show the attitude of humility, brotherhood, and equality, even admiration—the Christian ideals. Tucker seemed to walk between these two influences or adhere to both simultaneously.

Given that landscape watercolor was a particularly English form of art, what happens when this English form is exported to the peripheries of the empire? Wherever English forms of painting, such as landscape watercolor, are transported to the outskirts of the empire, a very subtle "generic and ideological shift [occurs]."[23] A painting of an English gentleman under an Oak tree, for example, is a specifically English genre; representing not only national identity, independence, vigilance and integrity but also a link with property and power. Yet when the Oak is replaced by a Banyan tree the formula breaks down. It becomes too evident leading to a questioning of its ideological foundations—a questioning of the casual link between land and power.

In Tucker's sketches of the mission stations, a link between land and power is implied. The link may not be one of complete ownership, but one of duty and influence. In the sketch of the Mochi Mission Station (Fig.4) the landscape sweeps away into the vast distance and includes Mt. Meru. The flag, in the foreground, higher than Mt. Meru, was used by the CMS missionaries to denote their presence in the station; it flies over the entire scene, almost in the attitude of staking claim on the vast expanse before the viewer. This sketch could be interpreted as reflecting or mimicking an attitude of empire. Yet the flag is not the Union Jack but the flag of the CMS, possibly implying a territory to be influenced not with temporal government powers but with those of a spiritual nature.[24] Tucker spells out this association in a letter to Carus-Wilson, a long-term correspondent: "We are

23. Tobin, *Picturing Imperial Power*, 20 and 21.

24. Minutes of conference of the Usagara missionaries with Tucker (Précis Book 3, Oct. 28, 1890) agreed not to fly flags of a national character as the mission was in the German sphere of influence. CMS wrote back for clarification ". . . we shall be glad to learn with regard to the question of flying flags, whether the Germans object to the use of ordinary (not national) flags such as the flag which the CMS vessels always carry. . .we should like to know what reason there is . . . that the Germans would disapprove of our using (should it be for any reason desired) our own mission flag." Lang to Tucker, Nov. 10, 1890, CMSA G3/A5/L6/42. Tucker responded that only the German flag was permitted so he instructed the stations to fly no flags. Tucker to Lang, Feb. 20, 1891, CMSA G3/A5/O/114.

ready to take possession of the country in the name of the Lord."[25] Here again is a tension between empire mind-set and Christian idealism.

Figure 4—Mt. Meru from Mochi Mission Station (Feb. 13, 1892)

In all the categories of the Durham collection there is a tendency toward preserving anthropological or ethnographic scenes. Ethnographic art includes sketches of porters or servants, the recording of customs, clothing, manners, or huts. These types of sketches are peppered throughout the Tucker deposit. Two examples can be viewed in illustrations Fig. 5 and Fig. 6. Sketches of this type gave people and their culture the status of objects of natural history inquiry. Ethnographic art collects information from the periphery to send to the center of empire for analysis and categorization helping to shift the balance of power as explained above. But also the collection, categorization, and analysis became a type of encyclopedic enterprise.

---

25. Tucker to Carus-Wilson, September 20, 1903, BGCA, 135/1/2.

Figure 5—The National "Shauri" Tree, Taveta (Feb. 10, 1892)

Figure 6—Rope Bridge at Taveta (Feb. 10, 1892)

There was an impetus on the part of missionaries and explorers to record these scenes out of appreciation before they completely disappeared in the wake of outside influences.[26] Ethnographic art could also be used to assess the abilities of the people as agriculturists, builders or entrepreneurs in order to appropriate these skills in a future colonial partnership that could involve domination. The sketch from Ruwenzori, "Threshing Beans" (Fig. 7) could have been used for this purpose. At the same time Tucker's encyclopedic and ethnographic recordings illustrate his obvious admiration and fascination with the people; as in the recording of the seemingly pleasant and peaceful village in Kavirondo (Fig. 8).

Figure 7—"Threshing Beans:" A Village of the Bakonja Ruwenzori (Aug. 1898)

26. Professor Jean Michel Massing interview, Kings College, Cambridge, June 3, 2004.

Figure 8—Kwa Sakwa's Village, Kavirondo (Dec. 7, 1892)

Another example of this tension can be found in the two sketches of the "sleeping bwanas" (Fig. 9 and Fig. 10). In both sketches the African subject takes the center of attention while the European is off to one side. This positioning might be interpreted in several different ways. The European sleeping in the presence of the Katikiro of Toro (Prime Minister) could be seen as dismissive; or that Europeans could take their ease while Africans do the hard work. On the other hand, Tucker may be presenting the European presence as being on the periphery (sleeping on the side) of the true center of African life, which is the African him/herself.

Figure 9—The Camp Taveta (Jan. 29, 1892)

Art as the Handmaiden of Empire

Figure 10—*The Rev. T. R. Buckley and the Katikiro of Toro (July 7, 1898)*

Consciously or unconsciously Tucker was collecting ethnographic information for the centers of power back home. At the same time, he objected strongly in his letters to appropriating African labor in any kind of plantation system owed by foreign investors. His position on the type of economy needed in East Africa was quite different from that of the colonial government. Corresponding to his view of the future church, he believed that the existing African economy must be recognized and not hindered from continuing to be independent, free from any subordination or dependence on an outside economy. The economy he preferred was built on production being in the hands of small African landholders for a domestic market. The colonial government favored the development of a plantation economy tied to the needs of the wider world market. Tucker's views are spelled out clearly in his letters to the Acting Governor: "Forced cultivation of cotton is wrong. The feudal system is being run for all it is worth in the matter of labour and the cultivation of cotton is no exception to the rule.

Economically unsound."[27] And three days later he writes: "The industry may suffer for a while, if the compulsory cultivation of cotton be abolished, but it is, I think, better that it should be so than that the people for whose sakes the land is being governed should suffer."[28]

Although Tucker was an Anglican bishop he was from a Quaker background.[29] He was not baptized until 1878 at the age of twenty-nine (at St. Aldates's by Canon Christopher) as Quaker families would not baptize their children and Anglicans are baptized in infancy. Possibly his close association with H. E. Fox could also be related to a Quaker background. Given a Quaker upbringing, with the emphasis this denomination placed on the equality of all people regardless of race, class, or gender, Tucker's views on the innate African abilities seem very much more comprehensible and understandable, as would his adamant anti-slavery views.

On the issue of forced labor, he pointed out to Baylis, then corresponding secretary of the CMS, the constant tension that he felt to "keep on the best terms with the Government and at the same time, . . . guard carefully the interests of the natives."[30] This statement could be categorized as one that, in keeping with his contemporaries, belies an attitude of empire—or at the least, paternalism. At the same time the role of a bishop ideally includes guarding the interest of his followers, especially those who are disadvantaged. Whether he was expressing an empire mind-set, or one related to Christian ideals, it clearly shows the pulling apart of the two positions as time progressed, with the missionaries caught between.

Additional sketches of the mission stations offer further glimpses into the interaction in Tucker's art of imperial impulse with the high ideals of love, appreciation and an equal place in the world. For example, the sketches of the view from Tucker's room (Fig. 11) and the interior of the Taveta mission station (Fig. 12) both use a framing technique. In both cases the beautiful landscape is framed and surrounded by a European style house. In order to see Africa one must look through the European structure into the scene beyond.

---

27. Tucker to Boyle, Dec. 20, 1909, CMSA, G3/A7/O/38. Also analyzed in Hansen "Mission and Colonialism," *Mission Ideologies*, Christensen and Hutchinson, 1982.

28. Tucker to Boyle, Dec. 23, 1909, CMSA, G3/A7/O/46.

29. Reynolds. *The Evangelicals*, 15.

30. Tucker to Baylis, May 31 1909, CMSA, G3/A7/O/219.

Figure 11—View from My Room—Baganda (March 10, 1893)

Figure 12—Taveta Mission (March 1895)

Africa is contained by a European viewpoint. And yet the structures are not entirely European; they are a combination of traditional African building styles (the reed walls) and traditional English ones (the pitched roof). Tucker appreciates the beauty of the African world, placing it in a prime position on the canvas where the attention is drawn to it, but it is seen as if through a telescope, a lens with a familiar order of home, dominating and bringing comfort in the wilds of Africa.

Another example from the mission station category is the two views of the Toro mission station. The first sketch looks outward from the station to the rugged mountains beyond (Fig. 13). A European style house sits on the left surrounded by a fence complete with an archway into the bush. Inside the courtyard the African bush has been subdued, there is order and safety. Outside the boundaries of the fence the grass and shrubby grow tall and wild and the mountain looms darkly A few Africans have been placed inside the fence sitting on the right and balancing the European structure. They appear to be performing various functions; maintaining the fence, preparing food, and sitting around a reading sheet.

Figure 13—Mission Station, Toro (Aug. 1898)

Again the theme of Europeans bringing order to chaos and inviting Africans to participate is discernable yet this theme is also augmented by the archway—an invitation to walk beyond. The second look at Toro (Fig. 14) is from the opposite viewpoint, from the mountain looking down on the mission station with a storm pressing in. The mission station is surrounded and dwarfed by the vast African landscape and the power of the storm is evident. The station appears only as a small wisp of smoke, dominated by the African setting leading the viewer to speculate whether the storm will wash it away or, like a tiny seed watered by the powerful equatorial rain, it will grow and take root.

Figure 14—*A Storm: Bethlehem (Mission Station), Toro (Aug. 1898)*

The contrast between the two viewpoints is engaging; presenting Africa first from the mission's perspective, and secondly the mission from the vastness of Africa, but the interconnectedness is unmistakable.

One final illustration of the friction between the imperial perspective and high ideals can be seen in the landscape/camp scene category of Tucker's work. On the way to his second stay in Uganda Tucker captures a scene from the caravan trail at Nzoi through present day Kenya (see Fig. 15). Again, the viewer is struck by the rugged grandeur of the African landscape which fills the canvas. Clinging to the side of the mountainous terrain are the tents of the European caravan, alien and temporary in nature. The camp is reminiscent of an army bivouac—the "soldiers of Christ" as it were, on mission in Africa subduing the heathen in imperial fashion and bringing light to the nations. But curiously the figures in the camp are indistinguishable, it is impossible to tell which might be European and which might be African, representing in an artistic way the egalitarian nature of this endeavor. All can participate equally in this joint effort and move together to accomplish the task.

Figure 15—Nzoi (October 20, 1892)

The above illustrations are representative of Tucker's work though not exhaustive. The artistic abilities of Tucker capture not only his own perspective but some of the mind-set of the time in which he lived. Through these artistic glimpses it is possible to uncover in a unique way the unwritten tensions involved when the idealistic mission project in East African unfolded in an imperial setting.

SUMMARY AND CONCLUSION

Artists played an important role in the Victorian Empire voyages of discovery in East Africa. Unlike Thomas Baines, who was attached to Livingstone's Zambezi Mission, Alfred Tucker was a professional painter who was also the director of the Church Missionary Society's efforts in East Africa and at the same time the Bishop of the emerging African church. Through his art we have a unique opportunity to examine the forces in play during the period when initial contact was made between East Africans and Europeans.

Tucker's micro-narrative, including his art, gives evidence to the theory that missionaries were often caught between two opposing forces; those of the empire in which they were completely immersed, and those of the ideals of their Christian faith. The transmission of information and images from the edges to the center of empire is clearly seen in Tucker's life and artistic expression, helping to shift power. At the same time, Tucker's Christian ideals were illustrated through his letters, speeches and his sketches, and it is easy to see the tension which existed due to these opposing forces. The nationalistic nature of English watercolor; Tucker's training, associations, and experience all reinforced the influences of empire thinking. However, when the essentially English genre of landscape watercolor met the African continent and culture in the hands of a Christian idealist, the jarring juxtaposition gives us a glimpse into the tension of being an English missionary; walking on the fault line between two great opposing rock walls of opposite ideas.

EXAMPLES OF ART CATEGORIES IN DURHAM DEPOSIT

Figure 16—Example of Camp Scenes—In the Camp at Unyanguira (Sept. 9, 1890)

Figure 17—Example of African Buildings—The Kings' House (Jan. 1880)

Figure 18—Example of Mission Station—Rabai (Jan. 26, 1892)

Art as the Handmaiden of Empire

Figure 19—Example of Landscape Camp Scenes—In Ugogo (Aug. 29, 1890)

Figure 20—Example of Landscape—Saadani (July 18, 1890)

Figure 21—Example of African Towns—Zanzibar

Figure 22—Example of IBEA Station—Fort Smith, Kikuyu (Nov. 12, 1892)

Figure 23—Example of People—Taveta (Feb. 8, 1892)

CHAPTER FOUR

Karibu Complexity
The Unwelcome Slavery Dilemma

THE DIVISION OF THE massive Diocese of Eastern Equatorial Africa began as early as 1897 when in October the CMS Committee of Correspondence confirmed the arrangement for a division in conjunction with the Archbishop of Canterbury, Frederick Temple.[1] Although Bishop Tucker began writing about the possibility of such an action almost from the time of his initial arrival in Mombasa, practically another two years passed from the time of its approval to the consecration of Bishop Peel (July of 1899) and then another three months before the communication arrived from the Archbishop defining the borders of the two new dioceses. Peel himself did not arrive in Mombasa to take up his post until December 18, 1899.[2] Therefore, until the beginning of 1900 Bishop Tucker was still effectively carrying out the confirmations and ordinations for the old administrative unit of Eastern Equatorial Africa.

On the verge of his departure to begin his work exclusively as the Bishop of Uganda, after an episcopate of eight years, Bishop Tucker took up a new and unexpected duty—that of legal counsel to a seventeen-year-old

---

1. Insert dated September 26, 1897 in Minutes of Committee of Correspondence, October 5, 1897, G3/A5.

2. "The brethren in Uganda" first mentioned the need for a bishop solely for Uganda through Archdeacon Walker in 1894 (Baylis to Tucker, December 21, 1894, G3/A5/L7/287). But Bishop Tucker himself raised the question as early as June of 1891. (Tucker to Baylis, January.8, 1895, G3/A5/O/1895, 44.)

female run-away slave named Keri Karibu.³ Just why he chose to take on this additional task despite the press of being Bishop of a huge diocese and the director of the mission as well, seems at first encounter somewhat of a mystery.

Sir Arthur H. Hardinge, the British Consul-General of Zanzibar (1895 to 1900) had his own theories. By extending himself from matters of the Church to issues wholly under the jurisdiction of Colonial government, Tucker was inserting himself into Imperial matters. Writing to Lord Salisbury at the Foreign Office after the debate in Commons in June of 1897 regarding the return of fugitive slaves to their masters, he postulates in a somewhat sarcastic fashion,

> The Bishop is, I fancy, so elated by what he regards as his victory over Her Majesty's Government on the fugitive slave question, and by the applause which it has won for him from the Anti-Slavery Society, that he is disposed to assume the character of a sort of African Hildebrand, or Thomas-a-Becket, and combine with his pastoral functions those of Commissioner and Consul-General, and indeed, to some extent, as far as the Protectorate is concerned, of Secretary of State for Foreign Affairs.⁴

Bishop Tucker's reasons for taking up the case, on the other hand, chose to emphasize the irony that he perceived of a Christian nation, such as Great Britain enforcing the policy of slavery on behalf of an Arab ruler.⁵ Privately to his friends he was even more explicit,

> Some people I know question whether it is the duty of a Bishop to take up questions of this kind. In my own mind I have no possible doubt as to my duty. When I was consecrated the question was asked me, 'Will you be merciful for Christ's sake to poor and needy people and to *all strangers destitute of help*' (emphasis his). I answered, 'I will by God's help.' If there is a stranger destitute of help in this world it is this poor slave girl Keri Karibu, and the poor and needy people are her fellow slaves.⁶

The above statement is admirable but why then did it take eight years from his arrival for this opinion to produce a substantial complaint or court case

---

3. The name is sometimes spelled Heri or Kherie, meaning "Blessing," and Caribou, meaning "Welcome" in Kiswahili.
4. Hardinge to Salisbury, January 16, 1898, PRO, FO 881/7024.
5. Tucker, "Bishop Tucker's Charge," *CMS Intelligencer*, February 1898, 89.
6. Tucker to Fox, February 23, 1898, BGCA, Collection 135/1/2.

in the cause against slavery? The answer to this question is complex and directly related to the tension between the cultural idealism involved in the matter of abolition, and the need to serve under existing laws and treaties of the expanding empire. That tension is embedded in his stated reasons for taking up the case (the cause of the poor) but Bishop Tucker also seems to have been fully emboldened to take a direct action against slavery by a decision of the English Parliament (April 1898) to finally bring to a full stop the lingering slave trade on the Coast. We will shortly see how complicated a process this was as the events leading up to this decision are given in more detail. But, until this decision Tucker's policy at the coast stations was the exact opposite of his unexpected action of harboring a runaway slave and arguing a case before the Imperial British East Africa magistrate. Initially his actions at Freretown were in cooperation with the Company representatives. He allowed the recovery of runaways and gave the appearance of one unable to work against the administrative powers and to oppose slavery. But behind this appearance, Tucker was quietly biding his time while seeking an opportunity; living a contradiction to his deeply held principles of abolition. But with Keri Karibu the door swung wide open to take action which matched his convictions.

A brief overview of the painfully slow progression towards the abolition of slavery in East Africa is very helpful at this point in order to understand this contradiction and to place the actions of the Director of the CMS mission within some context. In rehearsing this overview a careful distinction must be made between terms such as the "slave trade," the "legal status of slavery" and lastly, "slavery" itself. Also, within these categories a careful distinction must be made between illegality, abolition and the ability to enforce these rulings.

THE SLAVE TRADE

As early as 1807 Britain abolished the trade in slaves, making it illegal for British subjects to transport captive Africans for sale into slavery.[7] Later in 1822 and again in 1845 treaties with Said bin Sultan, of Zanzibar, agreed to abolish the overseas slave trade while leaving the domestic slave trade intact. Due to the extremely lucrative nature of the trade, these agreements were never successful and an attempt was made in 1847 to combat the trade anew by making a treaty with the Sultan of Muscat in Oman to prohibit

---

7. Shillington, *History*, 233; also Moorman. *A History of the Church*, 321.

the import of slaves from East Africa.[8] This treaty also seemed to have had no effect as three subsequent proclamations against the slave trade from the Sultan of Zanzibar (1862, 1864, and 1868) were issued.[9] Offered as appeasements towards Britain, they did little to stem the exceedingly profitable slave trade.

Fifty years after the initial Moresby Treaty of 1822, the Foreign Office asked Sir Bartle Frere (the Governor of Bombay having administrative oversight of Zanzibar) and Sir John Kirk (at the time Assistant Consul-General in Zanzibar, political officer and doctor) in 1873 to negotiate once again a treaty with Zanzibar to make the overseas slave trade illegal; this time with Sultan Bargash. As mentioned earlier, a naval blockade was employed to successfully accomplish the signing of a treaty and the slave market in Zanzibar had been closed. But the signing of a treaty and the enforcement of that treaty are two different things. The slave trade had resumed and three years later, in 1876, the Sultan, under pressure from the British, once again issued a proclamation to abolish the overseas slave trade in Zanzibar, Pemba, and the coastal regions of the Sultan's kingdom. The slave market in Zanzibar had re-opened, in a different location, within a year of its closing. The Sultan's kingdom was an independent one and any participation with British interests was purely voluntary. British ships, which began patrolling the coast after the 1862 proclamation, were too few in number to make a complete dent in the flow of human cargo and business had continued using overland caravans to the port of Kilwa, located two hundred miles south of Zanzibar on the mainland. Outright smuggling was also prevalent. Only a slight reduction of overseas slave shipment was noted by the 1880's.[10]

Not until 1890, the year Tucker arrived, was a similar action taken against the slave trade in Mombasa (located on a small island off the mainland). The Joint Powers Treaty was a sweeping bill from the British Parliament in conjunction with France, Germany, Portugal, and Italy, which sought to abolish and suppress the slave trade from the Suez to Madagascar. Just prior to his arrival the Imperial British East Africa Company, a business organization granted a charter by the Queen and therefore having a derivative authority, had established itself in Zanzibar. By a treaty with the Sultan (May of 1887) three years before the arrival of Tucker, it had been granted exclusive trade rights within the Sultan's Kingdom.[11] In 1890 an ad-

---

8. Liebowitz, *The Physician*, 132.

9. Ibid., 143 and 169.

10. Ibid., 222; Beachey. *The Slave Trade*, 261.

11. Liebowitz, *The Physician*, 200. On Sir John Kirk's advice, Bargash agreed to grant

ministrator, Sir Francis de Winton, established a presence in Zanzibar with a fledgling militia and legal apparatus which began to produce a systematic record for the handling of slavery complaints. Despite all these changes the holding of slaves continued to be legal, as was the domestic slave market; only import and export was banned beyond the Sultan's territory which was a ten-mile-wide strip along the coast from present day Mogadishu to Mozambique.

LEGAL STATUS OF SLAVERY IMPLICATIONS

Prior to the arrival of Tucker, it had been the practice of Mr. Price and then Mr. Binns who were in charge at the CMS coastal mission, in keeping with an arrangement made with IBEA, to detain runaway slaves at Rabai and Freretown and allow them to be re-claimed or returned to their masters. Guards were placed to prevent runaways from entering. Tucker arrived simultaneously to the IBEA Company Administrator in May 1890 and took up his official residence at Freretown. Within two months of his arrival he was pressured by the administration to return runaway slaves who were harboring themselves among the individuals rescued from slave ships and deposited at the freed slave colony of Freretown, and also at Rabai. Tucker seemed willing to let the situation ride without action as long as he could. However, when an official report from the IBEA administrator was presented to him, Tucker expressed general regret that any steps should be taken that required the return of slaves but felt honor bound to take action. Honor bound, first of all, to the IBEA administration, as agreements had been made with the Sultan's government to allow for the holding of slaves; and secondly to the Arab slave owners who were operating under existing laws. Tucker took four steps to remedy the situation.[12] First, he gave instructions that a *baraza* (business meeting) with the Arab masters should be held to explain how the runaway slaves came to be inside the mission estates. Secondly, the runaways would be counselled to return to their masters or work off their freedom. It is significant, however, that his action plan did not involve the return of the runaways by force. Although he made

---

the company the right to pass laws in the region they would be developing, the right to collect taxes to fund roads and wells, and to create a standing army or police force to protect their enterprise. The Sultan would benefit financially by receiving 20% of the company's profits and an additional 5% of mining profits.

12. Tucker to General Touch, July 9, 1890, CMSA, G3/A5/O/192.

no formal arrangements for the slaves to be reclaimed or returned, he set up a negotiation process with the owners and made a hopeful guarantee that no further runaways would be taken into Rabai or Freretown. It was a compromise born of the tension between an ideal and a political reality. Thirdly, Tucker instructed that the policemen, employed by the mission and stationed at the various approaches to Freretown to block the entrance to runaway slaves, were to be released from this duty and reprimanded. Lastly, Tucker reprimanded the African pastor at Freretown and CMS Agent, William Jones, whom he felt was responsible for the situation. Tucker explains,

> Before leaving Freretown a report reached me that runaway slaves were being harboured at Rabai contrary to the engagements with which we had entered. I at once wrote to Mr. Jones (Mr. Binns had just left) and asked him to tell me plainly whether it was true or not. In answer he told me that whilst there were a few such slaves at Rabai the report about there being 100 there was an exaggeration. Mr. Fitch was then at the point of going up to Rabai. I asked immediately to enquire about this matter and the report enclosed is the result. You will see that of Mombasa slaves we have over 100 at Rabai. We are thus face to face with the old difficulty and any hope that had been cherished (and I confess I have been indulging such hope) that the bitter feeling of the Arabs would die away seems likely to be dashed to the ground.[13]

Although in a settlement as large as Rabai it would be almost impossible to keep track of the comings and goings of residents, Jones was held responsible for the situation and Tucker wrote a reprimand instructing him of "his duty in the matter" as "I believe he has been guilty of a breech of duty."[14] A "breech" however, is not identical to a misjudgment of a moral issue which the Bishop never accused Mr. Jones of making. The Bishop was quite capable of splitting hairs as he juggled his ideals against the existing law. It was also necessary, in order to reinforce the compromise, for the Bishop to reprimand the pastor in charge of Rabai, Mr. Jones, for overlooking the runaway since the agreement was established before his arrival. In light of his staunch anti-slavery views, it was a finely drawn reprimand. The Bishop would have been hard pressed to distinguish Mr. Jones' position from his own.

13. Ibid.
14. Ibid.

The relationship between William Jones and the CMS missionaries is, in itself, an example of an emerging partnership with Africans, but one contained within a system of imperial supervision. It is certain, given the level of supervision from European clergy that was normal for African pastors, that Mr. Jones was operating with the knowledge, if not the explicit instruction, of Mr. Binns—the missionary in charge of Freretown. For an example of this level of supervision Tucker's letters give ample evidence. He writes, "We want men whom we can send forward into the regions beyond where they can superintend and organize the work of our native pioneers."[15] If Mr. Binns had not been in England, the reprimand would have been written to him. Since he was on furlough, it went instead to Mr. Jones. The fact that the reprimand went to the African pastor as the next in line of authority was an indication of the equal footing which Tucker considered Mr. Jones to hold in the CMS structure at Freretown. However, the fact that the first line of authority was always a European clergy is an illustration of the cultural milieu under which the missionaries functioned.

As Mr. Fitch was taking up his post at Rabai during the furlough of Mr. Binns the Bishop expressed his hope that the reprimand, together with European supervision, would be effective to prevent a repeat of the situation in the future.[16]

SHOWDOWN ON LEGAL STATUS

Seven years after the reprimand (1897 and 1898) a three-tiered change transpired which emboldened Bishop Tucker to reverse his standard operating procedure. Firstly, the legal status of slavery was abolished (1 April, 1897) on the islands of Zanzibar and Pemba (but not Mombasa and the coastal territory of the Sultan). Secondly, after a debate in the House of Commons (June 1897) regarding the legal status of slavery in Mombasa and its environs, the Attorney General stated that the return of fugitive slaves was illegal. Lastly, a year later (April 1898) a decree was issued reinforcing the original 1876 proclamation of the Sultan to abolish the slave trade on the coast, in Zanzibar, and Pemba. All imported slaves after that date were illegally held.

In order to understand more clearly the distinction between the slave trade and the legal status of slavery, but not slavery itself, it is helpful to

---

15. Tucker to Baylis, January 18, 1899, CMSA, G3/A7/O/62.
16. Ibid.

read the definition given by one of the pioneer proponents of the term, Sir John Kirk,

> The first thing to be done to remedy the state of things now existing at Zanzibar is to insist upon the abolition of the status of slavery as a condition recognized at law within the islands of Zanzibar and Pemba . . . I would not propose, however, to manumit slaves and so dislocate all the present relations of master and servant. I would simply insist upon the Sultan abolishing the recognition of slavery, leaving the system to die out as it did in India and as it is doing in the Portuguese possessions.[17]

In other words, no rights arising out of the relationship of master and slave would be enforced by any civil or criminal court, or any other authority. The legal status of slavery would cease to exist altogether in the law.

The abolition of legal status in Zanzibar and Pemba, debate about Mombasa, and the reinforcement of the 1873 Proclamation had two goals. First, it clarified that the present owners had no legal right to the possession of imported slaves introduced into the Sultan's kingdom after 1873, when Sultan Bargash had agreed to make the import of slaves illegal. Kirk reasoned that since slaves do not marry and have families "not one in ten of the slaves in Zanzibar and Pemba have been born in the islands, nine tenths have certainly been smuggled."[18] Therefore, those illegally imported persons were indeed free. Only those born in Zanzibar and Pemba would remain as slaves. Secondly, Kirk was proposing that the relationships between slaves born in the Sultan's kingdom and their masters should no longer be protected, regulated or recognized by the official legal system of Zanzibar; which, of course, was based on *Sharia* law. It was hoped that over time the relationships between slaves and masters would weaken as the parties gradually went their separate ways or moved into a voluntary situation.

The change of British government policy produced an immediate change in Tucker's overarching strategy when dealing with the operation of the coastal mission stations. Three months after the debate in the Commons which resulted in the declaration that the return of fugitives was illegal (June, 1897), Hardinge, who was opposed to the abolition of slavery, complained to the Foreign Office that the Bishop had given instructions to the missionary in charge of Freretown to "refuse absolutely . . . to surrender, or I believe, even decline to harbor any runaway slaves coming to

---

17. PRO, FO 541/33.
18. Ibid.

the Missions."[19] And four months later he complained again to the Foreign Office that the Bishop has become,

> most aggressive and pugnacious on the slavery question and seems determined, on the strength of the Attorney-General's declaration, to fight the Administration and the Arabs on every issue connected with it, at Mombasa as well as at Rabai.[20]

In the same letter Hardinge informs the Foreign Office that Bishop Tucker had chosen to "interfere" with the Karibu case.

TUCKER'S MISSION POLICY

In the unfolding of the events described above it is possible to see the basic outline of the Bishop's actions and the reversal of his policies based on the position of the British government. Whereas initially he took reluctant and limited action to permit slaves to be returned; he subsequently openly harbored runaways and refused to surrender them. However, a key phrase to understand the internal compass which guided the Bishop's actions in both scenarios can be found in a letter to the Corresponding Secretary of the CMS shortly before the abolition of the legal status of slavery in Zanzibar and Pemba. A survey of missionary opinion was sought by Hardinge as Parliament debated what action might be taken. Tucker wrote, "Feeling that it was our duty to assist the Government as far as we were able I consented to allow those who wished to do so to express their opinion on the subject."[21] Above all other considerations, "duty" to authority was always a heavy counter weight in Tucker's communications; so much so that duty prevailed "as far as we were able" even when the policy of the government was not in keeping with the Bishop's personal religious sensibilities. Rather than disobey, he readily engaged in lengthy and detailed letters to the Consul-General in Zanzibar, the CMS Secretary, or influential friends in England to have policy changed or challenged. Arguing the Karibu case was in keeping with this pattern. But adherence to what Tucker considered his duty often placed the Bishop, along with some of the other English missionaries, in the no man's land between their cornerstone beliefs and

---

19. Hardinge to Foreign Office, Sept. 14, 1897, PRO, FO 881/7032.
20. Hardinge to Salisbury, January 16, 1898, PRO, FO 881/7024.
21. Tucker to Baylis, March 19, 1896, CMSA, G3/A5/O/1896/180.

the imperial government at the time. Even Hardinge noticed the apparent contradiction.

> Mr. Price appointed a missionary at Rabai, with four policemen under his orders, to prevent any runaway slaves from entering the mission settlement ... [These are the ones Bishop Tucker dismissed.] So completely was this practice recognized as right and proper and acquiesced in by the mission that the by-laws of Rabai drawn up conjointly between Sub-Commissioner Pigott and the CMS provide that all runaways shall be detained at the station by the Missionary in charge until he received directions from the District Officer. It is open to Bishop Tucker to protest against the system, but it is not fair of him to create the impression that it is not one in which he and his brother missionaries have for the last seven years acquiesced, and to which the CMS East Africa representatives have solemnly promised to conform.[22]

Sir Arthur wished the missionaries to uphold slavery as a legal custom, pointing out that they had done so in the past. But Bishop Tucker's personal views against slavery are clearly and consistently expressed in correspondence dating from 1890 to 1898, prior to the Karibu case. If Tucker's views are understood in light of the overriding principle of obedience and duty, they are perfectly consistent, even though they appear to change. But they also belie the overall tension in which the Victorian missionary operated.

The abolition of slavery, Tucker wrote, is "a policy so righteous in itself."[23] Tucker was adamantly anti-slavery. So earnestly did he believe in this tenet that he was averse to return runaway slaves finding refuge in Freretown and Rabai. His reprimand of Mr. Jones for harboring runaways was delicately written and due only to pressure from the IBEA administration and coastal slave masters. Instead he hoped that the demand for their return would fade away with time. Almost whimsically, he writes, "I confess I have been indulging such hope that the bitter feelings of the Arabs would die away."[24] Committed to the training of African pastors and teachers at Freretown, his belief in the abilities of the African people to lead their own church was expressed in a rather backwards compliment involving the slavery issue. Tucker felt that the commitment to help the rescued slaves and the effort to train a group of African teachers had been confused together

22. Hardinge to Foreign Office, Sept. 14, 1897, PRO, FO 881/7032.
23. Tucker to Pigott, copied in Tucker to Baylis, Aug. 19, 1895, CMSA, G3/A5/O/1885/279.
24. Tucker to Touch, July 9, 1890, CMSA, G3/A5/O/192.

at Freretown and must now be made distinct. "The rescued slave element is the worst possible material, humanly speaking, that you could have to work upon. If you want native pastors and teachers as the outcome of your work choose the most promising material not the least."[25] The compliment is backwards because referring to human beings as "material" is not exactly recognizing their full status; nevertheless, Tucker was acknowledging that Africans were certainly expected to become leaders in their own church, making their own decisions and deciding their own future.

Tucker tips his hand as to his commitment to the abolition of the slave trade and slavery itself in other correspondence as well. For example, in describing to Mr. Stock his journey through Machakos (near present day Nairobi) he praises the IBEA officer in charge of the territory, "Mr. Ainsworth seems to have done a very good work . . . his influence in the direction of the suppression of the slave trade among the WaKamba has perhaps been the most marked feature."[26]

But most importantly, Tucker's excited letters to Mr. Stock describing the decision of the Ugandan chiefs to emancipate their slaves in the spring of 1893, and his role in this event, which he called "perhaps the most significant event recorded in the modern history of the continent of Africa," are evidence as well to his steady opinion.[27] Tucker was called upon to advise the chiefs and explain what he believed to be the teaching of the Scriptures on the subject of slavery. In his description we see not only his commitment to equality but interestingly enough, his commitment to authority as well.

> I said that without question as long as slaving was the law of the land they were bound to deliver up all runaways and more especially when ordered by the King and Katikiro. I added that if they thought the law a bad one they should try and get it altered. I then told them what I thought about slavery . . . I spoke to them of the law of love, the new Commandment, of Philemon and Onesimus, etc. . . . The movement has begun and none, thank God, can stay it.[28]

Sir Gerald Portal, the first Consul-General to Uganda, had a different interpretation of the emancipation event which he recorded in his private diary, "This seems suspicious, also rather too radical . . . it would make it

---

25. Tucker to Wigram, June 3, 1892, CMSA, G3/A5/O/237.
26. Tucker to Stock, Oct. 26, 1892, CMSA, G3/A5/O/504.
27. Tucker to Stock, April 16, 1893, CMSA, G3/A5/O/232.
28. Ibid.

impossible at first to get any work done by any one, and it is perhaps only a pretext to avoid work on roads, etc., by pleading as excuse no slaves."[29] Nevertheless, Tucker remained quite proud of the document for emancipation, and his role in its creation. A copy was duly sent to CMS headquarters in London, and visitors to his retirement residence in Durham recall seeing a copy hanging on the wall, along with other memorabilia from Uganda.[30]

Taking into account the consistent opinion from the correspondence cited above, but also Tucker's over riding need to operate under existing authorities, it then becomes possible to understand the reason for his seeming reversal, from an initial co-operation with the slavery system to one of outright opposition. The government itself had changed policy and Tucker was then able to follow in this wake.

A VARIETY OF POSITIONS

Tucker solicited a survey from up-country CMS missionaries opposed to slavery to bolster his own view in response to the government request for missionary opinion but there were missionaries and administrators who held views on the opposite end of the spectrum from those of Tucker and his fellow abolitionists. Those who disagreed with the "visionary impracticability of the evangelicals" chose to align themselves more closely to the government's attempt to conform to the existing culture, seeing this path as more realistic and practical.[31] Due to continual pressure from the Anti-Slavery Society, the government's policy became one of gradual emancipation, fearing that radical change would throw the traditional African society and also the Muslim culture on the coast into chaos and rebellion. Sir Gerald Portal, Captain Lugard, and Sir John Kirk were representatives of this position. Bishop Steere, the Universities' Mission Bishop of Zanzibar, had expressed a similar moderated acceptance with a gradual approach to abolition. He writes, "It is one thing to knock the fetters off a man's hand, it is another to free his soul . . . slavery is ingrained in the very nature of the people." Many believed that slavery was deeply embedded in the culture, and could not be eradicated by force until a future time when masters

---

29. Portal, *British Mission*, 227.

30. Hensen, Diary entry, Monday, March 3, 1913, DCL, Tucker Collection, 299, and Tucker to Baylis, April 8, 1893, CMSA, G3/A5/O/173.

31. Collister. *The Last Days*, 139.

and slaves alike could be slowly educated in how to conduct themselves in freedom.[32]

Sir Arthur Hardinge held a more extreme, ultra-traditional position. Being a great admirer of the culture of the East, Hardinge argued, some thought eloquently, to leave the system as it was. Seeing a basis for it in the pages of the Jewish scriptures and the Koran, Hardinge argued that the "Arabs had not been touched by Christianity and western civilization, their political institutions and family life were still that of the Books of Judges and Kings . . . and their ancestor Abraham" and, he pointed out as well, those of St. Paul![33] Lugard was concise on the subject, "An arbitrary and despotic rule, which takes no account of native customs, traditions and prejudices is not suited to the successful development of an infant civilization or, in my view, in accordance with the spirit of British colonial rule."[34]

Hardinge was fond of shining light on the benefits given to a slave under Islamic law; such as the requirement of kindness, the ability of slaves to own slaves, the practice of *"tadbir"* (freeing slaves for divine favor), or the equal inheritance of slave children with the children of the wife. How, Hardinge asked, could it be appropriate for Britain to impose its own sensibilities onto this culture when it worked so well?

Lest it be tempting to categorize Hardinge's opinion as one of enlightenment, his position toward the slaves and the Arabs within the culture that he admired so much was clearly one of degree. He did not believe in educating slaves and just as the Arabs ruled benignly over their slaves, so too those of Hardinge's birth and background were chosen to rule justly over the Arabs and Asians in East Africa. Hardinge's position is still a form of imperialism, though at times it would seem to appear quite accepting and contemporary.

There was no shortage of missionaries who agreed with this approach to leaving the institution of slavery in place. Mr. Binns, the Secretary of the CMS mission on the coast and much longer in the field than Tucker, did not favor emancipation due to the disruption it would cause, such as lack of support of the aged and provision for the young, and cost to the government in compensation to the owners. Although he regretted the return of runaways from his station, he also seemed to agree with Hardinge's over-all acceptance of the system. Binns writes, "good slaves rarely leave

---

32. Bishop Steere in Collister, *The Last Days*, 115.
33. Hardinge to Kimberley, March 28, 1895, PRO, FO 107/43.
34. Lugard, *Rise*, 651.

their masters: a slave runs because he committed theft, was lazy, or had questions with a woman. [I have] never come across a slave who has been cruelly beaten."[35]

As the debate to abolish the legal status of slavery in Zanzibar was gearing up, other CMS missionaries on the coast expressed their opposition, for various reasons, to emancipation as well. Joining Mr. Binns in writing a letter to the government to this effect were Mr. Taylor, Mr. Smith, Miss Grieve and Miss Lockhart.[36] Bishop Tucker objected to the use that Hardinge made of these "weak letters," which the Bishop interpreted as Hardinge attempting to paint the CMS with an anti-emancipation brush.[37]

It was possible to find missionaries both for and against emancipation; just as it was possible to find British administrators for and against. But a third position is also evident from the archives—that of compromise and tension; of accommodating practice against conscience. It might even be appropriate to call this position one of half-belief.

A further illustration of the tension of operating between two opposing views can be seen in the fact that Freretown was obligated by agreement with the government to receive liberated slaves rescued from the slave ships by the patrol off the coast, but not encouraged to harbor those who liberated themselves.[38] The fact that domestic slavery still existed legally in the Sultan's dominions was in itself a middle position cobbled by the government; which was, like the missionaries, straddling two positions. On the one hand, the dominions of the Sultan were regarded as an independent kingdom to be treated as partners, and on the other attempts were strongly made to force the Sultan to conform to the mores of Europe. It is not surprising that the missionaries walked with a similar stutter-step.

Other English missionaries in East Africa shared Bishop Tucker's tight rope walk. Favoring freedom and equality for African slaves, the Free Methodist missionaries took a clear position and protested consistently the return of runaway slaves to their masters. Even so, they felt compelled to carry out their return. However, they did so "with the greatest reluctance."[39] The other missionary groups in East Africa, The Universities Mission, the Roman Catholic mission, and German Protestant Missionaries, also felt

---

35. Quoted in Hardinge to Kimberley, Sept. 14, 1897, PRO, FO 107/43.
36. Tucker to Baylis, March 19, 1896, CMSA, G3/A5/O/1896/180.
37. Ibid.
38. Lang to Tucker, August 12, 1892, CMSA, G3/A5/L6/378.
39. Hardinge to Lord Kimberly, Sept 14, 1897, PRO, FO 107/43.

compelled to refuse runaways, sending them instead for hearings before the IBEA magistrate.[40]

Bishop Tucker was actively walking the same tight rope between these two positions a full four years before taking the Karibu case, when he wrote a letter of inquiry to Consul General Hardinge about the status of the rescued slaves at Freretown.[41] Tucker was obviously seeking to untangle all the various legislation, passed incrementally over the years, and to understand how it applied to the conglomerate of people residing with the mission; some of whom were from parts of Africa where slavery had already been abolished, such as Uganda. Others from African decent were born in India. And more confusingly, some were freed by HM Consulate General, some by IBEA, some inland, and some at the coast. It is safe to say that Tucker had familiarized himself with all of the various categories and therefore when he heard the story of Keri Karibu it was readily apparent to him that in light of the recent changes in government policy, coupled with the long-term legislation, he had a case that could not only highlight the cause of abolition but perhaps free him from the tension between his ideals and his government and bring final legal closure to returning runaway slaves.

THE KARIBU CASE

The first mention of the Karibu case to the CMS comes early in the year 1898, only one week after Hardinge mentioned it in a correspondence to the Foreign Office but one month after it began.[42] Embedded as the seventh point in a long letter, Tucker gives the details of how he became involved in the whole situation. The runaway slave, Keri Karibu, did not approach Bishop Tucker on the street and plead for his help. Rather it was Mr. Parker, a newly arrived missionary just starting his ministry in Mombasa to whom the girl ran, clinging to him and asking for protection from her master's representative who was publicly threatening to strangle her. Mr. Parker then escorted the girl to the mission house where the Bishop was engaged in a discussion with Mr. and Mrs. Burt. It was here that Tucker had the opportunity to hear the details of her position in the quiet of the mission house, weigh the possibilities and decide in a rather considered way if the

---

40. Ibid.

41. Hardinge to Pugott, August 29, 1894, and Lord Kimberly to Hardinge, November 15, 1894, PRO, FO 881/6538.

42. Tucker to Baylis, January 25, 1898, CMSA, G3/A5/O/1898/8.

situation could be used to force an examination of the status of slavery in Mombasa and the coast and ultimately move toward a more rapid acceptance of total abolition. In the last line of the explanation to Mr. Baylis of the CMS he writes, "The case is one which may possibly affect the position of thousands of slaves."[43] Tucker was no exception to the Victorian missionary propensity to "think big and build largely."[44]

The arguments in support of the legal case of Keri Karibu v. Sheik Uwe were written by Tucker and presented to the IBEA magistrate who operated under the auspices of the Sultan of Zanzibar. Bishop Tucker extrapolated the arguments from his understanding of the existing slave legislation, reasoning for the freedom of Keri Karibu and delineating the following points of argument:[45]

> 1. Heri Karibu is a fugitive slave asking for her freedom. Upon the word of the Attorney General in a telegram dated June 27th, 1897 to the Commissioner for the East Africa Protectorate a British subject is breaking the law if he restores a fugitive slave to his or her master. Therefore it is against the law for the British citizens of the court to order Keri Karibu to return to her so called owner.
>
> 2. Mr. G.S. Mackenzie's proclamation of May 1, 1890 declared that inland tribes, including the Wakamba of which Miss Karibu was a member, were under the protection of the Company and could not be held as slaves. Even though she was sold into slavery before this proclamation, it should be retroactive as there is nothing in the document that says it is not; and in the Company's original treaty with the inland tribes' freedom was guaranteed. It is morally reprehensible not to make it so.
>
> 3. Heri Karibu was brought from the mainland to the Island of Mombasa in contravention of the Sultan of Zanzibar's Treaty with Great Britain dated June 5, 1873 which outlawed the import of fresh slaves from the mainland of Africa.
>
> 4. Her importation was also in violation of the decrees of April 18, 1876 which reinforced the one of 1873; prohibiting the import of fresh slaves to the coastal districts and the movement of slaves by land within the coastal area.

---

43. Ibid. Also see Tucker to Fox, Feb. 23, 1898, and April 10, 1898, BGCA, 135/1/2.
44. Warren, "The Church Militant Abroad," in Symondson, *Victorian Crisis*, 60.
45. Tucker, "The Case of Heri Karibu," February 2, 1898, CMSA, G3/A5/O/46.

5. There was physical evidence of cruelty. And the greatest cruelty of all was to extort a monthly fee from her knowing that her only recourse was prostitution.

Even before knowing what the decision of the hearing would be, Tucker was positioning himself for an appeal. First he wrote to the CMS and asked if, in the case of a negative decision, they would support a continuance of the case even though he would be relocating to Uganda. Whether he meant by this question financial backing or even a barrister to be sent, seems to be a question lurking in the background. Secondly, he quickly began to set the stage for an appeal by finding fault with the Sub-Commissioner who heard the case, Mr. Cranfield, on the grounds that he was not a lawyer and was completely hampered by his position within the administration and the need not to make waves. The Bishop also arranged the outline of the argumentation in such a way as to separate the points of law from the facts of the case. This also was done, he stated, in order to set up a subsequent appeal, if necessary. It appears from the planning and determination given to this case that Tucker was intending to make an impact and was determined not to let that possible impact slip away easily.

Despite the detailed legal brief that Tucker presented, the outcome of the case (which reached him three months later in Uganda) was decided on a single point: that Keri Karibu was not born in Zanzibar but a "raw" slave imported from the inland territories after the Sultan's Proclamation of April 18, 1876 prohibiting the import of slaves to the Coast, Zanzibar and Pemba. Tucker was pleased with the result as it meant that the "majority of slaves now held as such in Mombasa and the coast district of the East African Protectorate are illegally in bondage."[46] He apparently agreed with Kirk's earlier assessment that most of the slaves in Mombasa were not born there. But he also sought to press home the implication of the ruling. Some of the major objections to the abolition of the legal status of slavery in Mombasa and the coast district, which was Tucker's true objective, came from those who felt that the compensation to slave owners (which the abolition of the legal status would require) would be too great due to the length of time slavery had been legal in the area, and the great numbers of legal slaves there as a result. But this ruling reduced the number of legally held slaves greatly, meaning no compensation would be required in those cases, and

---

46. Tucker to Allen, June 20, 1898, CMSA, G3/A5/O/1898/151.

therefore the amount that abolition would cost Her Majesty's government by "many thousands of pounds."⁴⁷

With this encouragement Tucker agreed with the Secretaries of the CMS who advised a question on the matter should be brought before the Parliament. Tucker seems to shift his direction from an appeal scenario to a debate tactic. Tucker was a master at adapting to the most direct and practical route to accomplish his goal; it did not have to be the one of least resistance. He devised the question to be asked, "Has a slave who repudiates the condition of servitude in which he finds himself no remedy in a Court presided over by a British subject holding the Queen's Commission in a country like British East Africa where the whole administration is carried on in the name of Her majesty?" ("The deputation is even being taken on paper embossed with the Royal Arms."⁴⁸) A "no" answer would incense the public leading to a clamor for it to be so; and a "yes" answer would result in practical emancipation, Tucker's goal. Other questions which Tucker proposed were, "What does the government propose to do to make this decision [of the Karibu case] operative?" Or, "Now that the chief objection to emancipation has been removed, what does the government propose?" But ten years were to elapse before questions of this nature were indeed asked in Parliament.

Although pleased with the immediate result of the Mombasa ruling, Tucker also had lingering objections which rankled. The judgment gave Keri Karibu her freedom and made a way for money to be saved, but it had not done away with the legal status of slavery—and this objective continued to command his untiring focus. His first objection was that although the ruling conceded that she was a raw slave it refused to acknowledge that she was a fugitive slave. It was quite clear in Tucker's mind that Ms. Karibu had run away from her master and sought to dissolve the existing relationship. Yet this did not seem to be possible under the present arrangement which led to a contradictory position, as Tucker pointed out, for English judges. Contrary to the common law of England, they found themselves helping to deprive people of their liberty against their will.

> "The Judge apparently contends that he can do as a Judge that which as a British subject he is precluded from doing. It seems to me however that the Judge is absolutely unable to rid himself of his obligations and responsibilities as a British subject . . . he is

---

47. Tucker to Fox, March 5, 1898, CMSA, G3/A5/O/1898/87.
48. Tucker to Allen, CMSA, G3/A5/O/1898/151.

precluded from ordering a slave who appeals to him for protection back into servitude."[49]

Exactly the conundrum the missionaries had found themselves in for some twenty years.

Tucker's second objection revolved around the fact that Keri Karibu's so-called owner was demanding payment of four rupees per month from his slave in exchange for her freedom to live independently. The payment was quite commonly obtained by prostitution. The court, rather than challenge this arrangement, ordered the girl to go back to her master's house if she did not wish to pay the fee. Tucker objected to this approach because Sheik Uwe offered no service or product in exchange for the payment—simply her continued liberty. "It was a defection of the girl's liberty by a British subject acting in the name of the Queen."[50] It is curious that Tucker did not use the Sultan's proclamation of December 9, 1888 which ruled that it was illegal to hire out one's slave to another party and receive their pay. Perhaps this would be to admit that Miss Karibu was involved in a lifestyle which would not have been flattering to the CMS, especially since she had been given refuge in the mission house!

The name of Keri Karibu never appears again in the Tucker archive. Before leaving the coast for his new responsibilities in Uganda the Bishop made arrangements with Mr. Binns "so that steps might be taken for the rescue of the former slave from her life of sin and I also wrote to Mrs. Pickthall in Mombasa asking her . . . to try and get hold of her to win her for Christ. . . . I have done what I honestly thought was right."[51] Mr. Hardinge, after extensive letters on the subject and wearied of the whole matter wrote flatly,

> "Now that Bishop Tucker is about to sever his connection with this part of his former diocese, it may be hoped that the last echoes of this wearisome controversy will die away. A new Bishop, who ought to have learnt in India to tolerate alien deed and social customs, has to deal with a new situation . . . it is not too much to ask of their future chief that he shall use the victory won with moderation."[52]

49. Ibid.
50. Ibid.
51. Tucker to Fox, April 10, 1898, BGCA, 135/1/2.
52. Hardinge to Lord Kimberly, February 9, 1899, PRO, FO 881/7400.

The legal status of slavery in Mombasa and the coast was not finally abolished until 1907. Domestic slavery continued in the coastal belt well after World War I. When the British took over the German territory, the terms in the mandate were to eliminate domestic slavery "as social conditions will allow" but even then servitude in various forms and in various places (such as Mafia Island) continued almost to World War II.[53]

SUMMARY AND CONCLUSION

Although pressed with the administration of a very large diocese and arrangements for a caravan to Uganda, Bishop Tucker took time to present arguments before the IBEA magistrate for the runaway slave Keri Karibu. The time invested and the tenacity of the Bishop on the subject was evidence to the importance that it held for him as he hoped it would lead quickly to the abolition of the legal status of slavery in Mombasa and the coast. But as was apparent through the many years of negotiations, the abolition of slavery in the Sultan's independent dominions in East Africa, would prove to be slow and tedious. Some residents, administrators and even missionaries were opposed to the abolition of slavery for a variety of reasons. Some preferred a gradual elimination of the practice, and others, such as Tucker, were "visionary impractical evangelicals" seeking the immediate conclusion of all forms of slavery.[54] The implications for the missionaries living and working among such mixed opinions and approaches tended to be confusing, resulting in compromise and tension. Bishop Tucker presided over an inconsistent, reluctant and weak acquiescence with the local practice of slavery, and the gradualist approach of the Foreign Office to abolition. However, relentless pressure towards abolition finally resulted in the elimination of the legal status of slavery on the islands of Zanzibar and Pemba. In addition, statements from the Attorney General against the return of fugitives, and the reinforcement of the Sultan's Proclamation of 1876 banning the import of "raw" slaves gave Bishop Tucker an impetus to take the Karibu case and use it to push for the legal status of slavery to be abolished in Mombasa and the coast, as well. Although consistently holding an abolitionist's opinion, Tucker was constrained by duty to an imperial British administration—and an Arab one as well. His actions against slavery became uncompromising only after the momentum at home made it somewhat acceptable to do so.

53. Beachey, *The Slave Trade of Eastern Africa*, 205.
54. Collister, *The Last Days of Slavery*, 139.

He then moved quickly from passive resistance, to the harboring of slaves and refusal to surrender runaways, to the active fight in a colonial courtroom. Although Tucker's advocacy was successful and Keri Karibu was given her freedom, he was not successful in his larger goal. The legal status of slavery continued on until 1907, well after Bishop Tucker had left the area for his duties in Uganda. In the slavery debate, the official government view and cultural mind-set of imperialism was continuously resisted and challenged by abolitionists within the Foreign Office and outside it as well. But, like a governor to a gasoline engine, the administration controlled the pace of change and the Sultan alone possessed the key to turn the engine off. The abolitionist missionaries, such as Tucker, could only ride along, periodically dragging their feet.

CHAPTER FIVE

Mission and Church
Struggle Within

As Alfred Tucker turned his attention towards Uganda and his new position as the first Bishop of the Ugandan Church, his focus would be drawn away from Mombasa and the various challenges associated with the coastal mission such as the organization of Freretown, the slave trade, the struggle to build a memorial church to the late Bishops Hannington and Parker, the spiritual needs of the growing British expatriate population and the frequent preparation for long treks inland to perform episcopal visitation to the interior mission churches. Matters in Uganda were apparently pressing, as the former Bishop did not linger in Mombasa to welcome or receive the new man appointed to take over from him as Bishop of Mombasa, William G. Peel, a missionary priest with long years of experience in India. Leaving Mombasa just five months after the division of the diocese was confirmed by the CMS General Committee (October 1897) and a full year and three months before Peel was even consecrated (June 1899), Tucker had already accomplished five visitation tours in his new diocese before the Archbishop of Canterbury sent seals, Letters of Orders, and the boundaries of the two new dioceses (October 11, 1899). Another additional visitation in Uganda was completed before Peel even arrived in Mombasa on December 18, 1899. Tucker wasted no time and seemed more than ready to leave behind the cares of the coast mission where he labored within a well-established Muslim milieu. Instead he surged forward to embrace the exciting possibilities of the Uganda mission with its high profile and vibrant "native" church.[1] He had expressed his frustration regarding Mombasa: "At the coast in days gone by we have gone on the principle of how *not* to do things and the greater part of one's time and strength is given up to undoing the doings of past days."[2] In contrast a notation in the CMS Précis Book reads: "no country or mission calls forth so much sympathy from Christians in England as the Uganda mission does and has done so far."[3] Missionaries from other sections of the diocese complained:

> I sometimes think that we who live here on the coast get little sympathy from the church at home; all their sympathy seems to be given to such missions as Uganda, which can speak of hundreds of converts and thousands of inquirers. I remember when I was at home, on one or two occasions when on deputation work, being asked if I came from Uganda, and upon my answering "no" there seemed to be very little interest in anything I had to say.[4]

Even if Bishop Tucker could shed his direct oversight of the Mombasa mission so happily his connection with the Church Missionary Society would not be set aside so easily. Not that Tucker wished for his dual responsibilities as Director of the CMS mission, and Bishop of the church created by that mission, to be dissolved in any way. With the change in personnel that the diocesan division would bring, the CMS Committee suggested that the time may be opportune to separate the position of Bishop from Director.[5] Tucker resisted this suggestion vigorously, seeing it as "a vote of want of confidence."[6] The discussion of the Committee on the subject failed to materialize into any action due to a clarifying report offered by Tucker's longtime friend, commissary and General Secretary of the CMS (1895–1910) Henry Elliott Fox. Fox explained that in fields such as Ceylon, Palestine, or even the initial contact with Usagara in what is now central Tanzania, the local Secretary acted as the Director or chief representative of the CMS Parent Committee, as in those settings the office of bishop was either non-existent or was a Colonial Bishop, completely independent of

---

1. This term is used consistently in all CMS communication as is "Native Church Council," the governing board of the indigenous church.
2. Tucker to Baylis, February 11, 1895, CMSA, G3/A5/O/61. See also Tucker to Fox, September 9, 1896, CMSA, G3/A5/O/272.
3. CMSA, G3 A7 P 1898–1907, 2.
4. Harry Kerr Binns, CMS Annual Report, 1898, 99.
5. Tucker to Fox, December 9, 1896, BGCA, Collection 135, 1-1.
6. Tucker to Fox, December 19, 1896, BGCA.

the mission. But where there was a CMS Missionary Bishop, such as in Yoruba, Niger, or Kiu-Shiu, the bishop was the Director of the Mission.[7] The desire to separate the two positions provides evidence that the CMS Committee in London recognized the confusion created by the insertion of the position of Director, which was only accommodated sporadically by the committee-based CMS structure.

However, Tucker's desire for continuance was not an indication that his relationship with the CMS headquarters was without difficulty. The partnership started well and ended well but the archives are filled with attempts to solve differences of opinion, confusion, competing approaches to ministry, lack of procedural guidelines, and difficulties. The letters are also punctuated with frustration and flashes of emotion. The tension between home and field, between mission and church was sometimes so acute that on four different occasions, and under four different sets of circumstances, Tucker offered to resign his post!

The first offer came only two years into his episcopate when CMS challenged his habit of openly articulating independent direction for the mission without consulting the home office. Tucker responded with equal irritation, that the CMS was making policy without consulting the Bishop of the diocese affected or the Director with on the spot insight. In 1892 he wrote concerning his desire to open new interior stations: "The Church Missionary Society under God was the instrument of my being called to this work in East Africa. It has only to intimate to me that its confidence is gone and the reins shall at once be laid down."[8]

One year later a similar offer was penned in reference to government inquiries into questionable behavior amongst the missionaries under his supervision:

> My chief ground of complaint is the state of utter ignorance in which I have been kept as to affairs in Uganda. So much do I feel this that I am constrained to say deliberately that if this state of things is to continue I must decline all responsibility and ask leave to resign my charge.[9]

---

7. Fox, "On the Directorship of the East Africa Mission," March 22, 1897, CMSA, GY A7 1/5.

8. Tucker to Wigram, July 4, 1892, CMSA, G3/A5/O/277.

9. Tucker to Baylis, January 20, 1893, CMSA, G3/A5/O/247.

Six years later, in the midst of the long drawn out procedure to divide the diocese and simultaneously negotiate sticking points in the constitution for the Ugandan church he wrote to Fox:

> Sometimes it feels that my duty is to say at once that the considerations which I have mentioned and especially that which has reference to the constitution, make it impossible for me to continue to hold my present position here . . . I have been strongly tempted at times to end it all by writing to the Archbishop and to the Committee to the effect that it is my duty to resign whatever position I hold here, if indeed I hold any, as soon as possible.[10]

And finally, four years later, after being promised certain boundaries for the new diocese and subsequently given different ones, he wrote privately to his friend, Mrs. Carus-Wilson: "I have told them [CMS] that if nothing can be done to undo this wrong I shall ask to be relieved of my charge out here. I cannot be responsible for the Church of Uganda when 'bribed, cabined and confined.'"[11]

PREVIOUS TENSIONS

The tension between the Episcopacy and CMS was not new on the scene in Tucker's time. In fact, various disputes had been played out across the empire since the 1830's, some fifty years before Tucker's tenure.[12] For example, Bishop Wilson of Calcutta (1832–1858) engaged in a controversy with the CMS over his right as a bishop to license and place clergy, even if they were recruited and paid for by CMS. This controversy would culminate in the famous "Norgate Case" in Calcutta in which the bishop reassigned a priest terminated by the CMS over the objections of the local Finance Committee. Venn, then General Secretary of the CMS attempted to offer a solution; writing "Appendix to the 39th Report," a set of guidelines which sought to bring CMS more in line with episcopal order. However, Archbishop A.B. Howley would be forced to intervene in order to bring a final decision, reinforcing the unlimited power of a diocesan bishop to revoke licenses and assign priests to particular places rather than using a blanket license for the whole diocese.

---

10. Tucker to Fox, September 15, 1899, CMSA, GAC 4/29/5675.
11. Tucker to Carus-Wilson, September 20, 1903, BGCA, Acc. 135/1–2.
12. Yates, *Venn and Victorian Bishops Abroad*, 22.

Other disagreements arose between CMS and Bishop Selwyn (appointed in 1841) in New Zealand over who would have the authority to terminate and supervise diocesan personnel. When the CMS Parent Committee in London overrode the local Finance Committee and terminated a surveyor they felt was overcharging, Selwyn objected to the interference, threatening to refrain from ordaining any further CMS candidates for ordination. CMS responded with a threat to withhold funds.[13] A compromise was reached by inviting the bishop to become chair of the Finance Committee and subsequently make joint decisions on such matters. However, a further disagreement over Selwyn's strict educational requirements for priests caused the CMS to organize a second and separate diocese, with more localized requirements, to enable Maori candidates to overcome the slow rate of progress toward leadership in the church.

Yet again in Madras, Bishop Spencer (1837–1849) tangled with the local Finance Committee of the CMS over their dismissal of W. T. Humphrey, a missionary who felt the structure and organization of the CMS needed to be reformed along high church lines.[14] Spencer objected to the dismissal on the grounds that the CMS was infringing on his prerogative, to evaluate fitness for ministry, and held to the belief that the CMS could not dismiss a missionary without the Bishop's permission. The CMS contended that it had the right as patron to withdraw finances from a missionary without questioning his priesthood, the rationale being that the missionary was an employee of CMS and could be terminated while not affecting the missionary's ordained status. The matter was eventually referred to the Archbishop who found that both sides had valid points, Humphrey was disconnected as a CMS employee, but the bishop still retained the right to give him an assignment in his diocese.

Other controversies surfaced in America, Australia, and New Zealand regarding the source of authority to supervise CMS missionaries. Did such authority derive from the colonial legislature and associated with government granted territory (called a Colonial Episcopate), or was it derived from a "consensual compact" among the associated congregations? (called a Missionary Bishop).[15] Eventually the stalemate was settled in favor of the latter by the actions of the Colonial bishops who consecrated a missionary bishop for Capetown without the consent of any legislature.

13. Ibid., 60.
14. Ibid., 78.
15. Ibid., 93.

Of course the most famous controversy arose in Sierra Leone between Bishop Crowther, the first African bishop, and his relationship with the CMS missionaries.[16] When CMS missionary Henry Townsend opposed the CMS appointment of an African Bishop (was he a missionary or part of the settled church?), Henry Venn, then Honorary Secretary, quickly deserted his low-church views of bishops who were elected from the grass-roots, in order to support the appointment of Crowther, preceding a fully formed church. Similar struggles between the CMS and episcopal oversight would play out in China and Madagascar as well which escalated to the attention of the Archbishop, highlighting rocky relations and differing viewpoints. These differing viewpoints find their genesis in the very beginnings of the CMS.

TWO ENDS OF THE CHRISTIAN STICK

The Church Missionary Society, began only eight years after the death of John Wesley. It was initiated by the evangelicals of the Church of England who were inspired by Wesley's ministry to the poor and disenfranchised. The beginning focus for the fledgling society was the spiritual needs of West Africa. The pioneer figures were "an older type of Anglican Evangelical who cared little for ecclesiastical regularity and [who] had many brushes with authority."[17] Its main goal was to extend the Gospel and not necessarily the church. Although the next generation of CMS leaders could not so easily separate these two things, the society still maintained a legacy from its evangelical roots—concern for individual conversion, pietism, a deep mistrust of bishops and a long tradition of rule by committee. The mission society had a reputation for dealing with bishops brought up through their own ranks "with a rod of iron."[18] Although Tucker was already a priest before his formal association with the CMS began, still he was selected and sent out to be a bishop by the CMS, and the attitude can be detected in letters from Robert Lang, the Corresponding Secretary (1882 to 1892) who wrote to Tucker with a slightly terse but revealing request:

> In the course of this morning's interview at the Company's office a copy of your letter to Mr. Portal was shown referring to the state

---

16. Ibid., 143.
17. Walls, "Missionary Vocation," 145.
18. Oliver, *Missionary Factor*, 12.

of things in Uganda, and suggesting that there ought to be a British representative there, which letter had reached them through the Foreign Office. We should be very much obliged if you could kindly let us have copies of all letters on political subjects which you find it necessary to write to the local officials.[19]

Even though the society was based in the center of empire and directed from there using imperial patterns, the organization had a more egalitarian mind-set. The CMS was administered by a committee, chaired by the General Secretary, who directed day to day operations, much as a Chief Executive Officer would do so today. The General Committee (also called the Parent Committee) was responsible for overall policy. Under the General Committee were various committees responsible for specialty areas such as medical, finance, and candidates. The Committee of Correspondence was one of these, overseeing three sub-committees relating to areas of the world where CMS maintained a presence—one of these was the Africa Group. Some serving on these committees were clergy, but the majority were prominent laity, well-connected and able to represent the goals of the CMS in various quarters of society, such as business and government. One of the founding principles of the Society was to keep clergy from dominating the organization. Hand in hand with this resistance was also an enduring tendency to keep a healthy distance from diocesan structure, also dominated by clergy. Clergy serving in other parts of the globe where CMS had a presence took note of this distancing: "For fifteen years I have been quite unaware that CMS had a policy which included such clear suspicion of and distrust in the diocesan set-up. It runs counter to all that I have believed in and have been working for during these years."[20] Creating a diocese in the mission field was often seen as an encumbrance to missionaries of the evangelical wing of the church.[21] The CMS saw itself as a manifestation of an idealized type of Christianity which drew its inspiration from interpretations of the primitive church of the New Testament: egalitarian with shared leadership, not necessarily tied to English church

---

19. Lang to Tucker, May 9, 1892, CMSA, G3/A5/L6/312.

20. Gurney to Milford, April 21, 1953, CMSA, AS/59/G2/E1/12/51–11/54. Also Rhodes, "The Anglican Church in Egypt, 1936–1956," Diss, University of Birmingham 2005, 194.

21. Cox, *Imperial Fault Lines*, 97.

structures, providing spiritual help for the poor in Africa who were brothers-to-be, promoting indigenous churches who were to be self-governed, self-supporting, self-propagating.

The CMS structure in Africa, as well, was also not to be dominated by a hierarchy but administered by a committee called the Finance Committee, chaired by a Secretary who kept the records and corresponded with the Parent Committee at home. Originally the Finance Committee consisted of all missionaries serving in the field. But as the work increased, it gradually evolved to include only senior missionaries. Various committees sometimes developed as local need required, such as translation, medical, or ladies work.

By contrast, the church actually taking shape in East Africa under the auspices of the CMS was an organization directed primarily by a hierarchy, and a clerical one at that. The structure modelled after the English church at home, with Bishops, Archdeacons, dioceses, and central administration, had its roots in Roman Empire bureaucracy. Just as the first century infant church had evolved into the official religion of empire, so the English church also maintained an official relationship with the state; with Bishops who were granted a seat in the House of Lords. So in this case the pattern of empire was reversed; the London based headquarters, while being very directive of local affairs, also maintained a very egalitarian approach, arriving at decisions in consensus.

The Diocese of Eastern Equatorial Africa was initiated three years before the presence of the British government in the form of the chartered Imperial British East Africa Company (1884). It did not have an official relationship with the government, still the pattern was set in the minds of the British administrators. For example, all letters to Tucker from the various residents in East Africa were addressed to "My Lord Bishop" as was the pattern in the Church of England, even though Tucker held no seat in the African administration and was "Lord" of no physical territory. At the same time the East African church followed a hierarchical pattern of administration, answering to the Archbishop of Canterbury regarding changes to the diocesan borders, warrants and licenses for ordination, the appointment of new bishops, communion regulations, etc. Bishop Tucker attended the Lambeth gatherings of all Anglican bishops in London in 1897 and 1908 as the Victorian church was comfortable being ruled from the center in a very familiar top-down organization. In this it reflected the style and mind-set of empire.

MISSION AND CHURCH

The two opposing philosophies and operating styles of an egalitarian-minded mission and a centralized imperial-style church produced a great deal of tension during Tucker's tenure as bishop. Having to operate in official positions in both organizations, as a Bishop and as Director of the CMS efforts in East Africa, Tucker did not have the luxury of keeping a low profile or operating independently while having a private opinion. A further complication in the dimensions of Tucker's role lies in the fact that he was also enfolded within the structure of the emerging native church; a phenomenon that would not be repeated once Africans filled the office of bishop.

LINES OF AUTHORITY

An example of the tension between mission and church can be detected in the correspondence regarding lines of authority. Much confusion arose around the questions of who was entitled to make decisions or to be informed regarding various pieces of information. Who was to be responsible to instruct missionaries, give them direction, or design structure—the Director of the Mission answering to the Committee of the CMS or the Bishop of the Diocese answering to the Archbishop of Canterbury?

CMS, aspiring to an idealized concept of rule by committee, was uncomfortable with any possible authority that a bishop might wield within the organization. Evidence of this stance came early in Tucker's tenure, only six months after his arrival in Mombasa to take up his duties. After an initial meeting with the missionaries who worked in the Usagara region on his way to visit Uganda, Tucker requested copies of all future official correspondence to and from the missionaries in that field to be sent to him. The CMS responded:

> The Bishop's request in the Paragraph on Official Correspondence is a right and rational request. But [we] thought it well to indicate that it is as Director of the Mission (in that capacity, that is, to which the Committee has entrusted administration of responsibilities) that this request for copies of official correspondence is rightly made. Not as Diocesan: the relation of the Diocesan to his clergy in the Diocese providing in itself no such claim. We are sure you will understand that there is nothing personal in this remark.[22]

---

22. Lang to Tucker, November 10, 1890, CMSA, G3/A5/L6/42.

A similar distinction was made two years later when, instructed by the CMS, Tucker set up an initial Finance Committee in the Ugandan part of the mission. This time with a more pointed reference to lines of authority:

> With regard to Uganda, we have been revising the letter of instructions given to our missionaries for that field, as to their being under the authority of the Finance Committee...we have told the men that the local representation will be, 'The Bishop, *as Director of the Mission* [emphasis mine] and the Finance Committee.' But with regard to the channel of Communication with the Parent Committee, we thought it sufficient to say the Finance Committee should be the channel. We of course shall try on our part to send you all necessary copies of our correspondence, and shall be prepared to tell the Finance Committee that they must keep you informed[23]

While keeping the lines of communication through the committee structure, the CMS did give additional power to the position of the director as an appeal step for missionaries who were unhappy with decisions made by the Finance Committee when the director was not present due to travel. This was a compromise by the CMS in order to "secure clear authority" to the director as their representative in the field.[24] Prior to this the usual appeal went from committee to committee up the ladder of authority.

The Finance Committees of the East Africa mission—Mombasa, Uganda, and Usagara—were not consistent in following through with the directive to "keep you informed" by copying official letters to the Director/Bishop. While consistently remaining within the organization, Tucker pressed the CMS structure toward a slightly more imperial style of administration, one in which the director would act similarly to a colonial governor representing the home government and having executive authority. During a trip home by Tucker (October 1893 to July 1894) with face to face communication with the Committee, a second memoranda was sent out to all Secretaries of the East African Mission reminding them to send copies of minutes and official letters to the Director.[25] An additional instruction went one step further saying that the Director should also be acquainted with any proposals of importance before they are brought before the Fi-

---

23. Baylis to Tucker, June 10, 1893, CMSA, G3/A5/L6/499.
24. Ibid.
25. Memo to Secretaries of East African Mission, February 16, 1894, CMSA, G3/A5/7/121.

nance Committee or higher committees.²⁶ This surprising last directive indicates that Tucker must have been persuasive face to face in arguing for more authority for himself. His travels to all the mission stations in the East Africa mission gave him a wider perspective of the whole effort with an ability to prioritize initiatives unavailable to regular missionaries. The idealistic committee-led CMS structure compromised at the insistence of Tucker and began to bend slightly toward an empire mode of operation.

In light of this confusion the Parent Committee conducted a review of policy regarding directors in other fields. A third memoranda on the subject shows that such a review was made, and a decision to allow even more authority to the director was incorporated:

> The enclosed copies of letters . . . will convey to you all the formal business decisions of the Committee with regard to East Africa since you left England. You will notice that by this mail instructions are sent to each of the Secretaries in the Mission to *give effect in your absence to any decision you may arrive at* [emphasis mine] in accordance with the Minutes of October 7, 1884, November 2, 1888 and July 30, 1889, which are the Minutes previously passed defining the authority of the Director.²⁷

Not only was the Finance Committee to keep the Director/Bishop informed, they were also obligated to carry out his decisions even while he was in another part of the diocese in the interim of any appeal to the Parent Committee. Yet these directives and intentions did not become reality in the field. The Parent Committee continued to operate as if the lines of authority went from central committee to local committee, with no role for a director, except as a member of the local committee. Tucker complained bitterly and concisely about the persistent tendency to ignore what he perceived to be his function—the ability to direct and to represent the Parent Committee. Upon receiving copies of instructions to the Secretary of the mission in Usagara he writes:

> I have the right to veto all or any of their [Finance Committee] proceedings . . . And yet except an incidental reference to myself which looks almost like an afterthought, there is no hint of its being the duty of the Finance Committee to consult and refer to me in any wise. I am supposed to be the chairman . . . I shall be glad if

---

26. CMS to Smith, Feb. 16, 1894, CMSA, G3/A5/L7/114 and G3/A5/L7/121.

27. Baylis to Tucker, August 3, 1894, CMSA, G3/A5/L7/187, also CMS to Binns, August 8, 1894, CMSA, G3/A5/L7/186.

you will kindly take an early opportunity of making it quite clear to the Usagara Finance Committee that as long as I am Director of the Mission, charged with solemn responsibility by the Parent Committee, I expect to be consulted in all matters affecting the general work of the Mission.[28]

Tucker put his finger on the pulse of the problem when he referenced the muddled duties of a local Finance Committee and a Bishop/Director:

You say that the duty of the Finance Committee is to take a general oversight of the work and workers in the district. No reference whatever is made to my responsibility in the matter of oversight, as Bishop (or even as Director of the Mission.) There might be no Bishop at work in the field, so far as your letter is concerned. There is no mention made of my responsibility and how it touches the responsibility of the Finance Committee on the matter of oversight.[29]

Tucker did not object to the simple oversights of the Finance Committees but felt that they sometimes lacked experience discerning direction and placement of personnel, especially ordained personnel. He was always very defensive of his status and protective of his authority. Also typical of his personality, he strongly refused to give ground on this point, pressing for clarity and asking for "a further statement of the relation of the Finance Committee to myself both as Bishop and also as Director of the Mission."[30] His final testy statement on the subject was a colorful flourish: "it would be well if some of our workers before they come out could have it impressed upon them that ours is a *Church Missionary Society*."[31]

The Parent Committee also held their ground and continued to insist that they must be trusted to administer the work through the Finance Committee in the absence of the director and only seek his advice when they needed additional insight; reiterating their promise to keep him informed.[32] They also recommitted to the procedure that any of Tucker's instructions to the Finance Committee would be carried out in the interim while the Parent Committee was consulted, but the Parent Committee retained final say in all mission related business. But the most revealing

---

28. Tucker to Baylis, February 17, 1896, CMSA, G3/A5/O/114.
29. Ibid.
30. Ibid.
31. Ibid.
32. Baylis to Tucker, April 24, 1896, CMSA, G3/A5/7/494.

Mission and Church

request came in relation to executive authority vs. committee authority. Baylis, the Corresponding Secretary, writes:

> When you are on the spot there is the question of your authority as Director, the only thing we should wish to ask being that you would, as far as possible, exercise that authority constitutionally, through the Finance Committee, who should act under your direction just as they would under that of the Parent Committee.[33]

Sounding slightly like a warning to use executive authority with a light touch, the CMS voiced their concern about heavy-handedness. It was a theme that was to resurface at regular intervals throughout Tucker's tenure, especially in private letters from H. E. Fox. For example, during the creation of the constitution for the Ugandan church he writes: "Constitutions cannot be constructed autocratically [but with] the cordial assent of all who are to be working parties ... we have been relying much upon the result of your influence over the conferences ... difficulties might be met with concession."[34] And also the same tendency was addressed by Fox one year later: "A Director is not an autocrat ... but the very extent of his power implies that he will use it only aportionately, (sic) and as far as possible on the official lines of the Society's working."[35]

It is not surprising that this concern would be fresh in the minds of the CMS General Committee given that a six-year power struggle between CMS and episcopal prerogative known as the "Ceylon Controversy" had finally been resolved only seven years prior to Tucker's deployment; well within the memory of all concerned.[36] A brief look at this previous situation is informative. Beginning in 1876 Copleston, a young "high church" bishop (having catholic theology and strong centralized administrative practice) was appointed by the Secretary of State for the Colonies to the Diocese of Colombo in Ceylon. An attempt was made to integrate the CMS missionaries, who focused on the native coffee workers, and the government chaplains, who focused on the European community, into a formal, integrated oversight structure. In addition, Copleston attempted to move the diocese toward a more catholic expression, much to the chagrin of the long-term CMS personnel and their converts. The conflict escalated to such

---

33. Ibid.
34. Fox to Tucker, November 29, 1899, CMSA, G/AC/2/593.
35. Fox to Tucker, February 17, 1900, CMSA, G/AC/2/594.
36 Stock, *The History of the Church Missionary Society*, 203–16, and Peiris, "Echoes of a Faded Memory," 173–91.

an extent that the Director of the mission was prepared to take his flock and move it under the authority of the Syrian Orthodox Church in South India. Copleston's method involved revoking licenses and shuffling assignments and oversight of the mission stations—two areas which Tucker would later hold to tightly as well. The CMS resisted control by the bishop in Ceylon until the entire debate needed arbitration by the Archbishop of Canterbury. The "Opinion" offered by the Archbishop in conjunction with the Archbishop of York, the Bishops of London, Durham, and Winchester (March 1, 1880) compared mission stations to benefices, which are independently funded. Cautioning bishops that licenses could not be withdrawn from clergy without just cause and avenues of appeal, it also reminded missionaries that they could not disassociate themselves from the bishop of the diocese.

The situation in East Africa was quite different from Ceylon because the missionaries had arrived fifteen years before the trading company with no restrictions on evangelization, as in India and no government chaplains to chafe against. Another difference was in the component parts of Tucker's diocese. The Ugandan part of the diocese became a British Protectorate (1893) three years after Tucker's arrival and bishops were therefore considered part of the Colonial Episcopacy. But in the part of the diocese which would later be Kenya, where Protectorate status did not arrive until 1907, the bishop was considered missionary in nature giving a bit more input to the CMS. Unlike Ceylon, where the CMS attempted to form a new indigenous church with a separate bishop to escape the unwelcome authority (and theology) of the government appointed bishop, Tucker's theology ran *parallel* to that of the CMS. In addition, an independent Native Church Council already existed in the Ugandan part of Tucker's diocese (1885) and had for five years before his arrival, making a clear organizational structure and chain of command which could not be withdrawn from his oversight. However, similarities did exist in the two situations; both illustrate the continuing concern over the delicate balance between episcopal authority and missionary society independence.

It was quite clear that some refinement was needed to solve this tug-of-war and Fox was forced to address the situation by writing his 1897 report, referred to earlier, to bring order to the situation. Stating flatly that he was not advocating an autocracy, but the Society must recognize at the same time that the Director *did* derive his authority from the Parent Committee

Mission and Church

and not from the Finance Committee in the flow of authority.[37] However, the home committee seemed to fall quite easily into the pattern used when the bishop was completely independent of the Society, as in Ceylon, and needed frequent pressure from Tucker "to remember that there is a Bishop out here whom you have made director of the Mission."[38]

PERSONNEL ATTITUDES

The consistent leaning and attitude of the Church Missionary Society was nearly always away from imperial patterns of administration, not only on the part of the committees in England but also by many of the individual missionaries serving in the field. The newly arrived bishop was not automatically saluted and obeyed but found that his office, much to his surprise, did not automatically entitle him to give directives to the missionaries, even if they were priests. For example, he complains about an unauthorized absence on the part of one missionary:

> My instructions to him [Mr. Deeks] were that he should remain at Nasa (sic) until he was relieved . . . It is possible of course that his health may have necessitated an immediate action to England, but I have had no communication from him to that effect . . . unless Mr. Deeks can give some good reason for a breach of my instructions some notice ought to be taken of what I regard as a grave failure of duty. We shall never get on if every man is to be a law unto himself. If instructions are not to be adhered to I shall cease to give them.[39]

The Bishop could be petulant.

Sir Gerald Portal, the first Consul-General to Uganda, observed the same inclination from the missionaries without giving the generous benefit of the doubt that Tucker gave regarding their behavior. He writes: "These missionaries are simply terrible, they have no common sense, they won't do what they are told and go like mules in the opposite direction to what they are advised."[40]

A dismissive, indulgent attitude toward the bishop was sometimes conveyed by the individual missionaries in CMS employment as in the case

---

37. Fox to Tucker, February 17, 1900, CMSA, G/AC 2/594.
38. Tucker to Baylis, August 31, 1893, CMSA, G3/A5/O/242.
39. Tucker to Lang, December 8, 1891, CMSA, G3A5O/332.
40. Portal to Lady Alice, May 2, 1889, RH, Mss Africa S/112/73.

of Douglas Hooper who wrote about Tucker; "the present man will reside at the coast and his diocese will not extend, I think, more than 200 miles up country—he is certainly too old to begin roughing it up country or on long journeys, but we all like him much."[41] Or a bit of irreverent poking of fun by the also newly arrived missionary for Nassa, John Percy Nickisson:

> The Bishop and I then went to explore the Village [Usonga]. It was strongly walled and ditched outside, and inside was divided by hedges through the small openings of which we had to crawl on our hands and knees, a very un-episcopal attitude for a Bishop, but while it is Africa here so it did not matter.[42]

Even the Committee in London could sound a condescending note on occasion which reinforced their reputation for disrespecting bishops. When Tucker objected strenuously to plans to develop an industrial school at Mombasa and threatened to have nothing to do with it, the Committee did not back away from their plans. Instead they asked for Tucker to hear them out. Fredrick Baylis, the Corresponding Secretary from 1892–1912, writes: "It is nice to get your plain spoken opinion, but I hope we may soon be rid of any misunderstanding that requires to be quite so vehemently dealt with; it quite strikes our committee to find how naughty they seem to have been unawares."[43]

ON THE EXTREME END

However, there were boundaries as to how far in the direction of equality and independent action that the CMS governing committees would allow the missionaries in the field. Just prior to Tucker's second visit to Uganda the missionaries in Mengo elected Robert P. Ashe to be "president" of their group, a position unheard of in the CMS structure. The Committee found this action to be a step too far in the direction of Presbyterian-style government and instructed Tucker to form a local governing body upon his arrival in Uganda in the form of a Finance Committee in accordance with the usual pattern, rather than this innovation. Tucker was also asked to appoint (not elect) a Secretary to perform administrative duties as was the

---

41. Douglas Hooper to Con Hooper, July 1890, CMSA, Acc. 336/F1.
42. Nickkison Papers, CMSA, Acc. 109.
43. Baylis to Tucker, Oct. 27, 1893, CMSA, G3/A5/7/48.

pattern established in other CMS missions, asking Mr. Ashe to lay aside his "presidency."[44]

As the missionaries were at odds about who would qualify to serve on the governing council, Tucker proposed that, in the future, only resident missionaries (those who had lived in the country for more than a few days and had already been assigned a post) would be eligible to serve and new members of the Finance Committee would be nominated by the present Finance Committee, but approved by the Parent Committee back in London.[45] It seemed a good compromise that gave expression to both styles, involving both the unanimity of a local committee and the approval of the head office. To this the London committee offered no objection. Even if the CMS, for the most part, maintained a more councilor style of governance, they were quite capable of combining this with Tucker's more imperial style if need be.

NOMINATIONS

However, by 1895, after only a few years, the compromise of how nominations were to take place began to encounter some snags. Since Tucker was the chair of three Finance Committees, one in Mombasa, one in Usagara and one in Uganda and moving about between them, he was not always present, aware of new nominations or able to vet them for the most appropriate candidate. To place a new member on the committee without his knowledge, in Tucker's mind, was to give him less of a voice on the committees than he felt was appropriate for the chair and director of the mission. He requested an input for nominations for any Finance Committee before the Parent Committee granted their approval.[46] The wording is important to note:

> May I ask you to be good enough not to confirm any nominations you may have made to you by the Secretaries of the Finance Committees now at work in the field without first being satisfied that I have been made acquainted with the fact that a particular individual has been nominated to serve on the committee. I am an official chairman of these Committees and it is I think only due

---

44. Baylis to Tucker, November 3, 1892, CMSA, G3/A5/6/422.
45. Tucker to Baylis, January 2, 1893, CMSA, G3/A5/O/245.
46. Tucker to Baylis, October 7, 1895, CMSA, G3/A5/O/342.

to me that I should at least be made acquainted with the fact of a nomination having been made.[47]

Although to Tucker the request must have seemed reasonable, allowing him only to be informed and to be a full-functioning member of the Finance Committee, the Parent Committee could not agree to the request and insinuated the idea that Tucker was asking to grant approval. The Parent Committee resisted.

> The Group Committee thought over your suggestion that they should only appoint to seats on the Finance Committee missionaries who were known to be *approved* [emphasis mine] by you in such office. They felt that your office as Director made it advisable for you to be consulted on the subject as much as possible, but as things at present are, with the possibility of your being at times practically many months out of the reach of consultation, they could not make it a matter of necessity to have your approval. Where you are on the spot the recommendation should certainly come home from or through you, but where you are not on the spot we think the usual course of forwarding all correspondence to you in duplicate should be followed and *the Parent Committee must then use their discretion as to the constitution of committees.* You probably know the rule we go by in such cases is to receive only the nomination made personally by the Secretary. At times of course, we might *initiate an appointment ourselves* for particular reasons.[48]

Tucker had not asked to approve the candidates, only to be informed. Not only did this standard way of operating the committee system place the Secretary in a direct power struggle with the Director, it also sometimes granted the London based Parent Committee close control over the membership of local governing boards.

This time Tucker did not press the Committee to allow him approval of candidates. Instead he sought to clarify his request, backing off his usual strong executive tendencies and reiterating that all he asked for was "an opportunity of expressing my opinion of the preferred appointment."[49] He acknowledged that the Society had a "right to appoint a member of the Finance Committee without any nomination from the field," possibly an

---

47. Ibid.
48. Baylis to Tucker, January 31, 1896, CMSA, G3/A5/7/466. Emphasis mine.
49. Tucker to Baylis, May 26, 1896, CMSA, G3/A5/O/246.

acknowledgement to memos created by the Ceylon Controversy.[50] But he also lamented the uncooperativeness of the Secretaries to provide information to him about nominations (which would allow him to offer input) and he lamented the assumption on the part of the Committee that this was being done.

The Society had made their case strongly for their right to appoint members of the governing boards without Tucker's approval, but surprisingly and without any explanation, they subsequently chose to ignore their own rule. Writing in August, a full month before the above lament arrived in September, Baylis writes: "Archdeacon Walker having nominated Mr. Martin Hall for membership of the Nyanza Finance Committee, the Committee have [sic] declared their approval of the appointment, subject to your approval."[51] Another compromise seemed to have unfolded in practice between the tendency of Tucker towards an executive, imperial style and the preferred bottom-up co-operation of the Society. This compromise gives a further illustration of how missionaries sometimes operated with a foot in both camps. The final word on the subject from the CMS, written in response to the lament letter, was a gracious one-liner: "We trust that with regard to appointments to the Finance Committee we have in recent cases done as you would wish."[52]

INDIRECT COMMUNICATION—A MARK OF DISMISSAL

The differences in world view, philosophy and approach between the Church Missionary Society and the Church, are evident in such matters as lines of authority, attitudes of co-workers, and nomination procedures. Another issue developed regarding the use of "indirect communication" style for which a similar trail can be found in the letters illustrating the use of this style by the CMS.

Tucker was sometimes capable of giving opinions and negotiating with different government authorities without consulting the home base,

---

50. Ibid. Also Stock, ibid, 208. An echo of "The Memorandum" adopted on June 27, 1877 by the Parent Committee in response to the perceived over reaching authority of bishops in India in the midst of the Ceylon Controversy which stated in its first point: "That individual Churchmen have a right to combine to carry on missionary work, and to control, within proper limits, the organizations created by them."
51. Baylis to Tucker, August 11, 1896, CMSA, G3/A5/8/30.
52. Baylis to Tucker, September 10, 1896, CMSA, G2/A5/8/35.

especially in the initial stages of his tenure but he generally was quite consistent at keeping Salisbury Square informed of his attempts and articulating an understanding of their veto power. The CMS, however, while maintaining a running barrage of letters with Tucker, regularly employed an indirect communication style, which left Tucker out of crucial decisions or communication loops. Such patterns serve to illustrate further the guarded approach to church hierarchy maintained by the Society and a commitment to shared, grassroots authority. But these patterns were also a source of aggravation to Tucker who seemed to strive toward functioning as a chief executive. At times he over-functioned in this area which his co-workers found exasperating.[53]

All of Tucker's offers to resign were a result of indirect communications patterns. They shed some light on the impetuous side of his personality. Yet even when given the opportunity to sever the connection with the CMS, his more logical side prevailed. He chose to remain within the organization, voluntarily straddling two opposing world views and forms of administration.

Tucker's first brush with the indirect style of the Society can be seen regarding a letter from Lord Salisbury at the Foreign Office to the CMS in response to Tucker's independent opinion (expressed to Gerald Portal, Special Commissioner to Uganda and sent up the line) that a British presence needed to be dispatched to Uganda as soon as possible in order to bring peace and security to the country in the midst of a political conflict. Ignoring Tucker altogether, CMS responded directly to Lord Salisbury's concerns without reference to the writer, which Tucker found not only discourteous, but an act of injustice because it removed from him the possibility of stating his opinions clearly.[54] Tucker's irritation seemed to derive from his perception that, as a bishop in the church, he was an executive in his own right and not just an arm of the Society, a concept not quite grasped by the CMS.

In a similar vein, Tucker complained about being kept in the dark regarding an investigation of the political activities of three missionaries in Uganda by the IBEA Company representatives just prior to the declaration of the protectorate. Although no charges were made and the explanation of the missionaries was found acceptable, Tucker inserted himself into the

---

53. Hardinge to Tucker, January 15, 1898, PRO Archives, FO 811/7024. "I am most unwilling to appear to take any step which could appear to you unfriendly; but I must really demur to your claiming, as you appear to do in virtue of your episcopal office, a right to exercise administrative functions in the East Africa Protectorate..."

54. Tucker to Wigram, July 4, 1892, CMSA, G3/A5/O/277.

communication loop between the CMS and the IBEA Company in the belief that the reputation of the CMS was at risk and, in his role as Director, it was his responsibility to find out the facts rather than be "kept in the dark."[55] A second offer of resignation then ensued due to a similar and repeated perception of executive privilege on the part of Tucker and lack of a shared view-point on the part of the CMS.

Three years later Tucker chides the CMS for questioning the decisions of the Mombasa Finance Committee using the "instruction letters," usually written by the Corresponding Secretary, and given to new missionaries. Rather than a direct inquiry, the instruction letter asked that the new missionaries call the attention of the Finance Committee "to the fact noticed by the Medical Board that a very large proportion of the work in Mombasa and Freretown seems to be carried on in the hottest part of the day."[56] Tucker's action again serves to illustrate the same tendency of Tucker to insert himself as a chief executive into communications between the Parent Committee and the Finance Committee, albeit through the individual missionary instruction letters.

But on a much more serious level, when a special sub-committee was formed by CMS to discuss parameters for a constitution for the church in Uganda on the eve of the division of the diocese, Bishop Tucker was not invited to attend the meeting, even though he was present in England at the time, quite specifically to discuss this subject. This could be seen as the ultimate exclusion from the communication loop. The minutes of the meeting note that, after listing those in attendance: "It appeared that by accident no notice of the meeting had been sent to Bishop Tucker."[57] The minutes also record that the concerns of the sub-committee revolved around the belief that a constitution should not be forced on the Ugandans against their will "by the CMS or its missionaries or by the English Bishop."[58] They were also concerned that the constitution be framed in such a way as changes could be made at a later date should it become necessary in the future to make it more adaptable to the Ugandan church. The sub-committee specifically stated that under such a future constitution it was their hope that missionaries and native clergy would be equal. To this proposal Tucker, had he been present, would have gladly agreed. But the proposal that the Ugandan

---

55. Tucker to Baylis, January 20, 1893, CMSA, G3/A5/O/247.
56. Tucker to Baylis, September 11, 1896, CMSA, G3/A5/O/274.
57. Special Sub-Committee minutes, July 19, 1897, CMSA, GAC4/22/4318.
58. Ibid.

Church would be considered a branch of the Church of England, which lost due to a tie vote 6 to 6, would have lost outright by a vote of 7 to 6 had Tucker been present, due to his fiercely held beliefs in the independence of the Ugandan Church. The meeting ended with the notation that a second meeting would take place the following week and that "for the purpose of consultation the Bishop is invited to meet the Sub-Committee."[59]

Certainly the most hurtful form of indirect communication involved the pattern of Baylis to communicate with Tucker through the Secretary of the Mombasa Mission, Harry Kerr Binns. Whether the subject was the secretary's power over clergy or the details regarding the draft constitution, Tucker expected direct and personal communication from the CMS in response to his inquiries regarding church matters rather than copies of letters to the secretary of the mission which contained the answers he was seeking. Being careful to distinguish church business from mission business, he considered the indirect form of communication about church matters a dismissal of his position by the CMS and refused to acknowledge this pattern as true communication. He wrote to Fox: "I have received no definite answer to any one of them [inquiries about the Secretaries' power over clergy]. A copy of a letter to Mr. Binns was forwarded to me and I was asked to take that as a reply. This I was quite unable to do and the questions still, to my mind, remain unanswered."[60]

Baylis was quite consistent in his pattern and Tucker was equally consistent with his feelings of disappointment:

> I am bound to say that in my opinion such a method of communication with regard to matters which have a peculiar relationship to my position as Bishop is not the most courteous, nor is it convenient. I am always glad to receive copies of letters which you from time to time address to the Secretary with regard to matters with which primarily the Finance Committee have to do. But with regard to matters like the Church Constitution and my powers as Licensing Bishop the case stands upon a different footing and I do not think I am unduly exacting or punctilious when I ask as I do very respectfully that the Committee will do me the honour of communicating with me direct and not through a third person. I am always most anxious to write to the Committee as fully as possible on all matters of importance which concern the work which we have jointly in hand, but if in reply I am to receive only a bare

---

59. Ibid.
60. Tucker to Fox, September 15, 1899, CMSA, GAC 4/29/5675.

Mission and Church

acknowledgement of the receipt of such letters, the real answer going to the Secretary it will become a matter of increasing difficulty for me to write at all.[61]

Fox entered the fray in an effort to bring peace and clarity to the situation. He assured Tucker that no disrespect was intended and that the committee continued to have full confidence in his abilities and wisdom. He acknowledged that confusion had been created due to the lack of a definition of the duties and power of a Director. But it was the normal operating procedure that the "Secretary at home communicates with that secretary in the field . . . copies of such official communications are supplied to you."[62] No recognition of a differentiation between the subjects to be handled by the office of bishop vs. subjects to be handled by the office of director seems to be realized by Fox; or that a different destination for communication might be required for different business. Instead he urged patience and a gentle touch owing to the immense authority Tucker held as the direct representative of the Parent Committee.

However, the distinction between the two offices held by Tucker was not lost on Baylis. Although acknowledging that there were occasions when correspondence with Bishop Tucker alone would be appropriate, he also pointed out that many of the affairs dealt with in day to day business and touched on both arenas—church and mission. When this overlapping occurred the head office would continue to use the Secretary as the main receiver of correspondence. Baylis' words, although very gracious, did not change the *modus operandi*: "In some cases the very same subject may have both aspects and may most obviously represent itself to our minds as Mission business rather than ecclesiastical, and when a thing is Mission business I hope you will still be good enough to accept as a rule copies of letters written to the Secretary of the Mission."[63] Baylis also pointed out that the correspondence about the Constitution came from the Secretary of the Mission acting as recorder of the conference; therefore the reply was sent to him. However, Baylis acknowledged: "I can quite see that care is needed and I shall hope to keep matters more distinct in the future . . . it is only a few cases that are practically concerned, and hope there will not be any difficulty in your requirements being met."[64]

61. Tucker to Baylis, December 14, 1899, CMSA, G3/A7/O/47.
62. Fox to Tucker, February 17, 1900, CMSA, G/AC/2/953.
63. Baylis to Tucker, March 9, 1900, CMSA, G3/A7/1/174.
64. Ibid.

No further mention was made of the subject in any of the subsequent correspondence. It is possible that Tucker was satisfied that he had put his point across, but also quite possible that he just abandoned the effort and resigned himself to the inability of the organization to alter its way of thinking. He expressed a type of resignation in his last letter about the problem to Baylis: "I must confess that it was with no little surprise and extreme regret that you had not found it possible to communicate with me direct."[65] It was just as well that Tucker was at this point moving to Uganda as a full time position. His transfer to a smaller diocese eliminated the necessity of being absent from the Uganda Finance Committee for the lengths of time that had been necessary for the supervision of three finance committees in a huge diocese and all of the problems associated with keeping the director informed while travelling.

ASSIGNING MISSIONARIES

In describing Alfred Tucker for a book review in the CMS Home Gazette, Doctor John Cook notes: "He was one of those rare characters which owe their richness to the blending of contrasted elements."[66] This is exactly the character trait displayed by Tucker and the CMS Parent Committee as they negotiated together to assign missionaries in the field. There was an ebb and flow between an imperial dictatorial approach and a collaborative style, ending in a clarification by Fox and finally an abdication by Tucker in favor of the egalitarian approach.

The blending of imperial initiative and collaborative attitude was the initial approach adopted by Tucker as he commenced his ministry in East Africa. Arriving in Mombasa on May 14, 1890, his first assignment of a missionary occurred just three weeks later, and it was a bold step. Tucker assigned A. G. Smith to open a new station in Jilore although it was the prerogative of the Parent Committee alone to decide the opening of new works. As if anticipating the response to his boldness he cushioned the blow of his independent initiative by explaining to the Committee that this was not really so much the opening of a new station as it was the moving of an old one at Mbugu to a new location. He also emphasized that the decision was made in consultation with both the Secretary of the mission in Mombasa and the Finance Committee who were together "enthusiastically

---

65. Tucker to Baylis, December 14, 1899, CMSA, G3/A7/1/174.
66. Cook, "Tucker of Uganda," CMS *Home Gazette*, November 1929, 167.

in favour of that field being occupied."⁶⁷ Blending independent initiative with consultation Tucker called the Jelore opening a tentative occupation and reminded the Committee that it was entirely up to them to negate the project if they chose by withholding their consent. But Tucker was not beyond acting in an imperial fashion without seeking to cushion the blow. In the same early stages of his tenure, and without any consultation, he assigned E. A. Fitch to Rabai and accepted as a missionary a young layman, Mr. Hunt, who was employed with the IBEA Company in Mombasa: "trusting that the Committee will endorse my action."⁶⁸ The Society did, but grudgingly, due to the fact that Hunt was breaking an existing contract with the government but his tenure with the Society was short; he died seven months later of fever at Usambiro.⁶⁹

A gracious and polite dance began between the Committee and Tucker with such phrases as: "maybe you will help us [the Committee] in deciding assignments."⁷⁰ or: "shall leave be given to the Bishop to [assign]."⁷¹ An initiative by Tucker was usually followed by an agreement from the Committee unless some special circumstances were evident, such as the assignment of missionaries with child-bearing age wives; in which case Tucker sought the decision of the Parent Committee. If initiative was taken by the Committee to make assignments, these were usually declined or modified by Tucker. A compromise in the egalitarian style of the CMS had been created by praxis, as their collective decisions began to flow through and be modified by the Director. Still, equilibrium had been reached which continued for three years.

All this was to change when Frederick Baylis attempted to define the duties of the Finance Committee, in a letter to the Secretary of the Usagara mission, without reference to the duties of the Director of the Mission. Tucker protested:

> Suppose it may seem good to them to move this or that ordained man from one district to another without my consent, I should object very strongly. Ordained men are licensed to particular

---

67. Tucker to General Touch, May 19, 1890, CMSA, G3/A5/O/134. Also Tucker to Touch, June 5, 1890, CMSA, G3/A5/O/158.

68. Tucker from Freretown, June 17, 1890, CMSA, G3/A5/O/157.

69. Lang to Tucker, January 9, 1891, CMSA, G3/A5/6/85, and August15, 1890, CMSA, G3/A5/6/4.

70. Lang to Tucker, February 10, 1891, CMSA, G3/A5/6/90.

71. Tucker to Lang, February 28, 1891, CMSA, G3/A5/O/114.

districts, e.g. one man is licensed to the missionary circuit of Mamboya. Now suppose it should seem good to the Finance Committee to move that man to Kesokwe (sic) without my permission, I should come down upon the Finance Committee for an explanation of their irregular action.[72]

The Bishop was equating the missionary circuit in Africa to a parish within any diocese in the Church of England. Within the English parish system, a priest must be issued a license by the Diocesan Bishop to officiate within the boundaries of that parish which is specific and exclusive to that parish alone. Only with the permission of the bishop can a priest move from one parish to another, at which time a new license must be issued by the bishop for the new parish. But the CMS was not making the same equation. Baylis writes: "It is usual for our missionaries [to have] their Bishop Licenses which allow us a very considerable amount of transference within a wide area, without change in the License. This I find in some cases is so wide as to be practically a License to officiate anywhere in the Diocese."[73] It is clear that by calling the area covered by the Usagara Finance Committee a "Diocese" Mr. Baylis was thinking along some similar lines as Bishop Tucker, but what was quite different was the thought that the Committee, not the bishop, would have the ability to move an ordained man in a way very similar to the Presbyterian system. Baylis added a sentence that surely would have been a red flag for Tucker:

> We should be grateful if you would kindly give to your licenses the more general form. Your authority as Director would enable you, in such cases as you refer, to deal with specific locations upon which the Parent Committee had not decided expressly; and we think you will see the advantage of leaving the Society a comparatively free hand in the matter of locations.[74]

There was no direct response from Tucker to this letter and it may be that he had not seen it before leaving for England on October 11 of the same year. At the time of its writing two episcopal visitations were squeezed into his schedule, ending in a month long hospital stay in Zanzibar. Never completely regaining his strength, he was invalided home a month later. Once home and recovered he threw himself into researching constitutions as the division of the diocese had already been proposed two months

72. Tucker to Baylis, February 17, 1896, CMSA, G3/A7/1/174.
73. Baylis to Tucker, April 24, 1896, CMSA, G3/A5/7/494.
74. Ibid.

prior to his illness and preparation was needed before writing one for the Ugandan church. Lambeth Convention took up the whole of the month of August and further arrangements for the division of the diocese also pressed before he departed once again for East Africa on November 25, where the letter quite possibly rested unread as Tucker immersed himself in the Karibu case.

Tucker's actions at this time give no indication of any change in style or philosophy as far as assigning missionaries is concerned. When knowledge of Miss Furley and Miss Chadwick's request to the Parent Committee asking for a pioneer assignment in Toro reached Tucker he was in-route home for recovery. He had already informed them in person that this was not possible and asked the Parent Committee to refer their request back to the Finance Committee, who made the assignments when he was out of the field.[75] Writing again three weeks later from Naples he again informs the Parent Committee that he has made arrangements for the assignments of the party of eight new female missionaries, assured that the Parent Committee would agree with his decision.[76]

However, there were limits to how far the Parent Committee was prepared to go in allowing a CMS bishop full rein. Assigning missionaries to open a new work, which required an outlay of cash, was a boundary not to be crossed as Baylis politely indicates:

> In our last mail from East Africa we hear from Mr. Binns that you have appointed 'Mr. England and Mr. Fincher to open up new work at the south of the Giryama Country.' You will no doubt be writing to us as soon as possible of the reason that led you to this step. I shall be very glad if you will kindly give them with some fullness, as I incline to think that without such help I shall be in a difficulty in submitting the matter for the Committee's approval.[77]

Once again there was no direct response, as Tucker was on his way home to recuperate and the matter, most likely, was addressed in person. While Tucker remained home, polite request went back and forth; the Committee seeking advice regarding new works, Tucker suggesting assignments or even requesting input for the location of new missionaries. But once back in Mombasa, the old pattern once again asserted itself as the Committee questioned the assignment of men: "we remembered that

---

75. Tucker to Baylis, October 15, 1896, CMSA, G3/A5/O/301.
76. Tucker to Baylis, November 5, 1896, CMSA, G3/A5/O/314.
77. Baylis to Tucker, November 6, 1896, CMSA, G3/A5/8/76.

you have authority to arrange for the locations of the men concerned when you see your way; but we also felt that we doubted the wisdom of putting Messrs. Heselwood and McGregor alone to work there, [at Kikuyu] and could not understand the suggestion that Mr. Binns might go"[78]

Finally, when Archdeacon Walker called Tucker's attention to a line in the instructions given to departing missionaries in which they were told that they would be assigned "by the Finance Committee and the Director of the Mission," it seemed to be the perfect opportunity for Tucker to make another clarification in his push for the individual power to assign missionaries:[79]

> [When home] I stated quite clearly and plainly what I considered to be my powers as Director of the Mission and also what my practice was with regard to the location of men. I interpreted the terms of my appointment as Director of the Mission to mean that I had full powers with regard to the location and movement of men. I have always acted (now for nearly 10 years) on that interpretation. My practice certainly in Uganda has been to hold myself responsible for the location of men and I have located them after conference with the senior missionaries in the field.[80]

Pointing out to the Committee that these assignments were made after consultation with the senior missionaries in the field was an indication of how Tucker was straddling, in the end, two styles of administration—one consultative and one executive. But consultation aside it was still his understanding that the power to assign was to be left in the hands of the executive. Once again, Fox stepped in to write a definitive instruction on who, after all, was responsible to assign missionaries. Quoting a letter from Baylis to Archdeacon Walker which had crossed Tucker's in the mail, Fox walks a delicate balance but ends by backing the Director:

> 'It is the custom of the Parent Committee to ask the local Committees in the general missions to assign particular posts to their Missionaries unless some special circumstances lead to a decision at home, and we assumed that the Finance Committee in Uganda as a rule consider all such cases. You know of course that the Director is authorized to assign and to change locations if he sees occasion. If therefore Bishop Tucker feels that it is essential for

---

78. Baylis to Tucker, January 28, 1898, CMSA, G3/A7/1/1.
79. Tucker to Baylis, September 2, 1899, CMSA, G3/A7/O/194.
80. Ibid.

him as Director to make the locations himself, he clearly has the authority to do so....' Mr. Baylis had no intention in his phrases which he has used in his Instructions... to make the Director and the Finance Committee coadjutant authorities: but he wished to imply that these are duties which fall as a matter of course to the Finance Committee, subject to the Director, who, no doubt, can veto any decision which they have done or take any matter out of their hands, as being himself the representative of the Society.[81]

But Fox could not help adding one more attempt to reason with Tucker toward a more consultative style:

You wrote that you speak of conferring with some of the Missionaries in deciding upon Location. I presume that these brethren are members of the Finance Committee. Would it not be a great advantage to the Finance Committee and, so to speak, somewhat more of a constitutional question, if they were the body with whom you conferred... we all know that the more which administrative bodies are trusted and brought to realize their responsibilities the more efficient they naturally become.[82]

However, the attempt failed and Tucker continued making assignments and moving missionaries as he had done in the past. Peace reigned on the subject for five years.

When the end finally arrived to this arrangement, it came quite quickly and without fanfare. Once again a missionary appealed to the Parent Committee for a reconsideration of an assignment made by Tucker.[83] R. H. Leakey wished to remain at Bulemezi, feeling that a move away from his present responsibilities was a type of demotion. By this time Fox had become ill and Leakey's letters were passed to Baylis for his attention. Tucker maintained that Leakey lacked the organizational and teaching skills necessary for such a large work and in addition was distracted by family responsibilities. Not only would a smaller sphere be more suited but, in Tucker's view, "fixity of tenure" was not something to be counted on in the mission field.[84] All missionaries should be prepared to move. However, with his mentor and protector, H. E. Fox, now absent from the scene and Baylis handling the complaint, Tucker seems to have lost all patience with

---

81. Fox to Tucker, November 3, 1899, CMSA, G/AC/2/469.
82. Ibid.
83. Baylis to Tucker, October 14, 1904, CMSA, G3/A7/1/491.
84. Tucker to Baylis, November 10, 1904, CMSA, G3/A7/0/226.

the continual struggle. Baylis, who had been at Oxford with Tucker, had been the instigator for the discussion of separating the Director's position from the position of Bishop, a proposal which Tucker had seen as a negative assessment of his abilities.[85] A certain amount of friction had consistently been present in the communication between them. Whether this friction goes back to Oxford dynamics or was simply due to the fact that Baylis was the main communicator for the Parent Committee and therefore took the brunt of Tucker's ready pen it is hard to know. However, it appeared that Tucker was not ready for another go-round regarding assignment of missionaries—especially with Baylis.

Only four weeks after the first communication from Baylis regarding Leakey's complaint, Tucker wrote to Archdeacon Walker proposing that beginning January 1, 1905 he planned to turn over the responsibility of assigning missionaries to the Executive Committee (formally called the Finance Committee), citing the increased ease of travel and communication as the reason. It was no longer only the Director who knew the situation at each station. However, even though the Executive Committee was now responsible to assign missionaries, he stipulated that the movement of ordained men must still have his approval and in the absence of the ability of the Executive Committee to meet and decide, all assignment matters could be referred to him. The long battle for control was at an end, and Tucker had acquiesced.

SUMMARY AND CONCLUSION

While serving as one of the pioneer missionary bishops of East Africa, Alfred Tucker's correspondence certainly captured one of the defining characteristics of the nineteenth century; the tension between central control and local independence, not only in Britain but also across the developing empire.[86] He was unique in the fact that he simultaneously held the office of bishop and director of the CMS East African mission. But he was not unique in his efforts to juggle two opposing world views—one imperial, dominating, and singular; the other plural, egalitarian, and idealistic. This struggle was also shared by members of the Church Missionary Society, both at home and abroad.

85. Reynolds, *Evangelicals*, 42.
86. Paz, *Nineteenth-Century*, ix.

Mission and Church

The tensions manifested themselves over lines of authority, individual missionary attitudes toward authority, organizational styles, nominating procedures, communication styles, and assignment of personnel. Due to these repeated struggles the question might be asked, who actually was the bishop of the native church—the mission board or the bishop? An attempt was made to keep separate the subjects properly addressed by the society and those to be addressed by the bishop on behalf of the native church; mostly due to Tucker's protective attitude toward Ugandan Church independence, but blind spots were common. Rather than attempting to function as a bishop per se, it could be postulated that the CMS Parent Committee was attempting to be a Presbytery. The tensions between church and mission concentrated themselves around the European personnel and funding rather than African clergy assignments or initiatives. However, a further question for consideration might include the role contributed by the Native Church Council. Who actually set the agenda for the indigenous church—the Native Church Council, the bishop, or the hierarchy in Britain?

At times Tucker approached situations using a shared leadership style, with Africans as well as British missionaries, using negotiation and compromise. Other times he chose to act the part of a fully empowered Diocesan, as in the decision to build a worship space for the European population of Mombasa, not waiting for approval from the CMS. Other times the lines of authority reached to the Archbishop of Canterbury; such as the decision regarding the division and borders of the diocese or the use of banana wine for communion, which Tucker and the Church Council approved but Lambeth prohibited and overruled.[87] The same phenomenon is true on the part of the CMS—sometimes imperial, most times seeking to devolve power and other times compromising. But through the pattern exposed by the correspondence, we catch a glimpse of the tension filled rift, that "space between" which was the purview of the British missionary.

---

87. Tucker's speech on the wine debate, August, 1897, LPA, LC 70.25–30.

CHAPTER SIX

The Mission and The Fort

As Tucker moved to become the Bishop of Uganda only, an assessment and evaluation of his eight-year tenure as Bishop of the Diocese of Eastern Equatorial Africa was a necessary step to bring closure to a term of office that, with the turn of the century, was passing into a new phase. Bishop Tucker chose to accomplish this assessment in the form of a parting sermon as he moved permanently to Uganda.[1] Taking each of the regions of the former diocese of Eastern Equatorial Africa in turn (Mombasa and the coast, Usagara, and finally Uganda) Tucker painted a picture of progress, using statistics and examples. With the exception of Usagara, which had suffered famine and unrest, the picture he painted was a rosy one:

> How great the progress of the work has been during the past seven years may be gathered from a perusal of the Church Missionary Society's Reports for the years 1890 and 1897 respectively. Let us briefly glance at these Reports and contrast the present with the past. But as we do so let us see to it that there be no thought lingering in the mind of self-complacency or self-glorification. The work from beginning to end, from first to last, has been the Lord's, and to Him alone be the honour and the glory.[2]

Growth in numbers of adherents, European and African workers, linguistic work and the diffusion of scripture, buildings, and the evangelistic outreach going out from the Baganda to neighboring people all were used

1. Tucker, "Bishop Tucker's Charge," 89.
2. Ibid.

to illustrate a positive and meaningful aspect to the endeavor for those gathered to hear his words. He was preaching to the choir, of course—to the Mission. But here we turn our attention to another major force in the imperial enterprise, the IBEA presence summed up neatly by the phrase "The Fort."

The Fort in Uganda was the military garrison employed by the Imperial British East Africa Company to guard supplies and transport links. Located on the hill called Kampala, the Fort sometimes had a slightly different opinion of the style used by the missionaries to assess their work. Ernest Gedge, initially a representative of the infant Imperial British East Africa Company (IBEA), and later East African correspondent for the Times (and interestingly the son of an English clergyman), records his impression at the beginning of Tucker's tenure: "In the evening went over to Freretown to hear an address on Uganda given by the Bishop. . . . There was a fairly good audience of Europeans and mission folks, but Lord how they do lave the butter on about their work."[3] Gerald Portal, as a young career diplomat, articulated much the same sentiment in an earlier evaluation, with slightly more bile: "I confess that I have little or no real sympathy with the English missionaries: a narrow-minded, quarrelsome, press-writing, conceited, self-advertising lot of men, who try to make themselves out to be martyrs (and I don't believe in well-fed, well-advertised martyrs, who are always writing to newspapers)."[4] Through the years Portal and other colonial administrators would conduct an uneasy relationship with the missionaries, and with their director.

If a similar assessment to that made by Tucker regarding the diocese could have been made of Tucker's relationship to the colonial government, one might have noticed different phases of that relationship as it changed over time. Missionaries were quite individualistic in their attitude toward the colonial presence and it is difficult to generalize. Scholars are careful to explain that "[t]he missionaries were not a homogeneous body. Their attitudes to colonialism varied enormously. Their reasons for supporting it, when they did, were equally varied."[5] And also, "The range of models in the relationship between missionaries and the early colonial state remained, nevertheless, considerable: from fawning subservience to deep

---

3. Gedge Diary, April 24, 1891, RHA, Mss. British Empire, S 290 / Box 6/3/74.
4. Gerald Portal to Lady Portal, May 29, 1889, RHA, Mss. Africa, 112/95–6.
5. McManners, *Illustrated History*, 460.

distrust and open disagreement."[6] The archives of the CMS missionaries in East Africa give solid evidence to these observations. For example, John Roscoe, at one time Secretary of the Uganda mission, held himself aloof and openly refused to participate in politics in any form; whereas Robert Ashe was heavily involved while working his assignment in Mengo. Robert H. Walker, who became the Archdeacon upon Tucker's arrival, tended to take the role of an intermediary and Mr. Borup, with an expertise in building engineering, eventually left the mission and signed on with the administration.[7]

Given this diversity it is unfair to try and characterize all the missionaries together. Tucker's views were part of the varied tapestry of the missionary presence. "The Mission and The Fort" was Tucker's own terminology, his way of seeing the world in Uganda with two prominent institutions in balance with one another. Yet there is no doubt that "The Mission" in his phraseology and in his thought always came first. Tucker's interaction with "The Fort" was complex, multi-faceted, and far from a monolithic support or resistance. Having a tendency to act as an advisor and sometimes a critic, his opinions evolved and changed over time, sometimes in reference to the personalities in power but more often to the evolving policies and growing formality of the administration. As Tucker began his service his relationship could be characterized as congenial. His duties as an ecclesiastical supervisor and director for the whole mission required that he move around a large area although he kept himself closely informed through correspondence. This prevented him from being mired exclusively in the intensely volatile blend of religion and politics taking place in Uganda. Others have described this blend on a social and institutional level, with great detail and insight, focusing primarily on the letters and diaries of Sir Frederick Lugard (IBEA representative & militia), Capt. W. H. Williams (Lugard's second in command), Robert Walker, and George Baskerville (both CMS missionaries).[8] But by focusing on Tucker's letters it is possible to discern, as time progressed, four distinct phases: a digression from the initial cooperative period, to a cooling-off phase which later evolved into friction and, finally to one that could be characterized by the term "loyal opposition."

6. Hastings, *Church in Africa*, 428.

7. Regarding Roscoe, see Tucker to Baylis, February 21, 1893, CMSA, G3A5/O/194; regarding Ashe, see Griffiths, "Bishop A. R. Tucker," 130; regarding Walker, see Walker to sister, February 2, 1900, CMSA, Acc. 88.473; regarding Borup, see Tucker to Carus-Wilson, December 31, 1904, BGCA, 135/1-2.

8. Hansen, *Mission, Church and State*, 29–57.

The Mission and The Fort

The four phases of Tucker's position toward the Fort closely coincides with the evolution of colonial rule in East Africa. As time progressed the British colonial structure grew strong and stronger. As Tucker's tenure lengthened, experience added a considered approach to his interaction with the colonial endeavor, but more changed as well besides Tucker. The archive shows that the political context changed and within this transformation Tucker's missionary project was increasingly pressed. During the initial period of the Northern European/African encounter when IBEA initiated a treaty of free trade, missionary cooperation was useful and possible. With the typical tightening of structures, exploitation, and occupation during high imperialism the space for missions was constantly reduced or fenced and the mission's strategies for dealing with this containment changed from accommodation to critical examination. This change can be observed in four different phases. In each phase Tucker was entangled with members of the imperial government and vice versa, sometimes against both of their wills in a rather forced but necessary partnership, and sometimes willingly for mutual benefit.

PHASE ONE—SHARING AND SOCIALIZING

The first letters of Tucker at the beginning of his tenure in East Africa to members of the British administration were very far from adversarial. The overall impression from both sides is one of partnership, sharing, and socializing derived from practicalities and a common cultural background. Frederick Lugard, one of IBEA's early representatives, captures the essence of this type of rarified fraternity as he writes: "I cannot speak too highly of the pluck and cordial spirit shown by both [the Rev. E. Cyril] Gordon and [the Rev. Robert H.] Walker, throughout all this period, especially in the very difficult situation which ensued immediately after my arrival, when they were the only two Englishmen in this part of Africa besides ourselves (sic)."[9]

Both organizations, the mission and the company, were worried about the factional unrest in the East African interior at that time between Catholic, Protestant, Muslim, and African Traditional Religionists. Their goals were intertwined, but for different reasons. Peace would enable the

---

9. Lugard, *The Rise of our East African Empire*, 59. From the annual reports in the Intelligencer, Gordon was alone in Uganda after the death of McKay in 1889 until joined by Robert Walker in 1890 then Baskerville, Pilkington, and F. C. Smith in 1891.

mission to initiate wider contacts and at the same time enable the company to engage in unhindered trade. No formal colonial administration existed at this stage beyond a few advisors, representatives of IBEA and a scattering of supply depots along the caravan route. Lugard's main objective was to build a road and to use an African hired militia with diplomatic persuasion to garner peace between the rival political factions.[10] The small mission was free to make contacts and evangelize wherever doors opened. Tucker shared intelligence on the situation in Uganda with Colonel Euan Smith, the Consul-General in Mombasa, gleaned from the intercepted missionary letters of Gordon and Walker to the CMS headquarters in Salisbury Square. Based on the information he had received in the letters he felt it was of the utmost importance for there to be a strong British presence as soon as possible to ease the tensions. He writes:

> The country lies open before them and if possible let a British Resident who will see justice done as between Protestants and Roman Catholics be appointed, we ask not and desire not a position of dominating influence but we do ask freedom to worship God as we think best and to teach as we please and this I fear we shall not get if Rome rules in Uganda.[11]

Lugard also voiced the same opinion and "in a letter impressed on Kabaka Mwanga the necessity of finally declaring himself to be under the British, thereby opting for the possibility that everyone could practice whatever religion he wanted without interference."[12] In the opinions of both Lugard and Tucker, only such a step could put a stop to the perpetual tensions and the constant threat of open war.

"Rome" was often used as a foil in Tucker's correspondence to push for CMS expansion, but also for a political appointee. He was advocating British imperialism to bring about equality of religion, and it is clear from the correspondence that his prejudice against Roman Catholics was pronounced. He also wrote to Robert Lang, who was then the Corresponding Secretary of the CMS, suggesting that the Committee do all in their power to influence the appointment of a good man by IBEA. Lang's response was agreeable but non-committal: "If only there be order and protection of life and property, and full effect of conscience, we should be thoroughly

10. Hansen, *Mission, Church and State*, 27.
11. Tucker to Euan Smith, September 14, 1890, PRO, FO 84/2066. Also Tucker to Portal, March 8, 1892, PRO, FO 84/2230.
12. Lugard to Mwanga, January 15, 1892, Hansen, *Mission, Church and State*, 45.

satisfied."¹³ But the reluctance toward political affairs peeks through in his following remark: "The danger, which the high position of warm influence now held by the Christians, brings to them incident."¹⁴

A reluctant partnership developed which seemed unavoidably necessary to both sides. Gerald Portal eventually became the "strong presence" requested by Tucker. He was sent to Uganda as a Special Commissioner to evaluate the possibility of establishing a Protectorate. After expressing his impatience with missionaries he writes to his mother:

> However, I quite see the necessity of keeping on good terms with the missionaries and I was on terms of the closest friendship with the Bishop [of Zanzibar] till he left and now his successor, Archbishop Bateman, thinks there is no one like me, and that I am an earnest, thoughtful, serious young man, with a sincere belief in the disinterested work of missionaries and full of hope for the regeneration of Africans by these means. This is the result of a good dinner or two with a few good cigars with the chief pillars of the church here. One must be a humbug at times, dearest, and I confess that it amuses me. At the same time when they lay aside all their professional manners and the sad sing-song voice affected by missionaries, the Archdeacon and some others are pleasant men of the world.¹⁵

The slightly forced socializing mentioned by Portal is also mentioned by other administration officers, such as Ernest Gedge, including his attendance at various church services: "yesterday I went to call on the Bishop. He and Gordon came back and had a cup of tea at my house. Have not seen the other missionaries who seem a very queer lot."¹⁶ Based on shared interest and experience, the contact continued in England. When Tucker returned home to muster recruits for the Uganda effort, a "rousing reception" was held for him at Exeter Hall that was attended by both Sir Euan Smith, the retiring Consul-General of Zanzibar, and Gerald Portal, who was to be his successor.¹⁷

Portal continued the assumption of partnership when both had returned to East Africa; writing letters from Zanzibar about the situation in

---

13 Lang to Tucker, December 6, 1890, CMSA, G3/A5/6/65.
14. Ibid.
15. Portal to Lady Portal, May 29, 1889, RHA, Mss Africa 112/95—6.
16. Gedge Diary, January 1, 1891, RHA, 6/4/411.
17. CMS Intelligencer, July 1891, 507.

Uganda which Tucker, although residing on the coast at Freretown, was reasonably informed about through letters from the missionaries there. Portal also wrote regarding the British missionaries in Mochi (now Moshi in Tanzania near Mt. Kilimanjaro) and their troubled interaction with the German administration of the area.

During this brief period of correspondence, Tucker suggested the idea of "spheres of influence" in East Africa for the two competing denominations. He suggested Uganda be occupied completely by English Protestants and the German territory given completely to the French Catholics. The suggestion evolved into a reality in the final stages of the Lugard administration, but only within the borders of Uganda, with eastern areas being assigned to the Protestants and western areas to the Roman Catholics.[18] This idea has been attributed to Captain W. H. Williams, Lugard's second in command, but Tucker's letter is dated a full year prior to the Williams' Memorandum.[19] Since Tucker, Lugard, and Williams met regularly together in Mombasa in August 1890 and Lugard and Tucker in September of 1892, it may have been an idea in common parlance.[20] Tucker lacked the authority to commit the CMS formally to any action; he could only offer a verbal suggestion and refer the matter back to CMS headquarters.

In the beginning stages of the British presence, Portal asked Tucker to help him acquire the signatures of the chiefs on the new peace treaty after an armed conflict in January 1892 which finally placed the Protestant party in ascendance in Uganda. Tucker was unable to assist in any significant way but the request serves as a further illustration of the friendly intertwined relationship. Tucker at the time was busy with coastal affairs during the whole year of 1892—a tumultuous one for mission, church and company in Uganda as it included the bloody skirmish of the Battle of Mengo.[21] Tucker, who was stuck on the coast with work and a lack of porters to travel, could only wait for news and worry. This same year was also a year of significant conflict for the English missionaries in the German sphere of Tucker's diocese, which is sometimes overshadowed by the much studied events in Uganda. Tucker encapsulates his feelings:

---

18. Tucker to Portal, March 24, 1892, PRO, FO 84/2230.

19. Williams' Memorandum, March 10 or 18, 1893, Hansen, 60.

20. Perham and Bull, *The Diaries*, 231, also Tucker to Lang, September 1, 1892, CMSA, G3/A5/O/354 and Tucker to Wigram, September 13, 1892, CMSA, G3/A5/O/383.

21. Portal to Tucker, April 18, 1892, RHA, Mss Af. S110 /15.

> There is so much to be done down here that I am most loath to leave it. Mombasa, Freretown with the enquiry and possible re-organization of things, to say nothing of the other stations on this line, are enough to keep one at work and hard at work here for months. I would give my right hand to be in Uganda at the present moment and yet I feel that I would give my left hand to be able to continue my work here.[22]

During this initial period, socializing and shared goals for peace did not prevent those of a similar cultural background from engaging in some spirited disagreements. Many are referred to in Tucker's letters and are also included in the diaries of missionaries and administrators alike; disagreements over treaties, over the "tone" of letters, over the treatment of Africans, over spheres of missionary influence, just to name a few. As one example: even during this period of cordiality one administrator records in his diary during Tucker's initial visit to Uganda problems with Lugard's assistant: "The Bishop and Williams had a most stormy interview. . ."[23] He does not elaborate on the subject matter and Tucker only refers to their meeting without any further description. He was returning to the coast, and encountered Williams who was five days' march coming into Kampala.[24]

This was not to be the last frictional encounter with Capt. Williams, who was left in charge of Mengo while Lugard travelled. His arrival in Uganda in January of 1891 was to be the beginning of what appears to be a cooling off period with the Company administrators. However, Tucker's relations with Sir Ernest Berkeley, the IBEA Company administrator on the coast, continue on unabated as evidenced by the offering to the CMS of a plot of land in Mombasa for the Hannington Memorial Church as well as the Company's abandoned station in Taveta.[25]

PHASE TWO—CHANGE AND COOLING

When Tucker reached Uganda in December of 1892 for his second visit, the full impact of the situation, which had been building for at least the previous two years, came into focus. Intending to stay only a few months he found it necessary to continue on in Uganda much longer than planned. He

22. Tucker to Lang, May 18, 1892, CMSA, G3/A5/O/197.
23. Gedge Diary, February 21, 1891.
24. Tucker to Sir Charles, January 14, 1891, PRO, FO/84/2147.
25. Tucker to Baylis, September 26, 1892, CMSA, G3/A5/O/401.

writes: "Before arriving here I felt that a sojourn of several months would probably be needed but from what I see and hear it will be hard indeed to get away. The work at the Coast is pressing, but the situation here is even more pressing."[26] Six months would elapse before Tucker was able to return to the coast. In that six months Tucker would deal with the impact, first of all, of finding a congregation of 5,000 Christians in Mengo led by an integrated Church Council but without episcopal oversight.[27] He writes:

> Today it was my glorious privilege to preach to a congregation numbering some 5,000 souls in an entirely new church. The order, the attention, the apparent devotion, the evident heart of the congregation was something quite remarkable. I doubt whether in the whole of Africa, and certainly in not many places in Europe, a similar sight would be seen. What wisdom, what even guidance is needed to deal with such a flock, to organize such a church! May the Great Shepherd himself lead on whither he would have us follow! Much, very much, prayer is needed for the Church of Uganda.[28]

In addition, he encountered the extremely strained relations between the mission, centered on Namirembe Hill, and the personnel of the IBEA Company fort, built on the hill called Kampala. Tucker records: "I am sorry to say that on my arrival here I found the relations between the Company's representative at the Fort and our mission greatly strained. Indeed, things were at a complete dead-lock."[29] He also experienced the disarray of the Finance Committee, the resignation of Mr. Ashe who was the Secretary of the mission; pressure for revisions to the Lugard Treaty of Peace signed just six months before, and serious questions from IBEA as to the missionaries' role in the political situation in Uganda.

In great contrast to his experience with the IBEA Company and the mission on the coast, Tucker realized relations between the two

---

26. Tucker to Baylis, December 25, 1892, CMSA, G3/A5/O/1893/146.

27. CMS Annual Report, Intelligencer, July 1896, 117. Due to the persecution of the Ugandan church members by Mwanga in 1885 and the anticipated forced departure of the missionaries, responsibility for the teaching and governance of the church had been placed in the hands of a church council which included Duta, Mukasa, Semfuma, B. Musoke and leading Protestant chiefs.

28. Tucker to Baylis, September 26, 1892, CMSA, G3/A5/O/401.

29. Tucker to Baylis, December 25, 1892. Tucker had already been informed of this by Baskerville and asked to come and help. Tucker to Lang, August 10, 1892, CMSA, G3/A5/O/325.

organizations in Uganda were quite tense possibly due to the personalities involved. He seems to acknowledge the contribution of the mission personnel to the problem:

> The relations between the Finance Committee and the Resident have been most strained. I will not say who has been to blame but it is the fact nevertheless. Let us suppose for the moment that the Finance Committee feels itself obliged to pass a resolution and to send it to the Resident! The latter naturally asks who are the members of this Committee and when he learns that the majority of the Committee is composed of young men who have come straight from Clapham or Islington or Cambridge [which Ashe did.] and who have spent a few days in the country he will not be disposed to attach much weight to such resolutions.[30]

Lugard himself had expressed concern about Capt. Williams' inability to get along with the missionaries.[31] Mr. Ashe, who had travelled to Uganda in 1891 and became the Secretary (and sometime "President") of the mission in 1892, also attracted controversy.

But beyond personalities, the tensions also involved the conflicting agendas held by CMS missionaries in Uganda and the infant administration. The missionaries, whose presence had preceded any British secular efforts by sixteen years, had been operating squarely within the belief of an evangelical mandate to preach the Gospel to all creation. In their view conversions to Christianity would eventually bring about peace in the midst of enmity. Lacking any British political presence, they were accustomed to seek invitations from African chiefs and to preach or teach where they found opportunity. The evangelism was driven on by a steady competition with the Roman Catholics and a desire on the part of the African chiefs to achieve any benefit that an association with Europeans could accomplish as their power grew. Walker explained: "Many are only followers of the Christian chiefs for the sake of the good they thus get in the country."[32] He coined this, "twilight Christianity."[33] The African Church Council was also anxious to extend their influence into adjoining areas such as Busoga although Walker openly wondered: "It is hard to tell how far this is prompted by a

---

30. Tucker to Baylis, January 2, 1893, CMSA, G3/A5/O/245.
31. Lugard Diary, Hansen, 505.
32. Walker to L. G. Walker, March 5, 1890, CMSA, Acc. 88.
33. Walker to CMS, Annual Report, 1891, 58.

love of souls: one fears that desire for power and wish to exclude Roman Catholics prompts them a good deal."[34]

With the arrival of Lugard and Williams in 1891 a new element of formal control entered the scene. Pressure was placed on the missionaries to follow the Company agenda, which was to bring harmony between the warring Catholic and Protestant political parties but not through personal conversion and societal transformation, rather through negotiation, appeasement, balance and fair play.[35] Access to new areas for evangelism was tightened to keep separate spheres for Protestant and Catholic missions and thus avoid competition and conflict such as that which occurred at the Battle of Mengo. When the missionaries began to look to the Company for protection, the Company felt justified in dictating conditions for missionary work. However, when the missionaries went out independently the Company still felt obligated, as any trouble would fall back on the Company for resolution.[36] Although IBEA could not compel the missionaries to ask permission when expanding their spheres of operations, they could appeal to them for cooperation. The objections of various missionaries to this curtailment concerned the freedom of their own mission and also religious freedom generally. But also there was the resistance of the local, independent, and consensus leadership of the CMS towards the more centralized and imperialistic approach proposed by the IBEA Company.

In the initial stages of the mission in 1891, the CMS lacked the resources and leadership necessary for any expansion. Therefore, denominational apartheid was a theoretical question, as the efforts were focused by necessity on consolidation and continuance in Uganda proper.[37] But despite the initial lack of needed personnel, members of the mission were thinking to the future and Lugard records almost daily rows with the CMS mission over treaty negotiations. The Company began to take a stronger hand in political arrangements. As spheres of influence were being negotiated between Catholic and Protestant the mission was quite aware that the

34. Walker to T. S., March 6, 1891.
35. Lugard Diary, Hansen, 41.
36. Hansen, *Mission, Church and State*, 34.

37 Lang to Tucker, February 3, 1892, CMSA, G3/A5/6/210. 'We shall be very glad if you will enforce with the weight of your opinion our views regarding the necessity of concentrating our efforts on centres, so far as our European Missionaries are concerned, where we can place little bands together who may support each other both in things physical and spiritual, rather than scatter our European forces in a thin line of detached units."

The Mission and The Fort

distribution of chieftainships and offices in their favor would give rise to open doors for their future work.[38]

The pressure over this issue continued to build during 1892, as Tucker, in Mombasa, was making preparation for a second visit up-country with reinforcements and also dealing with the forced evacuation of the CMS missionaries from Mochi [Moshi] in German territory. By this time the missionary presence in Uganda, in addition to Walker, Baskerville and Smith, included R. P. Ashe, J. Roscoe, G. L. Pilkington, Dr. Wright, and W. Collins; plus, two African Evangelists licensed by Tucker, Henry Duta and Sembera MacKay.[39]

The subject of the expanding control of the Fort in regards to the extension of their mission work continued to place the local committee of the CMS in a conundrum as seen by letters to Lugard from the Uganda Finance Committee:

> The question is this, do you refuse us as British Missionaries the right to extend our Missions anywhere in Imperial British E. Africa without your sanction? If you are unable as the Resident in Buganda to answer this on behalf of the Directors, we have only one course open to us, viz. to refer the matter to our Committee [in London] to be brought before the Houses of Parliament. As a matter of courtesy we should refer any extension to you but not as a matter of right.[40]

The missionaries involved were framing themselves within a much larger arena and debate which they articulated as religious liberty.[41] However the differences between the two organizations also involved a local collaborative assessment and governance style on the part of the CMS vs. the increasingly centralized, imperial-styled approach of IBEA through Lugard. With the addition of the strong personality of Ashe, the conflict had escalated into a head–to–head clash about the right of the mission and the Ugandan Evangelists to make their own decisions and move into extension based on their own assessment.

Even given the strong influence of Ashe, the English missionaries showed evidence of internal disagreement, with frequent reversals regarding IBEA's policy of curtailment, especially into Busoga, resulting in a vote

---

38. Hansen, *Mission, Church and State*, 508.
39. CMS Annual Report, 1892, CMSA.
40. Roscoe to Lugard, January 21, 1892, Hansen, *Mission, Church and State*, 36.
41. Hansen, *Mission, Church and State*, 35.

(11 February) to wait for the arrival of Bishop Tucker before making a final decision.[42]

Lugard had devised a treaty with Mwanga, involving an alternating chain of command between Protestant and Catholic office holders. This had become unworkable as it was incompatible with the existing Ugandan political system organized around a centralized patron with clients. He had been forced to revise the agreement around geographical *sazas* (political provinces) which would be allotted to Protestant or Catholic chiefs, based on the predominate creed held by the area's population.

When Lugard began negotiating directly with the Catholic chiefs and French missionaries and signed a treaty (5 April) which assigned Buddu to the Catholics, it prompted Ashe into action. Eight days later (13 April) Ashe wrote a defiant letter to Sir William Mackinnon, Director of IBEA and another to Lugard (30 April) resisting the policy of restriction vigorously.[43] He asserted the need for the independence of the missionaries in their relationships and their advice to the Baganda regardless of the directives of either IBEA or the CMS Committee in London; and he expressed extreme frustration that the company would not settle the situation in favor of the English missionaries, giving them special privileges to evangelize freely throughout the British sphere of influence.[44] Shortly after Lugard's negotiations with the Muslims (3 June) which assigned to them three *sazas* and the Protestants the remainder of the country, the local CMS committee reversed their earlier decision to wait for Tucker and sent Smith and sixty-eight Baganda teachers to Busoga, eight days east of Mengo.[45]

In the latter part of 1892, Williams proposed to revise Lugard's Treaty in anticipation of the arrival of Gerald Portal as a Special Commissioner (March 1893) to assess the feasibility of a Protectorate in Uganda. In this proposed revision the Catholics would be given more leading offices and land in exchange for the return to Mengo of Kabaka Mwanga's heirs, who had been held by the Catholics since the Battle of Mengo. Williams also sought to enforce more tightly Lugard's policy of restricting the evangelistic

---

42. Walker to Father, October 31, 1891. Walker papers, "Now we all do exactly as we like."

43. Ashe to Mackinnon, April 13, 1892, CMSA, G3/A5/8/342 and 343. Also Ashe to Lugard, April 30, 1892, CMSA, G3/A5/8/340.

44. Hansen, *Mission, Church and State*, 54.

45. Minutes of the Diocese of Eastern Equatorial Africa, CMSA.

efforts of both Protestant and Catholic missions.[46] The strength of "The Fort" was growing. In the midst of this effort, Tucker embarked on his inland journey to Uganda, informed by letters from on-the-spot missionaries and from CMS headquarters but not fully aware of the extremely intense situation awaiting him.

As Tucker tramped inland, he may have reflected upon what resources were available to him through his wide variety of friends, acquaintances and colleagues; peers of the realm, art contacts, Oxford classmates, CMS heavy-weights, fellow clergy, Keswick goers, anti-slavery activists, academics, missionaries and former parishioners from the *petite bourgeois*. A flavor of this can be seen from his description of events during his 1891 deputation in Britain: "Together with several warm friends of the Mission and one of the secretaries of the C.M.S., I was staying at a country house in the Highlands, when to our great delight it was told us that Sir William Mackinnon's yacht (founding trustee of IBEA) was steaming up the loch. He was coming to call on our host."[47] His broad interactions and travel throughout England, Europe, and East Africa gave him a breadth of experience and wider horizons than many of the missionaries who were mired, consumed and somewhat isolated within the day to day events in Uganda. As one historian writes: "Certainly the typical CMS candidate did not have the social and educational breadth of an Anglican Oxbridge clergyman."[48] Tucker, of course, *was* an Anglican Oxbridge clergyman. In a private letter to Lord Rosebery, Gerald Portal offers a blunt but descriptive statement: "With the exception of Bishop Tucker all the CMS missionaries were drawn from the lower middle classes."[49]

Sir Harry Johnston, a later Commissioner in Uganda (1899 to 1902), takes note of Tucker's people skills: "[He was] a leader but one who did not drive men along in a set groove but allowed each one full play for individuality of the special gifts which God had given him."[50] Gedge had a different impression of Tucker's light touch: "I had a long talk with him about Ashe

---

46. Hansen, *Mission, Church and State,* 504 outlines this policy of restriction. Although Roscoe may have been the main correspondent, he did not replace Ashe as Secretary of the Finance Committee until January, 1893. Tucker to Baylis, January 2, 1893, CMSA, G3/A5O/245.

47. Tucker, *Eighteen Years,* Ibid., 64.

48. Williams, "Not Quite Gentlemen," 306.

49. Portal to Rosebery, March 22, 1893, Portal Papers, Ms. Afr. S 109.

50. Sir Harry Johnston, Johnston Notebooks, Makerere University, Kampala, Uganda.

and impressed on him the necessity of speaking to that gentleman, but he is a very weak man and lacks the authoritative strength he ought to establish in dealing with his flock."[51]

The bishop had just returned from a visit home where his contacts and friendships had enabled him to almost single-handedly raise the funds to sustain the Company in Uganda for one more year. He felt their presence was needed in Uganda to settle the country—a peacekeeping force. It is not surprising that he would step into Uganda with a positive outlook toward the Company. Along with his experience in personal interaction coupled with a bit more diplomacy than the average missionary, he had a willingness to negotiate or compromise and even agree at times with colonial authorities. He was in short: "a newcomer with a broader perspective."[52]

At the same time, Tucker was committed to the goals and ideals of the Society: the conversion of souls, the preaching of the Gospel to all nations, the uplifting of those he perceived to be caught in darkness, the level ground at the foot of the cross. As IBEA's formal organization increased, the mission, according to Tucker, made inroads as well. He writes: "the whole aspect of the country is changing, specifically morally and materially, and this result I dare venture to say, under God, is due to the work of the Church Missionary Society begun some eighteen years ago."[53] He was anxious to open new stations whenever possible, seeing the Ugandans as natural evangelists and possibly the key to bringing the whole of East Africa under the influence of Christianity. He also shared with Ashe the incredulous reaction to the idea that the Company might lord it over the mission in any way. Just before leaving Mombasa he had met with Lugard, on his way home to England and expressed mild shock at the concept:

> I have just had the advantage of a long conference with Capt. Lugard who arrived yesterday. I have made an appointment for another meeting. May I ask you kindly to put before the committee or some legal authority the following question, "Has the I.B.E.A. Company any right to say to the missionaries of the C.M.S. 'we will not allow you to settle or carry on your work in this country or in that' within the sphere of our effective influence?" I shall be glad to know at the earliest possible moment exactly how the case

---

51. Gedge diary, February 20, 1891, RHA, Mss. Afr. 6/4/411.
52. Hansen, *Mission, Church and State*, 59.
53. Tucker to Fox, October 9, 1895, BGCA, 135/1/1.

stands. The Company through Capt. Lugard had claimed this right with respect to Busoga.[54]

The answer from the Committee placed Tucker squarely in the midst of a magnetic field of opposing forces; his loyalty and responsibilities to the state, his loyalty and responsibility to the Society, his responsibilities to the missionaries and the Ugandan church who wished to evangelize, and his loyalty to his understanding of the commands of scripture. Since Lang had retired, the new Corresponding Secretary, Fredrick Baylis writes:

> While the I.B.E.A. Co. are responsible for the Government of the Country, the Society's Missionaries are not at liberty to undertake work in any unoccupied district without the consent of the Company's representatives in the field, whose directions must be followed pending reference home ... the Committee were clearly of opinion the company's direction must be followed under the circumstances of the anxious position of the I.B.E.A. Co.[55]

Armed with this unsurprising directive as many members of the Society were also involved with IBEA, Tucker continued his steps toward Uganda. If he was troubled by the CMS response he gave no indication in his letters. His dual responsibility as director of mission but bishop of the African church could have served as a natural release valve for the tension of the situation: if he was unable to obey the evangelistic commands of the scripture through the mission, he could do so in his position as leader of the Ugandan church. Or perhaps he perceived the situation as merely temporary. As one of the missionaries serving with Tucker, Doctor J. H. Cook wrote, Tucker possessed "the calm forethought and clear insight of the statesman with the burning zeal of the evangelist."[56]

Drawing on this blending and having clear instruction from headquarters, on his arrival Tucker immediately attempted to continue the strategy of accommodation and arbitrate the yawning rift that had consistently grown larger between the local idealistic, independent-minded mission and the strong-minded Imperial British East Africa Company. Despite the challenges, he remained optimistic almost to the point of naiveté. Perhaps the first meeting with IBEA taking place on Christmas Eve influenced the interactions:

54. Tucker to Lang, September 1, 1892, CMSA, G3/A5/O/354.
55. Baylis to Tucker, November 3, 1892, CMSA, G3/A5/6/434.
56. Cook, "Tucker of Uganda," *CMS Home Gazette*, November 1929, 167.

> In company with Mr. Ashe the day after my arrival [23rd] I had an interview with Capt. Williams who is in command. The questions in dispute, complaints made on the part of the mission and complaints made on the part of the Company were gone into one by one. Each one was carefully and I am happy to say without temper, thrashed out with the result that both Mr. Ashe and Capt. Williams were satisfied. There seemed to have been misunderstanding on both sides. Explanations have been made with the result that harmonious relations are restored.[57]

Although Tucker was not aware of it, Ashe had already resigned his position with the CMS due to a difference of opinion with the Bishop over the disposal of CMS supplies in Usambiro. The letter of resignation passed Tucker on the road as he marched to Uganda but when he learned of it, he wrote an apology letter to Ashe for the misunderstanding. But on the same day as Tucker's arrival Ashe resigned a second time. This time for a wider reason:

> Thank you so much for your kind and considerate letter. I feel quite apart from any question between you and myself that I had no alternative but to send in my resignation to the C.M.S. were it only on the ground of communications from the African Secretary relative to the unfortunate incident of the burning of part of an Usakuma village. Also the general tone of the letters I receive is not calculated to make me wish to continue the connection. But still more I feel that the whole tendency of the C.M.S. policy is not one which I can heartily endorse.[58]

It was a policy of containment of the missionaries in the face of growing government influence. Tucker chose to bide his time as the relationship with IBEA cooled, and juggle these two forces; Ashe chose to resign.

However, it was not long before the call to expand, regardless of government policy and Committee admonition, began to pull at Tucker's compartmentalized position. The call came from a surprising source and gives a clear insight into the divided world traversed by missionary types:

> So far as Mengo, the capital, was concerned, the prospects were [of a] most cheering and encouraging character, and this in spite of the rancour of political controversy and almost daily alarms of war. But how about the country, the many counties of Uganda

---

57. Tucker to Baylis, December 25, 1892, CMSA, G3/A5/O/146.
58. Ashe to Tucker, December 23, 1892, CMSA, G3/A5/O/245.

absolutely untouched? Could nothing be done to extend the work of the Church into the regions beyond? This question we debated amongst ourselves over and over again. As usual in such cases light upon it came from the Church Council. Nikodemo Sebwato, who was Pokino (ruler of Budu) on the occasion of my first visit to Uganda, had recently, under the new settlement, become Sekibobo (chief of Kyagwe). He was most anxious that work should be commenced in his county as soon as possible and begged the Church Council to suggest it to us. The proposal was accepted with alacrity, and on February 13 I left Mengo, in company with Baskerville and Crabtree, in order to select a site for a Mission-station.[59]

Despite the tangle of loyalties and obligations, Tucker moved forward using Nikodemo Sebwato's invitation to take cover from the opposing tension of imperial oversight which discouraged expansion. Even the CMS home committee was tempered by caution. But the idealistic beliefs held by Tucker, the local committee and, in part, the Ugandan Church Council prevailed.

This new station did not raise a reaction from IBEA. However, a week later Tucker did receive a reaction as he proposed to open a third station in Singo, to the northwest but still within Uganda proper.[60] At this point IBEA, whose presence had been extended due to donations, was still negotiating a delicate peace between Ugandan political factions, while waiting for Gerald Portal's formal assessment as to whether Uganda should become a Protectorate. Bowing to their pressure, Tucker postponed his plans:

> In deference to your expressed opinion as to the advisability of not sending a mission into Singo at the present juncture and being anxious to avoid even the appearance of unfairness, I have decided not to ask Misters Gunther and Fisher to go into the MuKwenda's country. They will therefore remain here until after the arrival of Sir Gerald Portal. You will I have no doubt agree that this action of mine shall be without prejudice to the Protestant claim on Singo.[61]

59. Tucker, *Eighteen Years*, 118.
60. Tucker to Baylis, February 11, 1893, CMSA, G3/A5/O/133.
61. Tucker to Capt. Macdonald, February 20, 1893, CMSA, G3/A5/O/194. The Roman Catholic advance was a constant consideration in Tucker's letters. Tucker complains, "The Roman Catholics have followed consistently from the earliest days until now. I can mention case after case. At Buhili in Toro they have planted their station so close to ours that a single fence divides their property from ours. We had been on our present site four or five years before they put in an appearance. At Gayaza where we have been working for the last 15 years the Roman Catholics have at length followed and as of two

Portal arrived (17 March) assessed the situation and initiated a conditional British rule (1 April) pending approval by Parliament. The Fort was about to expand to include a Colonial government, with ever-widening power. Tucker felt free to proceed with his original plans and opened the extension into Singo (May 20) just two months later. The stutter-stepping of when and where to expand clearly illustrates the situation of the English missionaries who were plainly caught between an expanding imperialistic agenda, in themselves and others, and the religious values which called for equal opportunity for all to respond to the evangelistic Gospel.

PHASE THREE: FRICTION

Five months after Portal had arrived and gone, Tucker's correspondence with the English authorities began to display a negative and pessimistic turn, not only in Uganda, but on the coast as well. While Portal's report of the situation in Uganda went before the Parliament for final approval (20 December, 1893), the British government was now represented by a provisional presence and Tucker begins to complain about the "highhandedness" of the colonial administration. Stemming from an incident of robbery to the caravan of a leading chief called the Kaima, who was also a licensed evangelist, by two Nubian soldiers employed by the administration, Tucker attempted to mitigate the punishment dealt out to the Kaima for disarming two of Her Majesty's troops. The small colonial government began to assert its power. Since the incident occurred at a time of unrest which precipitated the evacuation of the IBEA administration and before the protectorate, Tucker argued that the case should have been referred to the King for settlement in accordance with tribal law, which allowed for an item to be taken from the accused for identification purposes. He succeeded in having the punishment reduced from imprisonment to a fine, which he promptly paid. He went on to complain about Portal's treaty signing with the Kabaka alone, ignoring the legally functioning institution of the council of chiefs. His detailed analysis of the interaction between Mission and Fort bears repeating at some length:

> The country has since the restoration of Mwanga enjoyed something of a popular government. The Government consisted of

---

years ago opened a station so close that here again our properties adjoin one another. At Kakanonzi we were followed, at Mitiana it was the same, at Koki still the same, and so on." Tucker to Baylis, CMS Archives, G3/A7/O/1910/30.

the King and chiefs. The autocratic power of the King had been abolished. The new order of things were (sic) recognized by the Company and both these treaties were signed by the King and Chiefs. The Consul General has ignored this Constitutional Government and has contented himself with getting the signature of the King alone to the treaty signed on May 29th, 1893. In other words, Sir Gerald Portal has smothered the first breathings of popular Government in Uganda and nominally re-established the tyranny of past days. I wonder what a liberal Government thinks of this? Of course, with this as a matter of politics I have nothing whatever to do, but underneath it all there is a policy which I believe will require very careful watching. This ignoring the chiefs, in my opinion, is the first step towards an attempt to break down the powers of the Mission. If this were merely the power of the Mission in the field of politics that was ending, nothing would rejoice me more heartily than such a consummation. But my belief is that unless a Resident is appointed with some sort of sympathy with Christian Missions we shall find attempts made more or less openly to cripple, or at any rate to hamper, our work. One's conflict of course in such a thought is that so far as it is of God it cannot be overthrown. But it behooves us to take every precaution possible for the protection of that which has cost so much.[62]

On the surface it is an illustration of the increasing power of the British administration as the Protectorate gained momentum and Tucker found it necessary to adjust his strategy. It also illustrates the internal conflict between Tucker's perception of universal Christian religious values and the imperial context of those values. Tucker criticized the heavy-handed, imperialistic style of Portal which ignored the blossoming Ugandan popular government, but this criticism is never voiced directly to Portal, instead he remains cordial. Tucker seeks to consult and protect the infant African Church but at the same time subjugates African clergy to European clergy. It is also ironic that Tucker would appeal to the power of the King to address the injustice of the Kaima's case, but also criticize Portal for attempting the same action. Tucker was pragmatic in his rhetorical style, whatever argument worked for the immediate need was the approach taken. But this leaves us with the question, where did his true energies lie: with the mission or with the Ugandans? Or was he unable to commit to either fully?[63]

62. Tucker to Baylis, August 31, 1893, CMSA, G3/A5/O/242.

63. It would be accurate to assess Tucker's perception of the African Christians as younger brothers and sisters. Brothers and sisters are equal in that they are all offspring

During this same period Tucker lamented, with growing frustration, the jumbled patchwork of local colonial arrangements. His complaints illustrate the preliminary nature of the British presence, but also the increasingly high profile of British influence in East Africa—more administrators, soldiers, and judicial responsibilities. As Col. H. E. Colville, Acting Commissioner in Uganda, finalized the Protectorate with Mwanga, Tucker complained that some of the outlying provinces were not being included in the Protectorate but returned to "slave raiding and slave trading" rulers. Tucker described the existing system; from a Sultan "puppet" ruler on the coast to an IBEA administrator in Mombasa, back to the protectorate of Witu answering to Zanzibar, cross the river and into the Kavirondo protectorate answering to the Commissioner in Uganda, cross the Nile and enter the Uganda protectorate answering to the Foreign Office, half of which was leased and the other half under the Commissioner in Uganda.[64] "When will the Government take the bull by the horns and bring the whole of this British East Africa under one head and administration? Not until they do so shall we have efficiency, economy or anything like a settled policy of either administration or development."[65] His concern to oppose autocratic power seemed to have evaporated and replaced with an irritation with inefficiency.

Termination of Company rule and the initiation of the Protectorate of British East Africa (1 July, 1895) had dispatched Sir Arthur Hardinge to Mombasa arriving six months later. The British presence had reached full flower. Tucker's discontent grew and the good relations with administrators on the coast, which had lasted for four years, began to unravel. The complicated issue of African Christian divorce cases within a Muslim state when the advisors to the Sultan were English Christians has already been addressed in a previous chapter but coastal relationships also suffered over the jurisdiction of Rabai. Because of its long history Tucker felt justified settling disputes between those living on mission land in Rabai, regardless of the subject matter. Rabai had been a mission station since 1846, having been founded by the legendary missionary team of Krapf and Rebmann.[66] So when tension arose between the Indian caravan agents and the African

---

from the same parents, but some are the eldest. Although the African Christians may have been equal to him, they were not Europeans and there was always a distance. He never "went native," maintaining a slight aloofness, but thought Africans could progress to the same level.

64. Tucker to Fox, July 31, 1894, BGCA, 135 /1/1.
65. Ibid.
66. Anderson, *Church in East Africa*, 2. And Anderson, *Biographical Dictionary*.

Wazee (elders) of Rabai, Tucker held a *Baraza* (town forum) and issued a proclamation addressing the problem areas and setting forth the rules to be obeyed.[67] But with the declaration of the Protectorate, these pioneer days of the missionaries acting as administrators for law and order were now at an end and Hardinge, now the Consul-General, took exception to the Bishop issuing orders touching on civil matters, regardless of the location. Civil disputes must be referred to the newly established civil authorities even when they occurred on mission land. Tucker was compelled to begin the transition from being an imperial power broker to being an imperial subject, a transition to which the Rabai Wazee could, no doubt, relate. Always sensitive of his status and touchy if encroached upon, he did not take this without complaint.

PHASE FOUR: THE LOYAL OPPOSITION

Perceptions of highhandedness, disorganization, confusion, and jurisdictional disputes were added to the slavery issue on the coast, to engender a position shift on the part of Tucker. The "hail fellow well met" comradeship of earlier years of European interaction with Africa, which included a bit of family feuding, seemed to give way to a more structured formalized dance which took on the characteristics of the loyal opposition. It was a situation similar to the relationship which exists between political power and the watchdog press.

Four years of relative peace had passed since the departure of Hardinge from Mombasa and Sir Ernest Berkeley from Uganda, replaced by Sir Charles Eliot and Sir James Hayes-Sadler respectively. However, some of the friction was still present between the mission and the colonial administration, even after the departure of specific personalities. Tucker refers to this tension when placing a missionary in Entebbe to minister part time to the ex-patriot community: "We *must* have a missionary in Ntebbe (sic) and we *must* have a chaplain there, and there is not work for two men. Mr. Willis since his arrival at Ntebbe has done a great deal to break down that prejudice which exists in the minds of many government officials against missionaries in general."[68] Another example of this abiding tension can be found in a letter of introduction for W. E. R. Cole who became the Assistant

---

67. Wazee and Hindis Proclamation, December 10, 1897, PRO, FO 881/7024.
68. Tucker to Baylis, May 8, 1903, CMSA, G3/A7/O/96.

Treasurer at Entebbe: "He is well inclined to Missionary work, but may be drifting into society in which little is made of our work."[69]

Regardless of this discounted position, Tucker clearly sees his responsibility as one which includes being alert to abuses of power on the part of government officials, even when the government personnel were "thoroughly in sympathy with us," as in the case of Col. Hayes-Sadler, who arrived as Commissioner of Uganda in 1902, and received Tucker's complaint regarding the shooting of an African in a fit of rage by the Resident of the Nile Province:[70]

> To my surprise and sorrow (sorrow for humanity's sake) he practically admitted the whole thing. He told me that he got angry at the man refusing to come to him and fired not intending to kill him . . . I felt that one's responsibility towards these poor helpless people made it absolutely necessary to bring the matter before him. This I did without loss of time. The chief was called and repeated the story and the Resident acknowledged the main facts of the case. He was therefore suspended and has been sent to the Commissioner at Ntebbe where I suppose he will be put upon his trial . . . One result, I feel sure of my recent journey will be better government for the Nile Province[71]

Tucker also felt that this duty to be a watchdog also extended to keeping an eye on government policy as in the case of the formation of the "Uganda Association." The original idea for a group of people having an interest in Uganda was sent to Tucker by his long-time friend and correspondent, Mrs. Carus-Wilson. Tucker floated the idea to Sir H. M. Stanley, Sir Fowell Buxton, Sir J. Kennaway, Rev. H. E. Fox and other influential men associated with the CMS. But Sir Harry H. Johnston was the most enthusiastic about the association and agreed with Tucker that a group was needed "to help the Baganda and to stand between them and any arbitrary action on the part of the government . . . acting as a check on the government"[72]

In the same vein Tucker comments on newspaper clippings sent to him by Carus-Wilson regarding a new commercial company forming to grow and harvest rubber in Uganda:

69. Baylis to Tucker, January 20, 1905, CMSA, G3/A7/2/14.

70. Tucker to Baylis, May 24, 1904, CMSA, G3/A7/1/446 and Tucker to Carus-Wilson, May 8, 1904, BGCA, 135 /1/2.

71. Tucker to Carus-Wilson, May 8, 1904.

72. Tucker to Carus-Wilson, October 11, 1902.

The Mission and The Fort

> I have seen the advertisements of the Mabira Forest Company. Many questions arise out of it. One is the right of the government to alienate the forests from the Buganda to whom they are secured by treaty. Another is whether the government ought not to prohibit this company from employing Buganda to collect rubber in these parts of the forest where the Tsetse fly is found . . . that is how the sleeping sickness is spread, by Government negligence and culpable complicity. Money is being made out of the lives of the Buganda. I only saw the advertisement yesterday or I would have moved before.[73]

Tucker also put pressure on the government to abandon the plan to resettle Asians in Busoga which was depopulated by famine and disease:

> Since my return I have been engaged in getting up my case against the Governor's [Bell] proposal to immigrate Indians to Busoga . . . instead of giving the people a chance to recover themselves and repopulate their own country the Governor proposes to import Indians. This will really mean the blotting out of the Busoga from the list of nations and to my mind to take advantage of their present condition of distress and sorrow. To hand their lands over to an alien people is to inflict a cruel wrong upon them . . . given a chance the Busoga can recover themselves. I have just returned from visiting Busoga and have had the advantage of a conference with some of the principal chiefs. My case is now complete and it goes by this mail to the Commissioner . . . They shan't be blotted out if I can help it.[74]

Nearing his retirement, Tucker's tendency to crusade on behalf of the Africans became even more pronounced as exploitative maneuvers increased. But in keeping with his well-established pattern of having high ideals and also an official place in English imperial society, he goes through the proper channels to try to bring about change and rectify what he judges to be a wrong.

The government was not insensitive to the criticism of the watch-dog missionaries. They were well aware that at this time the missionaries were connected to a wider arena which included individuals of wealth, power or influence. CMS also had a large support base informed with newsletters, slide shows, public meetings, letters to newspapers, sermons, prayer meetings, small gatherings, etc. Therefore, the administration was careful

---

73. Tucker to Carus-Wilson, September 19, 1906, BGCA, 135 /1/3.
74. Tucker to Carus-Wilson, September 9, 1909, BGCA, 135/1/3.

to continue Gerald Portal's approach of keeping the missionaries appeased as can be seen as late as 1906:

> As the matter at present stands, it seems uncertain whether a Christian marriage can be dissolved by the local Kathie according to Mohammedan (sic) law, but even if such is the case, it is inexpedient that such a practice, or potential practice, should continue, as it would undoubtedly lead, should it become general, to complaints by the missionaries.[75]

Sometimes this appeasement led to defeats for proposed colonial legislation as in the case of the Liquor Bill in South Africa:

> You will be glad to hear that I got the Archbishop last night to (sic) in the House of Lords the question of the Liquor Bill in South Africa with the result that I have got all I wanted. The government caved in completely. I was on the steps of the throne and suffered the brief for the Archbishop. He did the whole thing very well indeed and made a good speech.[76]

The government adhered to a policy of appeasement and negotiation with the watch-dog missionaries but some missionaries, such as Tucker, had an approach which could be described as "keep your opposition within your own tent." When the colonial office proposed an amalgamation of the Uganda Protectorate with that of East Africa and moving the capital to Nairobi, Tucker reveals an attitude of apprehension to the idea in a letter to Carus-Wilson on Sept. 9, 1909: "I am afraid we shall suffer if the final authority is at Nairobi instead of being here [Uganda]. One has felt a large amount of security in having the Governor at hand and in being able to approach him at any moment of difficulty." Close but not too close, he was part of the imperial system but yet not overtaken by the agenda.

SUMMARY AND CONCLUSION

An assessment of the relationship between one of the leading missionaries of the high imperial era in East Africa and the colonial administration reveals diversity among fellow missionaries but also a progression or evolution of this interaction. Four stages are discernable: cordiality, cooling,

---

75. Barrington to Acting Consul-General Sinclair, November 20, 1906, PRO, FO 881 / 9102.

76. Tucker to Carus-Wilson, June 23, 1908, BGCA, 135/1/3.

The Mission and The Fort

friction, and opposition. These stages are a result of personalities but also of the expanding colonial powers. They represent a shift of strategy from easy accommodation to guarded opposition. During the cordiality stage a reluctant partnership developed due to mutual benefit, peace for both trade and evangelism. Gradually a cooling of this cordiality took place as day-to-day interaction revealed differing agendas. The CMS believed peace came from a transforming Gospel whereas IBEA utilized negotiation, appeasement, and curtailment. The IBEA policy of missionary restriction came to a head during Tucker's second visit which finally resolved itself with African initiative and administrative permission. Friction replaced the cooling period as personalities played a significant role in handling issues during the transitional period from pioneer presence to protectorate. Finally, Tucker settled into a role which could be described as the "watch dog" missionary or the "loyal opposition;" part of the imperial system but not necessarily of the same opinion especially in regards to the rights of Africans.

In all of these phases of interaction with the IBEA Company personnel and later with the administration of the various protectorates in East Africa, Tucker displayed the characteristic of keeping a foot in two opposing camps—straddling that wide rift between two powerful forces. On the one hand he shared the opinions of the imperial party, that a strong British presence was needed to force peace and progress and no one could do it better than Britain. On the other hand, he recoiled from too much force in pressing this agenda, preferring to consider strongly the opinions and approaches of the indigenous Christians informed by his own sense of justice. Based on almost twenty years of interaction, long-term CMS missionary in Uganda George Baskerville's observations, are revealing: "As a guest he was charming. He liked to hear about you but he never invited confidences, though he was always ready with advice and commendation."[77] Balancing spheres to the very last, Tucker succeeded in operating with a slight distance from all parties; political, missionary, and indigenous.

---

77. Baskerville memories, no date given but collected by Carus-Wilson for a biography eventually published in 1929, BGCA, 135/1/5.

CHAPTER SEVEN

"Dusky Brethren"
Consultation with The Africans

FIVE YEARS AFTER TUCKER'S arrival in Africa, an increasing number of European female candidates began to offer themselves for missionary service, out of all proportion to male candidates. The Victorian custom of providing constant female chaperoning by males began to curtail the ability of the CMS to place female missionaries in the field. Fredrick Baylis, Corresponding Secretary of the CMS from 1892 to 1912, in writing to Tucker addressed the problem with a surprising yet characteristic suggestion coming from the CMS:

> there are several women candidates who seem particularly fitted for East Africa work and some of them we should much like to send, but what is to be done with them? . . .We have ventured to look forward to such work in West Africa, and having made some trial of the plan have felt that it is quite possible for say two or more ladies to settle in an African town or village, where there is no European male, but where some native, perhaps a trusted catechist, can in some degree act as a support and defence for them . . . We are faced by the problem of an inadequate proportion of men workers.[1]

Entrusting the female missionaries to the care of an African catechist expressed a certain amount of trust and social recognition toward the

---

1. Baylis to Tucker, May 7, 1895, CMSA, G3/A5 /7/374.

African Christians. At the same time, a European male to chaperon the ladies would have been so much better! Here is found simultaneously the blend of egalitarianism and imperialism which characterized the Victorian missionaries.

Most scholars acknowledge that a type of partnership with the Africans existed during the high imperial period, which Tucker's tenure in East Africa closely parallels, but the nature of this partnership is sometimes in dispute. Some scholars attribute such alliances to relationships formed for exploitation whereas others acknowledge the profound respect and intimacy that some missionaries acquired.[2] Still others acknowledge the intimacy and complementary roles between missionaries and Africans but place emphasis primarily on the translation project.[3] In any event, necessity caused the theory of partnership, long held by the CMS, to be applied in the East African setting in sometimes unanticipated circumstances, such as in the case of women candidates cited above.

The Tucker correspondence reveals joint decisions and sometimes the opposite, non-partnership, on the part of Africans and Europeans. Opportunities for consultations between Europeans and Africans took many different expressions: diverse partnership arrangements; outright consultation with the Africans; African initiative; and European imperialism. Occasionally several different approaches are referenced in the same letter, some in a paradoxical way.

DIVERSE PARTNERSHIPS

The partnership which Europeans and Africans developed can be found in various attitudes and practical approaches as things got off the ground in the initial encounter. British personnel were not averse to appreciate African spirituality, practical skills, underlying philosophy, financial arrangements, evangelism, and teaching and translating skills.

---

2. Cox, *Imperial Fault Lines*, 16, and Kevin Ward. Also Stanley, *The Church Mission Society*, 4. Tucker reveals the intimacy some missionaries acquired when he writes that Mr. Wray mastered the language of Taita so well "that the report was spread abroad some time ago that there was a white Mtaita living on the mountain." Tucker to Stock, March 22, 1895, CMSA, G3/A5/O/152.

3. Sanneh, *Abolitionists Abroad*, 173; also "The CMS and the African Transformation," in *The Church Missionary Society*, 174.

SPIRITUALITY

Out of the forty-three letters which describe various partnerships there are fifteen references (roughly 34%) which communicate a belief on the part of Tucker of a type of spiritual parity between African and European Christians. For example, Tucker writes of his admiration for the abilities of some of the African Christians, and a desire to imitate some of the innovative practices of the African church:

> Last Sunday (March 12th) we had two remarkable sermons—one by Yairo (candidate for ordination), and the other by Nathannaeli, who I trust may be ordained when he is a little older; at present he is under age. The latter sermon breathed a true missionary spirit . . . As a rule, just before the commencement of the service, the whole of the Church elders (or Council) meet the clergy in the vestry for ten minutes' prayer . . . I cannot help thinking that such a plan would be most fruitful at home."[4]

Another letter states: "I have been greatly cheered by the intercourse which I have had from time to time with the [African] candidates . . . I am glad to say that it will be with the utmost confidence that I shall ordain them on Sunday."[5] He then lists the names of all six candidates in full, together with the names of the four European missionaries being ordained at the same service. Not only does Tucker express admiration for the spiritual attributes of African clergy, for example Nikodemo Sebuwato, whom he describes as "devoted . . . earnest . . . faithful . . . true hearted , , , a lesson to come in contact with,"[6] but when travelling on confirmation trips with a mixed company of European and African ministers, all shared equal accommodations: "They have two large houses, one of which was placed at our disposal during our stay of three days; I occupied one room, the Archdeacon a second and Henry Wright Duta, who was also of the party, a third."[7] Adding to the impression of spiritual equality, if not linguistic superiority, was the decision to publish a commentary on Matthew's gospel

---

4. Tucker, March 13, 1893, *Intelligencer*, Vol. XLIV, Vol. XVIII, New Series, 684.

5. Tucker to Stock, May 20, 1893, CMSA, G3/A5/O/233.

6. Tucker to Baylis, June 18, 1895, CMSA, G3/A5/O/203; Also on hearing of the death of "Old Isaya," the oldest Christian convert, Tucker wrote, "He was one of the most earnest and simple hearted Christians I have ever known. He sheltered in the days of persecution those who were being sought out for death and this at the risk of his life. We are all conscious of a great loss." Tucker to Baylis, May 24, 1904, CMSA, G3/A7/O/126.

7. Tucker to Stock, December 3, 1895, CMSA, G3/A5O/96.

written by Ham Mukassa: "The historical allusions of course are mostly from notes taken at the Archdeacon's lectures to his Divinity Class. There is, however, a good deal of original work in the book."[8]

African evangelists, teachers, and clergy were recognized as the sole representatives of Christianity in the rural areas, and were also referred to frequently by the title "missionary" as in the case of Petero and Marko, "the two first missionaries to Toro, [who] were men full of love and zeal, and with a will they set themselves to the task of making Christ known to the Batoro."[9] On an earlier occasion Tucker expresses not only his delight at the dedication in Mengo of the first African lay evangelists, who would later become the first ordained Ugandans, but also the feeling of family and belonging:

> On that memorable 20th of January those six lay evangelists, together with the seventy who had been confirmed on the 18th, and the European missionaries, all gathered round the table of the Lord. . .What joy to kneel with those dusky brethren and sisters, and with heart and soul repeat that wonderful prayer of self consecration[10]

The poetic style was typical of Tucker as he attempted to capture the sense of oneness and equality. He goes on to describe the missionaries' determination, with a large infusion of idealism, that despite the unrest that sometimes threatened violence, they would "share the lot of the church of

---

8. Tucker to Baylis, June 3, 1899, CMSA, G3/A7/O/149.

9. Tucker, *Intelligencer*, January 1897, 35. Also Tucker to Stock, December 3, 1895. Other references to the term missionary include Henry Mukassa, "one of the first band of Missionaries sent to Nassa and by his steady good qualities has earned the respect and regard of all who know him," and "Nua Kikwabanga. . .Missionary to Buroga," Tucker to Stock, June 6, 1896, CMSA, G3/A5/O/271. Tomasi Semfuma to Koki, Nua Nakiwafu to Toro, Yosua and Jokabedi Kiwavu to Busoga are named as missionaries in Tucker to Baylis, June 3, 1899, Ibid; and Joeri Wamala to Nasa in Tucker to Baylis, May 20, 1900, CMSA, G3/A7/O/121. Apolo Kivabulaya, ordained by Tucker is then called "missionary to Toro" in Tucker to Baylis, January 5, 1901, CMSA, G3/A7/O/62. Tucker articulates his commitment to the evangelization of Africa by African missionaries in his "Speech by the Bishop of Uganda at the Church Congress, Brighton, 1901," 3, NLS, BY 26520. To distinguish, the British were called "European missionaries," as in Tucker, "Statistics of the Work in Buganda," October 5, 1896, CMSA, G3/A5/O/276.

10. Tucker, "Bishop Tucker's Reception," *Intelligencer*, July 1891, CMSA, 521. The six were: Henry Wright Duta, Sembera MacKay, Mika Semolimba, Paulo Bakunga, Zakaria Kizito and Yohana Mwina. Tucker to Wigram, December 30, 1890, CMSA, G3/A5/O/124.

Buganda whatever that lot may be."¹¹ Yet bound up in the term "dusky brethren" are hints of an oxymoron that the sharing would not always be equal. For example, at the monthly missionary meetings the Africans and Europeans reported equally, and while African evangelists sometimes operated independently, it was more often the case that the Africans were placed under the supervision of a European missionary.[12]

JOINT SKILLS

Another category of partnerships is found in letters which document joint skills and services to accomplish the work of the mission or church (approximately 14%). Typical of this category would be the descriptions of the training for African evangelists and priests. In a partnership approach, candidates were selected, supported financially and given title (position) by the Native Church Council which was already established by the time of Tucker's arrival. Nevertheless, the candidates were endorsed and trained by the missionaries, both formally in a class room setting and with field supervision.[13] Another example of joint efforts would be the provision of land, dwellings, and food by the chiefs for mission use or the building of dormitories for schools while the missionaries provided, for their part, training and instruction.[14] Despite these partnership arrangements, the articulation of joint endeavors with the Africans carried with it the definite connotation that one partner was the elder and one the younger, as illustrated in Tucker's contributions at Lambeth as he describes the general mind set held by many:

> We are pretty convinced in our mind that we have everything to give and nothing to receive; everything to teach and nothing to learn; moreover we find it very difficult to believe that there is anything of good in the pagan races of Africa, — that they have nothing to give; that they have nothing that they can contribute to the common weal; that they have no message for us at all. Is it

---

11. Tucker to Stock, May 20, 1893.
12. Tucker to Stock, October 14, 1895, CMSA, G3/A5/O/1896 / 60.
13. Tucker to Wigram, December 30, 1890, CMSA, G3/A5/O/124; Tucker to Baylis, February 9, 1899, CMSA, G3/A7/O/74; Tucker to Baylis, May 8, 1899, CMSA, G3/A7/O/113.
14. Tucker to Baylis, October 8, 1907, CMSA, G3/A7/O/243.

so? Nay, I believe it to be far otherwise. Many, I believe, have much that they can teach us.[15]

Tucker went on to explain that the "whole of our church organization has been based upon a . . . native method of administration" which was financially independent and employed a "native ministry" with their own illustrations and methods, educated in the vernacular and living their lives "as Buganda with all their racial and national characteristics adorned and beautified with Christian graces and virtues."[16] At the same time Tucker refers to the Africans as "the child race of the Baganda" or "our own child races of Central Africa" and insists that it is the obligation and duty of the missionaries, and not the Africans themselves, to "enlist, lay hold of and utilize to the very utmost these influences" which would bring about a church on national lines. The missionaries were encouraged to deny their own "masterful Anglo-Saxon temperament," much as an older brother would, and allow the qualities which were appreciated in the African full-play such as, childlike faith, simplicity, gentleness, patient capacity for teaching, and belief in the reality of the unseen.[17] There was recognition that each nationality had a share in the church, but at the same time an admonition that it was up to the missionaries, as the superior power, to make room for others to play their parts. Tucker added prophetically: "Uganda is a kingdom with a nationality of its own; and a time will come when it will pass from the stage of childhood . . . and it will claim for itself the freedom to do as it pleases in these matters."[18]

UNDERLYING PHILOSOPHY

A very small number of letters display simply an attitude or philosophy toward the work which could be termed egalitarian. For example, the Bishop's Charge to the Diocese in 1898 addresses the "brethren beloved; men and women, Native and European" and reminds all that missionary dominance in the design of church governance, architecture, or style of leadership will not bring about a healthy church.[19] Another example would be the insis-

---

15. Lambeth Speech, August 1897, Lambeth Council Records, LPA, LC 66, 132–38.
16. Ibid.
17. Ibid.
18. Ibid.
19. Tucker, "Bishop Tucker's Charge," February 1898, Intelligencer, 98.

tence by Tucker that annual letters of the African clergy should properly be sent to the Native Church Council as the supervising authority and not to the CMS, seeking to emphasize the autonomy of the African church.[20] A further illustration of this attitude can be found in the fact that African testimony regarding abuses on the part of missionaries and government officials was regarded on an equal basis with European testimony. For example, Tucker took into account both African and European observations concerning the conditions at the Freretown dormitories, the complaints about treaty arrangements, the shooting of an African in the Nile providence, and the request to move a European missionary from Gayaza because he was "impeding the work there."[21]

JOINT FINANCIAL ARRANGEMENTS

The fourth sub-category of various partnerships gives evidence to joint responsibility in financial arrangements. In the early stages of the mission the Bagandan Christians provided substantially for the upkeep of the missionaries as Tucker explains:

> In no other part of the world is there to be found a native church which is so disposed to support itself and its ministry as the church of Buganda. The land occupied by the missionaries is a gift from the people, the houses occupied by Messrs. Gordon and Walker were built for them by the Christians . . . everyday the Christians bring us food in such quantities that we have more than enough for sustenance.[22]

Although it could be observed that the initial provision of houses and food might represent cultural responsibilities of hospitality, within a short period of time the Native Church Council was providing for Baganda evangelists as well, as Tucker describes: "Most earnestly do I ask the prayers of all Christians at home for this band of native evangelists. They will be supported entirely by the native church and will I hope be so trained by Mr. Walker . . . that the whole land will be blessed through them."[23] Again

20. Tucker to Baylis, November 7, 1900, CMSA, G3/A7/O/2.

21. Tucker to Wigram, June 3, 1892, CMSA, G3/A5/O/238; Tucker to Baylis, January 17, 1893, CMSA, G3/A5/O/246; Tucker to Carus-Wilson, May 8, 1904, BGCA, 135/1/2; Tucker to Baylis, July 10, 1899, CMSA, G3/A7/O/164.

22. Tucker to Wigram, December 30, 1890, CMSA, G3/A5/O/124.

23. Ibid.

we see a pattern of partnership, financial support from the Africans and training from the Europeans who were supported from home.

A system of patrons and clients was (and is) an integral part of the African political and social system. Kabaka Mwanga (King, 1884–1900) established a new system of clientele after his enthronement as he sought to engender loyalty and consolidate political power moving away from the clientele system of his father, Mutesa.[24] Both Catholic and Protestant missionaries, as well as the Muslim teachers at court, were caught up in the power struggle as they and their converts became incorporated into competing lines of patronage. The financial commitment of the chiefs, in order to be fully understood, must be placed within this context.

It was Tucker's consistent opinion that the African church should be financially independent believing that foreign financial investment invited foreign control. This he expressed at every opportunity through speeches at Lambeth, addresses to the diocese, warnings to both missionaries and the CMS committee, and suggestions in administrative reporting practices. Tucker's financial views have been analyzed chronologically emphasizing his commitment to the self-supporting African church. Yet there was also a partnership in financial arrangements, especially in regards to support for large projects such as schools and hospitals; which extended to England, but also outside of Christian circles to the wider African community due to the overwhelming financial burden.[25] However, in Tucker's strong insistence on self-support he consistently overlooked the fact that he himself was an officer of the native church but supported by overseas investment.

When the CMS Parent Committee informed Mr. Binns, Secretary of the Mombasa mission, that offerings collected in the "native" Mombasa congregations were considered to be CMS funds, Tucker challenged the CMS, feeling that their arm had become too long and threatened the partnership understanding. Tucker protested: "Allow me to say that while I quite grant (as I said in the house the other day) that so long as the CMS pay the stipend of the pastor they have a right to a certain measure of control, I cannot agree to the statement that these funds are absolutely CMS property."[26] Quoting back to the Committee the regulations of the Society, he bolstered his opinion: "The part which the CMS should play in the matter of this fund is I think stated in the regulations of the Society where native admin-

24. Hansen, *Mission, Church and State*, 14.
25. Griffiths, "Bishop Alfred Tucker," 261.
26. Tucker to Baylis, June 28, 1897, CMSA, G3/A5/O/161.

istration is spoken of, that 'administration *to some extent* [emphasis his] is controlled by the Society, so long at least as the fund receives a grant from the Society.' This is not the absolute control which your letter seems to me to suggest."[27]

Tucker preferred a grant-in-aid understanding which would be in keeping with his partnership approach to an autonomous African church. In addition, he called for a Native Church Council to be created in Mombasa, as in Uganda, to oversee African clergy stipends.[28] Mombasa, lagging behind the integrated governing style of Uganda, managed mission business using only the exclusively European Finance Committee which not only controlled CMS funds, but the funds of the African congregations as well. This form of European control led to a blow-up with William Henry Jones and Ishmael Michael Semler, the African priests at Rabai and Freretown, over a pay raise.[29]

The story of Ishmael Semler is less well known than that of William Jones. In his story we see a commitment to an egalitarian approach to clergy management and a remarkable resemblance to the approach of Ajayi Crowther, CMS Bishop of the Niger mission eighteen years earlier.

Originally from Mozambique, Semler was abducted as a small boy and forced to serve on a sailing ship. He was rescued by the British in 1850 and resettled in Bombay where he received a full education first at the Indo-British Institution, then the Robert Money School and finally at Nasik. After returning to East Africa in 1864 and serving with Johannes Rebmann, Bishop Hannington ordained him to the deaconate in 1885.[30] Tucker ordained him to the priesthood on June 30, 1895 and described him as "a very worthy man." To Semler he wrote: "We have a great regard for you and your whole family" and assigned him to be the pastor at Freretown.[31]

Almost one year after William Jones received a pay increase, Semler also requested a similar consideration from Harry Binns, the Secretary of the Mombasa Finance Committee, and threatened to resign. In response Binns dismissed the African priest with the opinion that he was "not in a

---

27. Ibid.

28. Tucker to Baylis, December 29, 1897, CMSA, F/PY/A5 /12.

29. Sundkler and Steed, *A History*, 554. Sundkler gives a summary of the problem of pay for Mr. Jones.

30. www.dacb.org/stories/mozambique/semler_ishmaelm.html, June 15, 2016.

31. Tucker to Baylis, September 24, 1898, CMSA, G3/A7/O/184; and Tucker to Semler, September 25, 1898, CMSA, G3/A5/O/191; *Register of Missionaries (Clerical, Lay and Female) and Native Clergy from 1804 to 1904*.

right spirit."[32] Tucker, very distressed at the situation, relays a response to the CMS:

> Has Mr. Binns power to suspend any man in the coast district of my jurisdiction who in his opinion is not in 'a right spirit.' If he has the power to suspend a native under such circumstances, then he has equally the power to suspend a European. Is this so? I think it would clear the air if you would kindly tell me. If it be so then I should like to know whether Mr. Binns possesses this power because he is the Secretary simply or solely. In that case it might chance that the Secretary was a Layman. It has been so at Freretown in days gone by. Has a Layman then power to suspend a clergyman in Priests Orders on his own initiative, as was done in the case of Mr. Semler.[33]

It is possible to compare the above statement to the words of Bishop Crowther to the CMS when The Rev. F. N. Eden, Secretary of the Niger mission, dismissed fifteen African clergy after a similar assessment. Crowther asks whether Mr. Eden was "alone empowered to dismiss and suspend and do everything in the Mission . . . will you write down, say please, Bishop Crowther expresses surprise at the statement of the Secretary that he has power as the representative of the CMS to suspend any clergyman from his duty."[34] The two opinions bear a striking similarity, but unlike the Niger, in the Mombasa mission Semler relented and returned to his position.

The indistinct mixing between the mission, the church, the Company, and the government was so typical of the early days of the British presence; and this mixing caused irritation and confusion. Binns certainly may have had the power to suspend a clergy's association with CMS, but not to suspend the ministerial functions of a licensed priest. However, one year after Tucker's question, the matter was still unsettled as to the power of the CMS Secretary.[35] Fox brought some clarity to the question when he agreed that the Secretary of the mission has only the ability to sever the clergy's employment with the CMS and not his function as a priest, but goes on to remark that "in such a Diocese as that of Mombasa he may have few if any places or opportunities in which to exercise his existing license." There were

---

32. Tucker to Baylis, September 24, 1898, CMSA, G3/A7/O/184.
33. Ibid.
34. Sanneh, *Abolitionists Abroad*, 139.
35. Tucker to Baylis, September 24, 1898, CMSA, G3/A7/O/184 and Tucker to Fox, September 15, 1899, CMSA, GAC 4/29/5675.

no congregations except those associated with the CMS. He also instructed unnecessarily that it was not within the purview of a bishop to insist that the CMS employ a particular clergy.[36]

But Binns had done more than suspend Semler from CMS employment, and Tucker, like a bull seeing red, was not about to back down; especially since he had the ability to place Semler in another part of the diocese. Appealing to the Lambeth Advice regarding superintending missionaries he makes the case that Binns had exceeded his authority in suspending an ordained man from his ministerial office.[37] He goes on to express his commitment to acting toward African clergy with a sense of equality:

> I may say that I have felt intensely the case of Mr. Semler . . . he is given his three month's wages in lieu of warning and dismissed just in the same way as your office boy at Salisbury Square would be dismissed. No! I am wrong. I am quite sure that your office boy would be dismissed in a very different way. Thank God! No native clergyman in Uganda can be dealt with in this way; and this brings me to what I said in the beginning that the whole subject of the relations of the CMS Secretary in the field over native clergy has an intimate bearing on the development of native churches. If, as is apparently considered, the Secretary has absolutely autocratic power in dealing with native clergy, then I think we need hardly look much further for the cause of much of the slow progress which many churches in the mission field seem to be making towards independence . . . Has he [the Secretary] power to suspend any European clergyman thus licensed . . . Of course the answer to my question may be to the effect that the European is in a different footing to the native who has been ordained, licensed and is paid in exactly the same way. . .If so then I would point to this difference of treatment and show its ultimate bearing on the great question of the development of native churches.[38]

Tucker expressed this problem as being a systematic one rather than one of individual attitude but Tucker was not unaware of imperial opinion among the missionaries. As Tucker was then on the verge of moving to Uganda, the matter was put on hold until the new bishop could take it up. No further mention of the question appears in the correspondence.

36. Fox to Tucker, November 3, 1899, CMSA, GCA 2/469.
37. Tucker to Fox, December 11, 1899, CMSA, GAC 4/29/575
38 Ibid.

"Dusky Brethren"

EVANGELISM AND INVITATIONS

Another expression of the diverse forms of partnerships with the Africans can be found in joint evangelistic efforts and invitations to evangelize. The evangelization process was often a team effort. Two Ugandans were partnered with European missionaries to open a new outstation in Singo (north-western part of Uganda) early in Tucker's tenure: "Messers. Gunther and Fisher start tomorrow for Singo to commence work at our third station. One of our native teachers, Stefano, will go with them as one of the permanent staff . . . Tairo, whom I hope to ordain Deacon will also join in the work."[39] This joint effort could also be seen ten years later when Tucker proposed a team to open up the Nile Valley to Christian influence. The team was composed of nine experienced European missionaries and a number of Baganda Evangelists and Teachers.[40] There was partnership but there was also a back and forth rubbing of opposites. The European missionaries were placed in a supervisory position at new stations, but it was a joint African/European decision to send them. Tucker writes: "Our brethren both European and native press the importance of an out-station at Chagwe."[41] Or again three years later: "On my arrival here I found that the Christians (or rather the readers in Koki) were eagerly looking forward to a missionary being sent to them . . . The Missionaries here as well as the Church Council agreed in this account of the pressing nature of the call. I have therefore asked Mr. Leakey to go to Koki."[42] Of course, the building of a patronage system was inevitably a part of the African participation. Having Europeans as a patron or client meant schools, hospitals, employment, and vocational training. But "movement and influence were never in one direction only."[43] The European missionaries benefited as well back home from the prestige of perceived accomplishment so the "unconscious absorption of the exotic" was a two-way dynamic.[44]

---

39. Tucker to Stock, April 16, 1893, CMSA, G3/A5/O/232.
40. Tucker to Baylis, December 30, 1904, CMSA, G3/A7/O/19.
41. Tucker to Stock, December 26, 1892, CMSA, G3/A5/O/1893/104.
42. Tucker to Baylis, November 11, 1895, CMSA, G3/A5/O/1896/49.
43. Marshall, *Cambridge Illustrated History*, 185.
44. Ibid.

TEACHING AND TRANSLATING

The final illustration of various partnerships deals with teaching and translation efforts (18% of the references). When Tucker first arrived in Mombasa the "native pastor" at Rabai, Mr. Jones, had two hundred candidates prepared for confirmation. As Tucker made plans for holding a service of confirmation, there was no mention of re-teaching or examining the candidates prepared by Jones. When Tucker returned from the service, for which Jones had translated Tucker's sermon "admirably," he expressed his satisfaction with the "faithful work and service" and the quality of the work done at Rabai. As Mr. Fitch, the English missionary who would be assigned to Rabai had only just arrived; Tucker could only have been referring to the efforts of William Jones.[45] Not only does this passage reveal the team effort which was operational upon Tucker's arrival, it also shows the roles occupied by the two participating members of the team. The Africans were involved predominately in evangelism, teaching, translating, and pastoring while the Europeans were involved in supervising, organizing and managing. But this arrangement did not preclude friendship.[46] It was a partnership in which the Europeans were deeply involved in the African sphere. Africans being heavily involved in the European sphere was less prevalent, but not unheard of.

For example, on Tucker's first journey to Uganda he met with the Native Church Council. He records that he:

> Spoke to the members on these points: First, their own spiritual life and suggested as a help that they should meet together at regular intervals for prayer and the study of God's Word. Secondly, the Confirmation which I propose holding very shortly, and I pointed out how very much they as elders in the church could assist their members in the work of preparation. Thirdly, I spoke to them very earnestly with regard to the Supper of the Lord and the Communicants classes that must be organized in connection with the confirmation."[47]

---

45. Tucker to General Touch, June 5, 1890, CMSA, G3/A5/O/158, reports the arrival of Mr. and Mrs. Fitch and the confirmation service was held just ten days later.

46. Walker to CMS, Annual Report 1891, CMSA, 61 "Sembera is a right down good man in heart and soul, an earnest Christian, in life a gentleman and affectionate friend. I am thankful to say he is one among many of the same sort." Sembera and Duta translated the Baptism, Marriage, and Funeral services.

47. Tucker to Wigram, December 30, 1890, CMSA, G3/A5/O/124.

"Dusky Brethren"

Training, organization, and preparation were, at this stage being accomplished by the Ugandans. This is not surprising as Gordon and Walker were the only European missionaries present. Inevitably, as more European missionaries arrived, more responsibility shifted to their hands. By 1895 preparation for Baptism was being done by the African teachers, but examination of the results by European missionaries had been inserted into the process.[48] Translation work and evangelistic work continued to be a joint process, but Tucker reports that: "churches are springing up in every direction and congregations are being formed with miraculous rapidity" as the Ugandan evangelists took the initiative, making complete European supervision of all aspects quite difficult.[49]

By 1896, in Tucker's statistical report of the diocese, the pattern seems to have become solidified into a planned procedure:

> [There are] seven hundred and twenty-five native evangelists and teachers. Although a noble band for whose work and devotion one has only thoughts of praise and thankfulness, [they] are altogether unable to cope with the growing needs of such a mass of seeking souls. Although men full of love and zeal, they need instruction and guidance. Whence are these to come? Without force and consolidation at the base, extension will be but the fritting away of our strength. A little band of European missionaries sent now to Buganda would do a work in the way of organization and instruction that will tell on the Church's life down through all the ages.[50]

The distinction of roles cannot be dismissed: Africans evangelize and teach the people, Europeans organize and instruct the teachers. An echo of this same pattern can be observed coming from headquarters as Baylis writes of the effects of the lack of a steam launch on Lake Victoria:

> There was some feeling too that Archdeacon Walker was probably right in a view he has himself expressed, that although the

---

48. Tucker to Fox, October 9, 1895, BGCA, 135/1/1.

49. Ibid.

50. Tucker, "Statistics of the Work in Buganda," October 5, 1896, CMSA, G3/A5 O/276. Compare this to Crowther: ". . .as rough quarrymen do who hew out blocks of marble from the quarries which are conveyed to the workshop to be shaped and finished into perfect figures by the hands of the skillful artists, in like manner native teachers can do, having the facility of the language in their favour, to induce their heathen countrymen to come within reach of the means of Grace and hear the Word of God. What is lacking in good training and sound Evangelical teaching [would be supplied by others more qualified.]" Ward and Stanley, *The Church Mission Society*, 188.

absence of better communication between the islands may prevent some itineration, it may have its counterpoise in encouraging the Missionaries to more settled methods of work, training at their stations Native Agents who can do perhaps better than the Europeans the pioneering evangelistic work.[51]

By 1899 the preference had become a reality as Tucker reveals in his request for personnel: "We want men whom we can send forward into the regions beyond where they can superintend and organize the work of our native pioneers. Nearly all our pioneer work is done now by natives but still the European missionaries who follow them must be men who are prepared to forego the comforts of home."[52] Yet Tucker reveals during a nostalgic recollection about the early days that the European instructors were themselves at one time instructed by the Africans:

> Nua Kikwabanga, one of our Native Clergy (who is in Priest Orders) has sleeping sickness and there is no hope whatever of his recovery. He was the first Muganda whose acquaintance I ever made. He was Mr. Pilkington's first instructor in Luganda and he as you remember really saved Mr. Weatherhead's life at the time of the mutiny. He has done splendid service to the church and as minister in charge of a District proved himself to be faithful as well as able.[53]

It is significant to note that Nua Kikwabanga had risen to the level of management and supervision of a district, a position that was predominantly held by Europeans at this stage. The archives offer strong antidotes to the misperception that Europeans were always in charge. African leadership had arrived quite early in the effort.

DIRECT CONSULTATION

The various forms of partnership exhibit the confrontation between idealism and imperialism and the practical ways in which these two forces played out. But beyond questions of partnership, there also existed outright consultation on the part of both the Europeans and the Africans which exhibits very similar dynamics. For example, as the IBEA military attaché

---

51. Baylis to Tucker, June 29, 1903, CMSA, G3/A7/1/359.
52. Tucker to Baylis, January 18, 1899, CMSA, G3/A7/O/62.
53. Tucker to Baylis, May 24, 1904, CMSA, G3/A7/O/126.

"Dusky Brethren"

Capt. R. A. Williams awaited the arrival in Uganda of Sir Gerald Portal, the Special Commissioner, after the departure of Lugard, he sought to re-negotiate the Lugard Treaty, giving the Catholic Party more power, as outlined in a previous chapter. Due to the influential position the missionaries held at that time and owing to their longer tenure, Williams solicited Tucker's help in convincing the Ugandan chiefs this step was needed. Tucker was initially against changes but hoping for a lasting peace he writes:

> Of course the only way in which it is at all possible for us to touch such questions as the last treaty is in the way of advice given to the Christian chiefs who come to us seeking counsel . . . Although I considered that Capt. Williams had not shaken the sufficiency of my reasons against any revision at present of the treaty, still I felt that possibly there might be in his memorandum a possibility of a final settlement being arrived at. I therefore undertook to sound the Protestant chiefs on the subject. This I did and was greatly pleased with the conciliatory spirit displayed.[54]

After consultation, the opinion of the African chiefs helped to sway Tucker toward a revision of the treaty which was, in essence, an imperial rearrangement of their society. In this particular instance the chiefs initially sought the advice of Tucker and later he consulted them in return. The revisions eventually stalled out due to the Roman Catholics' appeal to the Pope.

There is church business in the same letter as Tucker contemplated the ordination of the first "native brethren" to the deaconate after prayer and consultation with "the brethren here." He mused:

> I cannot give you their names at present as they are still under consideration . . . I find I have to curtail the power at present exercised by the Church Council with respect to the presentation and acceptance of candidates for Confirmation and Baptism. But by laying a measure of responsibility upon those selected for ordination the difficulty will be surmounted.[55]

Although it might be tempting to see this curtailment of power as a lording over the Africans in an imperialistic fashion, Tucker was in fact devolving power from the diocesan level of management to the parish level, as the Church Council was responsible for many congregations. Interestingly, it is possible to see hints of the patronage system as the chiefs seemed to be using a selective granting of full church membership to consolidate power.

54. Tucker to Baylis, January 17, 1893.
55. Ibid.

Whether Tucker perceived this and sought to circumvent the practice by devolving power is not clear. Possibly he was only acting as any diocesan would in any setting.

At the same time in the political arena, in addition to the revision of the Lugard treaty, Tucker also consulted the Africans as a direct agent for Portal in the signing of the Protectorate treaty; becoming, as well, an intermediary for the Africans. Tucker describes his activity:

> Difficulties arose on a question of double chieftainships. This question aroused the greatest opposition, and the arguments against the adoption of the scheme seemed to me so strong that I wrote Sir Gerald a letter . . . After a good deal of negotiation Sir Gerald sent to me a draft treaty and asked me to lay it before the chiefs and if possible get their signatures and he would then try to get the signatures of the Roman Catholics and the King.[56]

Tucker found himself in a diplomatic position, explaining the objections of the Africans to the British and the wishes of the colonial administration to the Africans but engaging in direct consultation on both counts.

In addition to political matters Tucker also consulted the Native Church Council, primarily on church policy. For example, in the arena of church business in 1893 Tucker decided to open a new mission station at Chagwe "in consultation with the senior missionaries and the church council."[57] Tucker's consultative style can also be seen in his intentions for the future organization of the church in the interior section of his diocese. Walker proposed to organize the church along parochial lines, as those in England. But Tucker was keen to incorporate African styles of organization. He writes:

> In my opinion any decision of at all a binding character which might be arrived at on these points would at present be premature. I should much prefer to leave these matters until a Bishop for Uganda has been appointed who in consultation with native priests and deacons and representative laymen might frame a constitution for the church suited to the characteristics of the people and the peculiar political arrangements of the country. Things are developing themselves gradually and what is specially needed at the present time is a watchful eye and a moulding hand with respect to things native rather than any attempt to pitchfork

---

56. Tucker to Wigram, April 24, 1893, CMSA, G3/A5/O/241.
57. Tucker to Baylis, February 21, 1893, CMSA, G3/A5/O/194.

a foreign organization into conditions which will supply neither nourishment nor strength.[58]

Long before the phrase "Africanization of Christianity" became fashionable, the CMS pioneered the concept of adapting their familiar outlook to a different setting; however, a "moulding hand" is quite different from a "hands off" approach as the African church accomplished its own organization.[59] Rather the CMS took a blended approach; one which recognized the autonomy of the African church but at the same time acted from a position of superiority.

In the early years of interaction there is a mixture of political matters as well as church matters in the consultation with the Africans. Consultations about the modification of the Lugard treaty, the double chieftainship issue, and the emancipation of slaves are mixed with consultations about ordination candidates or the opening of new stations.[60] As time moved forward, less and less consultation was carried out by Tucker in regard to political matters as the government, gaining organization and formality, began to do its own consultation.[61]

Early consultation also involved soliciting invitations from chiefs to send teachers and evangelists, sometimes against the wishes of the colonial administration. A typical example of this form of interaction can be seen in Tucker's vivid description of the council at Taveta, in what is now southeastern Kenya, when Tucker asked if the elders of the WaTaveta would consider sending more numbers to school including the women:

> I arranged to meet the Taveta elders under the great Shauri tree ... It was interesting to notice how each man seemed to take his proper place. First of all the twelve chief councillors rose up and slowly walked away to a neighbouring tree where they consulted together. Then the married men moved off to another spot some

58. Tucker to Baylis, January 14, 1896, CMSA, G3/A5/O/102.

59. Sanneh, "The CMS," 174.

60. CMSA, G3/A7/P/1911/102. By 1911 there existed a Native Church Estates Board which managed the use of church property.

61. Commissioner Sadler to Marques of Lansdowne, June 11, 1903, FO 881/8192. "In dealing with a kingdom like the Kingdom of Uganda, whose Kabaka we have recognized as the native Ruler, and for the governance of which we have, most wisely, allowed a system of autonomy which provides for the direct rule of the people by the Kabaka under our guidance I consider we should uphold native laws and customs; advising the Lukiko to amend them when necessary, but being cautious of superseding them by our own laws except when necessity is clearly shown."

> distance away and lastly the young warriors took up their position under some trees in our front. In about a quarter of an hour the seniors having apparently made up their mind were joined by the married men and a further conference took place. While this was going on the young warriors were seen. . .to take regular orders. This went on for some time until . . . the council had made up its mind and was returning to give an answer to my address . . . Then the spokesman rose up and delivered an address which was supposed to embody the results of the conference and to be an answer to my speech.[62]

Although the WaTaveta could not be forced to attend school and the decision was left to them, the arguments used by Tucker to convince were, by today's standards, daunting. Tucker reminded the WaTaveta that the message brought by the missionaries was from God, who loved them and wished to bless them but the message "could not be rejected without guilt and future punishment."[63] The combination was one of an exterior coating of egalitarian practice but with a hot molten center of what could easily have been interpreted as a veiled threat of force. However, the WaTaveta were not entirely intimidated. They agreed to schooling but only on certain conditions: that it fit into their own priorities (such as cultivation) and that run away wives would not be allowed to attend.

There was a subtle contrast between consultation with rural pastoral groups, such as the WaTaveta, and those in Mengo in the center of the Ugandan kingdom. In Uganda itself (exclusive of the tributary kingdoms later incorporated) the decisions were not about the initial presentation of the message but about supervision and management of an emerging structure. Here in the center Tucker occasionally consulted the Native Church Council on the placement of European missionaries, a practice which may have given pause to the British missionaries if they had been made aware of it; especially given the fact that this very practice was the sticking point which held up the finalization of the Ugandan church constitution for eleven years.[64] On the placement of Rowling, a particularly prickly missionary, Tucker writes: "I had of course then to consider whether it was possible for him to go to any other part of Uganda and I mooted the idea to several members of the Native Church Council but every one of them shrunk from

---

62. Tucker to Stock, March 22, 1895, CMSA, G3/A5/O/152.

63. Ibid.

64 Tucker to Baylis, August 15, 1904, CMSA, G3/A7/O/172. ". . .they will not submit to have their qualifications for this or that post discussed in the presence of a native."

the possibility of his being located in Uganda. It was said that he would 'kill the work.'"[65] As Rowling was eventually assigned to Kyadondo, a Saza in the south-eastern part of Buganda, the opinion of the Native Church Council was apparently initially discounted.[66] However the Church Council's evaluation of Rowling proved correct as Tucker eventually requested his re-call on theological grounds.

A very interesting use of consultation with the Africans occurred in reference to this theological dispute with Rowling. Rowling had developed a theory regarding the nature of the Trinity in which the Holy Spirit was seen as a "separate personality."[67] This view Tucker considered to be heretical: "Mr. Rowling has strained his theology to fit a linguistic theory . . . as to the use of the word '*omwoyo*' [spirit or heart]."[68] In the process of seeking to explain and clarify his position, Rowling called together the members of the Native Church Council and presented his case. Appalled by this impropriety of order and the fact that Rowling had left his district without permission to meet with the Council, Tucker asked the Parent Committee to antedate his furlough and return him to England immediately. Tucker does not ask the Native Church Council to evaluate Rowling's theological linguistics. Instead he asks Dr. J. H. Cook, as chair of the integrated Translation Committee, to address the matter. Based on their earlier negative opinion of Rowling and his recall to England, it is apparent that he did not received a positive hearing from the Council.

IMPERIAL PARTNERSHIPS

Regardless of the many examples of various forms of partnership and consultations between Africans and Europeans, the opposite behavior was also simultaneously present. At various times the Europeans refused to participate in (or even understand the necessity of) joint efforts. These tendencies were evidence of imperialism. But in the same way the Africans, as well, displayed an independent mind in regards to various decisions and actions. This tendency could be categorized as African initiatives.

---

65. Tucker to Baylis, May 8, 1899, CMSA, G3/A7/O/113.

66. "List of Missionaries and Their Stations, January, 1909," *Uganda Notes*, CMSA, G3/A7/O/1909.

67. Tucker to Baylis, July 12, 1910, CMSA, G3/A7/O/1919/88.

68. Ibid.

AFRICAN INITIATIVE

By far the largest grouping of correspondence documenting African initiative within the joint European CMS/East African mission effort pertains to the skills involved in launching a church. These skills, such as evangelism, teaching, initiating new congregations, leading services, pastoral care, designing and building worship space, are abundantly described by Tucker in relation to his African co-workers. Decisions to embark on evangelistic endeavors took place on both an individual level and on an institutional level. Tucker describes one of his early encounters with an individual evangelist while visiting A. R. Steggall in Taveta, now south-eastern Kenya:

> Four Taveta boys have already been baptized one of whom it was my privilege to confirm on February 7th. The name of this lad— (he is almost a young man) —is Johanna. He is very earnest, faithful—a true witness for Christ among his own people. Nearly all those at Taveta who have been brought under instruction have been induced to come through Johanna's influence.[69]

On an institutional level Tucker describes the official sending out of evangelists by the Native Church Council as early as 1894: "The missionary spirit in the Church seems to be increasing and teachers [used then interchangeably with evangelists] in large numbers are being sent forth by the native church into un-evangelized parts of Uganda, the isles and even the regions beyond."[70] Five years later Tucker records that the same pattern had spread beyond the capital to more remote areas even outside Buganda, such as Mboga just southwest of Lake Albert: "It will be well now if I attempt to give in brief outline some account of how Christianity came to this out-of-the-way place—some three hundred miles from Mengo, and on the outskirts of the Great Forest. . . . The instrument has not been the European missionary, but the Native evangelist from Buganda."[71]

Teaching was another area where African initiative was respected. The practice of students becoming teachers in an informal way and through their own decision is explained and described during Tucker's initial visit to the islands in Lake Victoria:

---

69. Tucker to Lang, March 9, 1892, CMSA, G3/A5/O/134.

70. Tucker to Fox, July 31, 1894, G3/A5/O, CMSA, and BGCA, 135/1/1. Griffiths notes that Baskerville mentions evangelists as early as February 1891.

71. Tucker, "The Spiritual Expansion of Buganda," *Intelligencer*, February, 1899, 108.

"Dusky Brethren"

> It is remarkable how the system of those who are taught teaching others has taken hold on the minds of the people. In Buganda the taught are fast becoming teachers and so in this far off island of Bugaya. Although the people know so little, many of them only the alphabet yet even these are teaching their fellows what they themselves have learnt. I found in this church the two Baganda teachers at work it is true. But I also found some dozen people belonging to the island at work as teachers. Be it remembered that the people have only once seen a European...[72]

In areas where the local chief was opposed to Christianity, the spontaneous teaching took place underground, such as in Busoga under Chief Matanda where people "read more or less in secret."[73]

A similar description of appreciation of African initiative comes from Tucker's first visit to the frontier of Bunyoro. The work had spread without European leadership through the efforts of African teachers and Yafeti, the chief of one of the sub-divisions of the Toro region. Tucker writes:

> Mr. Fisher [is] to accompany me with a view to the complete organization of the whole field of labour . . . four churches have been built in the district, and for some time the work of teaching has been carried on by our Native brethren. Mr. Fisher was the first European to visit Kijungati and to organize our operations... Yafeti, a member of the Royal family of Bunyoro, who had been taught and baptized in Mengo some years previously, was the living agent used by God to bring the Gospel to this far away country. He had been appointed chief of the great province of Mwenzi. At his request reading sheets and books were sent to him together with two Christian teachers..."[74]

The African initiative was greatly admired but in keeping with the pattern the Europeans then stepped in to superintend. But such was not always the case as the mission continued to expand. By the early 20th Century the pace of new missions had outstripped the number of European missionaries to superintend. In the case of Gondokoro, then the northern frontier

---

72. Tucker to Stock, December 28, 1895, CMSA, G3/A5/O/1896/101.

73. Tucker from Mengo, October 4, 1895, CMSA, G3/A5/O/341.

74. Tucker, *Intelligencer*, September 1897, 35. In other instances, the European missionaries initiated evangelistic work and gradually brought into existence a Native Church Council who then sent out teachers and made themselves responsible for their maintenance as in the case in Toro in western Uganda. See Tucker, "A Missionary Journey through Nkole," *Intelligencer*, July 1900, 506.

of Uganda, the Native Church Council at Mengo sent Baganda evangelists in 1906 to serve a colony of Baganda who had already been teaching the local people. They turned to Mengo for books and teachers and promised to build a church building and maintain the teachers.[75] In this project the Europeans acted only as messengers of events.

Another area of launching Christian faith which was taken into the hands of the Africans was the startup of new congregations. Tucker gives evidence of this as he writes of his first visit to "Mondo's" in Legumbwa, four hours west of the Nile in Uganda: "where we were most joyfully greeted by the Christian teacher and his flock. A small church has been built here, regular services are held, classes for Christian instruction. Took part in evening prayers at the little church . . . No European has ever taught at this place; the work has been entirely that of the Natives."[76] Four years later the reed structures were beginning to be replaced by more permanent buildings but still built without European assistance.[77]

Not only did Africans take the initiative in starting new congregations, but also in designing, building and maintaining church buildings. On Tucker's second visit to Singo, fifty miles west of Mengo and the country home of the Gabunga (chief of canoes), he describes his astonishment at finding a large congregation of 600: "The church which is a thoroughly well-built one (but of course reeds) stands in a fine situation on the top of a commanding hill. The whole of the work connected with the structure has been done absolutely without any European supervision."[78] Five years later a similar situation was found in Jungo, sixteen miles southwest of Mengo where Yairo Mutakyala, placed as a pioneer African district supervisor of forty congregations in 1896, built a structure seating one thousand. Tucker writes: "It has been built entirely by the Natives, and absolutely without European superintendence. It is a substantial structure and will, I doubt not, stand many years. It is extremely well lighted and ventilated. It has two capacious vestries and a deep verandah (sic) all round."[79]

From the very beginning of Tucker's ministry in East Africa he records his observations of Africans taking the initiative in the leading of worship, prayers, and liturgical ceremonies. The assumption of this type of

---

75. Tucker to Baylis, March 1, 1906, CMSA, G3/A7/O/78.
76. Tucker from Mengo, October 4, 1895.
77. Tucker to Baylis, May 8, 1899, CMSA, G3/A5/O/113.
78. Tucker to Stock, December 3, 1895, CMSA, G3/A5/O/1896/96.
79. Tucker, "A Confirmation Tour in Uganda," *Intelligencer*, November, 1900, 838.

leadership was accomplished not only by African clergy, such as Jones and Semler who had been ordained since 1885, but also by ordinary people — porters, church elders, or hospital workers. Tucker writes as he camps on the shores of Lake Victoria preparing to leave Uganda after his first brief visitation, of hearing murmuring voices all around his tent, which he finally recognized as The Lord's Prayer and the Benediction coming from the houses of the near-by inhabitants as they engaged in evening family devotions.[80]

During his second visit to Uganda on his initial visit to Singo, he writes of his porters:

> It was very delightful to find that my Waganda Porters were readers and many of them Christians. Both night and morning prayers were said and generally conducted by one of their own numbers. Before daylight the murmur of voices told me that the men were engaged in prayer, not in my presence, but at a distance in their own sleeping place. It was interesting to notice how one was chosen by the rest, and that without any formal election, to be the leader in this devotional exercise. He seemed naturally to fall into the proper place. I called him the 'minister' and certainly he deserved the title. He truly served his people.[81]

In the same letter Tucker describes the liturgical ceremony of the Restoration of a Penitent under the direction of the church elders at Mengo: "At the morning service at Mengo a member of the Church who had been excommunicated on account of notorious sin was publicly readmitted to the enjoyment of Church privileges . . . A time of probation had been given, and the church elders were all satisfied as to the reality of his repentance."[82]

Another example of African initiative is the very rare example of a written prayer, composed by Semei, one of the hospital workers at Mengo, to be used regularly in the visitation of the sick:

> Our Father in Heaven, we Thy servants and handmaidens kneel in prayer and praise to Thee. We thank Thee for preserving us during the night and causing us to look upon the light of this day. Clothe us with Thy grace and strength. Guide us in all we do. Help us. Save us from sudden death and heal us from the pain of sleeping-sickness, small-pox, and every other kind of illness.

---

80. Tucker, *Eighteen Years*, 56.
81. Tucker to Stock, May 20, 1893, CMSA, G3/A5/O/233.
82 Ibid.

> Continually save us as Thou didst save Daniel from the lions' teeth, and as Thou didst save Shadrach, Meshach, and Abednego from the tongues of fire. Save us too, night and day continually. And we pray for all the sick. Preserve and save them day by day, from the oldest to the youngest. And we pray for all who are in darkness that they may obtain the faith, that we may be one fold. Father, save us, because healing comes from Thee. Our Father, we have prayed for everything in the name of Jesus our Lord.[83]

Although much initiative was taken in prayer, so rare is the recorded African voice unmediated by Europeans, that Dr. Howard Cook chose to print the prayer in the CMS newsletter to give insight into the thought patterns of African co-workers.

Africans took the initiative in several other ways such as choosing their own leadership for the fledgling church, asking advice of the missionaries, and invitations to build mission stations which are sprinkled throughout the letters. However, references to these subjects are less frequent in the Tucker archive than the previous examples. Nevertheless, they are significant as documentation of the emerging African leadership. After ordaining the first deacons for the Ugandan Church Tucker also set apart ten lay evangelists. This would be one of the various steps on the road to the priesthood after lay reader and the teaching office. He writes: "At the afternoon service I set apart and licensed ten lay evangelists." He then lists their names in full and states that: "All these men were recommended to me by the Church Council, and the recommendation was endorsed by the whole body of the missionaries."[84] It is important to note that the recommendations originated with the Native Church Council and not with the Europeans and the authority to function was again given by the same council.[85]

Missionaries sought out the advice and consulted with the Africans on various political and church related subjects. The Africans, as well, initiated consultations but these were very few in number and seemed to revolve around issues of injustice. An example would be the complaints that came to Tucker over perceived favoritism of the Catholic chiefs over the Protestant chiefs by Macdonald: "the protestant chiefs came to the missionaries complaining of a gross act of injustice, the advice given to them was go to

---

83. "Uganda," *Intelligencer*, October, 1903, 767.

84. Tucker to Stock, May 20, 1893, CMSA, G3/A5/O/233. Also Tucker to Stock, October, 14, 1895.

85. Tucker to Baylis, December 26, 1898, CMSA, G3/A7/O/48.

"Dusky Brethren"

Kampala and ask for justice."[86] Other examples would be the disputes over salaries and treaties already mentioned.

The Ugandans also took the initiative to consult the missionaries on subjects that were both religious and political, such as the emancipation of the slaves in Uganda. Tucker describes his role: "I was asked to meet the chiefs in order that this matter might be brought before me and so I might be in a position to advise them. . .I recommended them to pray over the matter and to talk it over amongst themselves with constant reference to the word of God. Should they come to any conclusion on the subject, I said that I should be glad to know what it was."[87] To Baylis Tucker explicitly states: "I begged them to pray it over and with the word of God in their hands to talk it over amongst themselves. I refused to advise them one way or another.[88] In this subject Tucker took a more hands off approach and was delighted with the outcome as the chiefs then signed a document of their own composition to release their slaves.

But by far the most intriguing decisions undertaken by the Africans were the ones in which the direction taken was the complete opposite of advice given by the missionaries. Hints of a strongly independent mind-set appear in Gerald Portal's exasperated comments regarding his negotiations with the warring factions in Uganda: "They have been nearly at each other's throats, haggling and bargaining; the Protestants refusing altogether to carry out what their Bishop promised for them and the Frenchmen getting crusty."[89] Clear indicators of strong, clear-headed opinion, running the opposite of missionary advice, can be found in regards to the assignment of missionaries. The problem with Rowling's assignment has already been described and the assignment of Crabtree was very similar. Tucker confides:

> I may say that the Church Council petitioned me to remove Mr. Crabtree from Gayaza on the ground that he was impeding the work there. I have solved this difficulty by relieving him of all spiritual work. His work is now purely linguistic. . .There is a native pastor now at Gayaza but he is entirely independent of Mr. Crabtree and in any difficulty refers to Mengo not to Mr. Crabtree.[90]

---

86. Tucker to Baylis, January 20, 1893, CMSA, G3/A5/O/247.
87. Tucker to Stock, April 16, 1893, CMSA, G3/A5/O/233.
88. Tucker to Baylis, April 8, 1893.
89. Portal to Gedge, April 21, 1892, Gedge Papers, RH, Mss. Af. 1/2/13–15.
90. Tucker to Baylis, July 10, 1899, CMSA, G3/A7/O/164.

Although Tucker had assigned Crabtree to his location, respect for his position did not hinder the Church Council from pressing their disagreement and effecting change. Not only did the Church Council have something to say about the assignment of European missionaries, but individual African missionaries at times had something to say about their own assignments. It was not always assured that candidates would fulfil the requests of the bishop of the diocese, as the European missionary in charge of theological education at Freretown writes:

> I had an interview with the Bishop this evening. He wishes Thomas [Sereze] to go to relieve Rev. James Deimler of the school at Rabai . . . The Bishop came up to afternoon tea and by arrangement Thomas came. I had previously told him of the Bishop's wishes, and was puzzled by his reference again to difficulties regarding food and clothing. . .The Bishop was most kind and patient, and was very grieved at finding this difficulty crop up after two years teaching . . . The Bishop offered Thomas the chance of going to Rabai and seeing for himself how things went. This he did not accept.[91]

The Church Council also disagreed with Tucker as to the language of instruction in the province of Toro in the extreme west of Uganda. Tucker felt that Luganda rather than Lunyoro should be used even though most in Toro could not understand it although the two dialects were very similar. In fact, many believed that Lunyoro was the mother language of Luganda. Since most instructional material had already been translated into Luganda time would be saved. He observed that Lusesse and Lusoga had already yielded to Luganda and felt that eventually it would become the dominant language. But the Africans did not agree. Tucker details the situation:

> It was discussed in the Finance Committee and it was decided to refer the matter to the Church Council. The Church called to their assistance the Buganda teachers who had laboured in Toro. They one and all testified to the fact that the mass of the people do not understand Luganda. After a long discussion it was decided to refer the matter to the principal chiefs in Toro for discussion. The King was asked to call the most representative men together and submit the question to them. They unanimously decided to ask that Lunyoro might be the language of instruction.[92]

91. Journal of John Edward Hamshere, October 8 and 9, 1896, ACKA, Language School Library, Nairobi, Kenya.

92. Tucker to Baylis, August 10, 1900, CMSA, G3/A7/O/170.

"Dusky Brethren"

Forced to compromise, Tucker agreed that elementary education would be in Lunyoro and higher instruction in Luganda but added that: "I have fought against Lunyoro being adopted in Toro just as I fought against Lusoga for Busoga, but circumstances were too strong for me and so far I have yielded" but he confessed the hope that Luganda would ultimately triumph.[93]

However, Tucker was incorrect. Seven years later he observed that "year by year the demand for Lunyoro has been growing steadily stronger."[94] Ultimately Tucker changed his mind and authorized all evangelistic work to take place in Lunyoro along with the printing of the scriptures in their entirety.

The missionaries have been portrayed as constantly wielding an unstoppable power which at times crushed the indigenous culture in its path. There is quite a bit of evidence to show that this did frequently happen. At the same time there is also evidence that the Africans accommodated only the amount of change which they felt comfortable with or which gave some amount of benefit.[95] At times, playing the missionaries off the colonial authorities, proved to be a strategy of freedom such as declaring one's conversion to Islam or traditional beliefs in order to divorce a Christian wife in the secular court, or changing from Protestant affiliation to Catholic in order to appeal ones legal case to a judge who would render the most satisfactory outcome (in the days of double chieftainships). It is good to remember the strength of the African culture and character which is not easily flattened. When the Africans solicited missionary support in 1889 during the ousting of Kabaka Kalema for Mwanga "Walker and Gordon's advice to the Protestant chiefs...was heard and ignored... they were by no means inclined to follow any given advice, which did not correspond with their own thinking."[96]

---

93. Ibid.

94. Tucker to Baylis, August 9, 1907, CMSA, G3/A7/O/213.

95. Marshall, ibid, 206. The attractions of conversion could include food, jobs, land, education, or advancement in addition to the psychological reassurance and intellectual consolations.

96. Griffiths, "Bishop Alfred Tucker," 127 and 128.

TUCKER'S NON-PARTNERSHIP

There is very clear evidence of the partnership and egalitarian approach which Tucker employed not only in the forced labor debate but his role in the creation of the Ugandan church in particular. At times he is referred to as an "impassioned advocate of racial equality."[97] Some acknowledgement is also given to his imperial side. For example, Tucker's campaign to keep IBEA financially solvent on his visit to England in 1890 and the appointment of a European, rather than a Ugandan, as his successor.[98] The European missionaries mention the fear of Tucker's authoritarian tendencies and his lack of consultation before writing the draft constitution. But still more pointed examples of Tucker's imperial opinion have not been fully aired and the very real dynamic of the tension between the egalitarian ideals, clearly embraced by Tucker, and the mind-set of empire that was ever present as well, is in need of more illustration.

It is clear from Tucker's letters that he believed the African church needed supervision as it evolved into maturity and that Tucker's admiration of the innate abilities of the East Africans did not include an across-the-board reliance on their organizational ability. Even though he modelled the structure of the Ugandan church along indigenous lines and certain individuals and groups emerged into leadership, this was a gradual occurrence, something to be earned. Whether racial characteristics played a role or only experience, somehow the supervision of the work seemed to fall most often to the Europeans as was the case for the work in Bugaya, an island off the north-eastern shore of Lake Victoria. After praising the initiative of the two Baganda teachers, Sira and Sambili, he writes: "I trust that something may shortly be done to bring this truly interesting work under proper supervision and control . . . I hope to make arrangements as soon as possible for Mr. Rowling to visit the island periodically."[99]

A similar pattern can be seen in Tucker's letters describing his trip to the Ssese Islands off the north-western shores of Victoria Nyanza. He praises the believers as being "lovers of the truth for truth's sake . . . there is a simplicity about them which is very impressive."[100] The native teacher

---

97. Stanley, "Afterword," *Church Mission Society*, ibid, 350.

98. Ward, "Taking Stock," 28–29. Griffiths disagrees, pointing to Tucker's reference to an African successor in Tucker to Jackson, September 19, 1900, UNA, A22/1. And Tucker to Lang, April 5, 1892, CMSA, G3/A5/O/161.

99. Tucker to Stock, December 28, 1895, CMSA, G3/A5/O/1896/101.

100. Tucker, "The Island of Komi, Victoria Nyanza," CMSA, G3/A5/O/118.

was also impressive: "His sermon was on Romans 6 and a very striking one it was. He is evidently a man of considerable ability and spiritual power."[101] Also impressive were the church buildings: "There are, I am glad to say, fine churches on the island. The central one is at Mamere and accommodates some 500 worshipers. It is beautifully built with communion table, rails, pulpit, all entirely of native workmanship."[102] But despite all this Tucker felt the existing leadership was not sufficient as he writes: "All that we need is a teacher of experience to organize the work and carry it on" and he plans for a native priest to be assigned to visit but under the direction of Mr. Gordon who lived on the main island of Bukasa.

Even two years before Tucker's retirement, after the church was no longer in the beginning stage, with experienced African leadership in place, the same approach was outlined. In the efforts to open new stations in the untouched Lango and Teso sections of Bukedi, an area northwest of Mt. Elgon, Tucker concluded that "an effort should be made at once to send out a strong band of Buganda evangelists . . . But these men cannot be sent unless we have [European] stations from whence they can be supervised and helped."[103] To his friend Mrs. Carus-Wilson he is more explicit: "I cannot send them until we have the European to supervise and guide them as well as control them."[104]

It is possible, and even quite frequent, to find references in Tucker's letters that contradict one another in regards to equality and consultation with African Christians. Tucker expresses frustration with the female European missionaries and their lack of ability to consult the African women about training programs:

> Apparently they have not the faintest idea of training native women to do Christian work in any organized or regular way. They cannot even see their way to call the native sisters together to talk over the work to be done or the best way to do it. The prejudice which one notices in the memorandum of the contrasted term, 'European ladies and native women' has found expression in a letter from Mr. Baskerville to myself.[105]

---

101. Ibid.
102. Ibid.
103. Tucker to Baylis, March 22, 1909, CMSA, G3/A7/O/137.
104. Tucker to Carus-Wilson, March 26, 1909, BGCA, 135/1/3.
105. Tucker to Baylis, September 24, 1898, CMSA, G3/A7/O/184. Also Tucker to Baylis, January 18, 1899, CMSA, G3/A7/O/62.

But at the same time, an argument from silence would note, there is no reference to any consultation on Tucker's part with the Africans when the division of the diocese was contemplated or when the curriculum for formal intermediate schooling was designed, with a very great emphasis on English and English literature.[106] It is not unusual to find, in the same letter, contradictions to the idea of racial equality. For example, after criticizing the female missionaries Tucker proposes: "I have drafted a resolution which affirms the necessity of equality of workers and the impossibility of making race distinctions, distinctions between European and natives."[107] But several paragraphs later in the same letter he makes a racial distinction in regards to assignments of missionaries at Jilore:

> For some time I have had grave doubts as to its being a fit place for European life . . . I would suggest that the Committee should pass some resolution to the effect that European workers must be withdrawn as speedily as possible from Jilore and no more be sent there. The work need not be given up. It can still be carried on by natives and the station be regarded as an outstation.[108]

After four European deaths from Blackwater fever they must be removed, but still the station remained acceptable for African workers even though they were not immune from the same disease! The idea that he was discriminating according to race most likely never occurred to Tucker. But the distinction only serves to highlight the tension between opposing viewpoints in Tucker's mind and in the day to day operation of the mission. Once again a year later a very similar occurrence appears in a letter regarding the struggle to adopt a constitution for the Ugandan Church. Tucker laments the immovable opinion of the European missionaries:

> Here we have a Church—young in years it is true—but full of life and vigour. It is a Church which has its own ministry of 21 native clergy, 36 licensed Lay Readers, and 980 teachers (male and female). Its communicants number between 5,000 and 6,000. Its baptized members are over 20,000 in number. Its adherents number more than 100,000 . . . It maintains its own clergy, readers and teachers. It builds, maintains and repairs its own churches and reading houses. It is sending missionaries into Busoga, Bunyoro, Toro, Koki and Ankole. It is all this and does all this, and yet is not

---

106. Tucker to Baylis, May 8, 1903, CMSA, G3/A7/O/95.
107. Tucker to Baylis, September 24, 1898.
108. Ibid.

to have a legal Constitution, and that mainly because European Missionaries shrink from a remote possibility of being controlled by natives. Oh the pity of it!!![109]

Yet in the very next paragraph he writes: "The second alternative, that of having two separate organizations—one for the European Missionaries and one for the Native Church, is to my mind an absolutely impossible one . . . It would not be safe to give at present to a purely native governing body the power of enacting laws for the church."[110] Tucker's ideal of having a truly integrated church still maintained a racial distinction regarding governance. The Africans seemed, in Tucker's view, to be perfectly capable of governing the European missionaries but at the same time not capable of governing themselves. A further contradiction occurs in the integrated church ideal when the subject was worship services at the yet to be built Memorial Cathedral in Mombasa. Although Tucker's hard push for integrated structures is well documented at the same time in Mombasa he speaks of the European inhabitants as a separate and distinct group, having its own worship needs. He explains:

> In dealing with this matter I ought, I think at the outset, to disabuse the mind of the Committee of any idea which they may entertain of the Government, by any possibility, providing for the spiritual needs of the white population in Mombasa . . . I took in hand immediately the work which seemed to be so pressingly necessary. A church has been built at a cost of between 400 and 500 pounds in which, for nearly 12 months, a regular service for Europeans has been held with an average attendance of something like 60 persons . . . it is the duty of the Bishop to provide services for Europeans . . . it is not, in my opinion, the duty of the CMS.[111]

Tucker then proposed that the Memorial Cathedral building would be shared by both the Africans and the Europeans—but in separate services. Tucker stated that: "The natives would be unable to maintain it and certainly the Europeans would refuse to do so were they prevented from using it. By a joint use an easy way would be found for the maintenance both of the fabric and the services."[112]

---

109. Tucker to Fox, June 7, 1899, CMSA, G3/A7/O/149.
110. Ibid.
111. Tucker to Baylis, February 6, 1899, CMSA, F/PY/AF/12
112. Ibid.

For all of Tucker's advocacy of African approaches to church government and leadership, he still maintained an easily distinguishable separateness. When negotiating with the CMS and the missionaries about the place of the Europeans in the formal constitution, he took the position that it was "useless to consult the Natives on the above matters until the European Missionaries are agreed among themselves."[113] But why this would be the case is not exactly clear. Certainly when helping to negotiate government treaties or women's ministry assignments with the Africans, the missionaries had not agreed among themselves so why agreement would be necessary on this particular issue could be explained by the innate sense of separateness of the Europeans and the African Church to begin with. The separateness is also apparent as Tucker speaks of his duty to "guard the interests of the natives."[114] However admirable this may be, it was still a duty which was approached from a separate and superior position. This separateness is thrown into stark relief by Tucker's personal letters to friends: "The rains were on and I caught a severe cold and had a touch of bronchitis. This when you have to spend your time in a wet tent is anything but pleasant. I got into rather a sleepless condition and as I was terribly alone, that is without a European companion, things were anything but lively"[115] Consultation with the Africans did not necessary mean companionship with the Africans and an equal standing did not always mean an identical one.

SUMMARY AND CONCLUSION

The British efforts in East Africa which included the Mission, the Native Church, the Company, and the Colonial administration was a blended affair. But the nature of that shared enterprise is where the debate lies. Examining the Tucker archive reveals an egalitarian approach to the Africans in the areas of spiritually, skills, philosophy, finances, evangelism, and teaching. Tucker admired certain qualities he observed and considered spiritual in the East Africans. No doubt his Quaker background provided an underlying philosophy of egalitarianism from which he drew heavily in his bid to produce an autonomous African church. In Tucker's view the abilities of the Africans in areas of evangelism, financial self-support, and

---

113. Tucker to Baylis, October 15, 1899, CMSA, G3/A7/O/4.
114. Tucker to Baylis, May 31, 1909, ibid.
115. Tucker to Carus-Wilson, September 9, 1909, BGCA, 135 /1/3.

teaching merited not only respect and support but independence: Echoes of Bishop Crowther are sometimes very apparent.

Yet even when Tucker's approach was placed into operation with a heartfelt appreciation for African abilities, two attitudes were frequently and simultaneously present; first, that the Africans were the back-up personnel to be used when there were not enough Europeans, and secondly that the Africans needed tutoring before they would be ready to take on responsibilities alone at which time it was the duty of the western missionaries to allow them their part. It is possible then to see together a juxtaposition of equality, admiration and an unequal interaction from a perceived superior position.

Direct consultation with African authorities was generally a part of the equation for Tucker whether it involved political matters, such as treaty revisions, or church matters, such as ordination candidates, new mission stations, governance, or evangelism opportunities.[116] Surprisingly, he even consulted the Native Church Council on the placement of European missionaries! At the same time Tucker approached these consultations with a mind to mold the church and the culture into shapes that he considered acceptable. At times it was possible to use African approaches to accomplish the transformation, at other times they must be discarded.

African initiative in evangelism, teaching, church building and worship played into Tucker's egalitarian hopes but at times pulled in directions contrary to his own opinion. He supported these initiatives by agreeing with them, such as the language question in Toro or the removal of ineffective European missionaries, but at other times "support" came in the form of European supervision, such as that in the Sese Islands. Tucker's tendency to carry in the same letter a message of equality and solidarity together with a sense of distance and superiority is sometimes striking but in every respect illustrative of the two opposing world-views held in tension by a western missionary in a non-western world.

---

116. In the interior the consultations tended to be with strong African political and church authorities, but on the coast where the Muslim faith prevailed and the English government presence was well established, the mission was small and struggling. There consultation was with individuals and tribal chiefs.

CHAPTER EIGHT

Conclusion

STANDING ON THE HILL overlooking the small village of Kisokwe, in central Tanzania with the ruined foundation of the mission chapel at one's back, the eye sweeps over a great distance across a broad valley. Protected on three sides by hills, the site of the old mission station is now a church training center. Nestled high in the descending folds of Mt. Kiboriani, a clear fresh spring bubbles down to the collection of new buildings. But on top of the hill old pathways lined with stones wind between the various old foundations of the original buildings. They are overgrown with tall dried grass and shrubs but still visible. It is here that the original English missionaries grew vegetables from their homeland, built a clinic, a school and dormitories, taught reading and baptized the first converts. It is here that Bishop Tucker came on visitations to confirm, baptize and ordain. Down the hill in the less rocky valley, not more than 200 yards below the chapel, near the *wadi* and completely hidden from sight, lay the graves of several pioneer missionaries baking in the hot African sun. They are marked with no headstones or names but only simple piles of local rocks, in the middle of a dense corn field. Those who keep the records at the CMS headquarters in London are unaware of their existence. They are hidden from most passersby. Only the few who know the story can guide the visitor to the spot.

It is not unusual for European visitors to ponder why those early missionaries went to Africa and to wonder what they were trying to accomplish. Perhaps if the location of this particular mission were in a bustling trade center it would be easier to understand. But standing in the almost

Conclusion

unchanging hills of rural Tanzania with the afternoon peace broken only by the sound of the wind or the distant chopping of wood, it seems a puzzle. Their stories, like their graves, are hidden from view and known only to those Africans or Europeans who intentionally seek them out.

This study began with just such intention; to discover the why and how of a European encampment in the Tanzanian *porini* (wilderness). It also began with an initial tentative assumption: that the story of those early Europeans in East Africa was not entirely hidden, there would certainly be some letters, diaries, minutes of meetings, and other materials to find. And, there must be stories passed down from person to person, whether among the Africans or Europeans. Academia would certainly have something to say about the whole colonial endeavor. Imperialism has left a big stain in history books and most studies have included a mention of the missionary's interaction as part of this story. Countless undergraduate lectures ring in the memory as verification. Yet, in spite of these possibilities at discovery, there are many untold stories, lost records, forgotten legacies, and unnamed graves covered with rocks.

Untold narratives have a certain power to draw questioning researchers, regardless of nationality, to dusty archives; and archives are curious collections of information—they can be read and interpreted in different ways. Some scholars attempt to approach archives with a seemingly open mind, with the intention of allowing the recorded information to organize itself according to its own internal categories. Others may arrive with an assumption and seek documentation for this assumption until proven or disproven. Some insist that it is quite impossible to achieve the former and that the latter is generally the only possible approach—and even then the whole picture will never be known. Regardless of the debate, my beginning research assumed complicity on the part of Tucker, and missionaries in his jurisdiction, with the imperial juggernaut. However, after completion of this study this assumption has been found to be only partially the case. The initial impression was countered by an intimate interaction with the primary sources.

Another assumption at the outset of this study was that quite possibly Tucker and other missionaries in his grouping may have been slightly unhinged from reality. What else could possibly prompt an Oxford educated, successful artist and fully-employed curate to live apart for long periods of time from family, loved ones and familiar surroundings and tramp through the African wilderness experiencing very unstable social conditions? There was no lack of opportunity for him at home and surely the roughly six hundred pounds a year (plus allowances) which he received for this service was not an overwhelming factor.[1] The archives produced a firm and consistent record that Tucker did have some very high ideals, even when the reality of the situation did not always entirely match these visions. For example, Walker, Tucker's Archdeacon in Uganda, opposed an exclusively rosy portrayal of the Uganda mission often given in CMS publications, which he felt was not being balanced with reality. He writes: "The Church Council have (sic) handed in the names of 80 so-called Christian men who are known to be public drunkards. More are women but they drink at home. [There is a] grievous state of morals on the part of many of the Native Christian women."[2] Yet this darker side of the mission efforts is never acknowledged in Tucker's communication, although he does acknowledge the challenge posed by the non-Christian environment, as in the Freretown situation. His response to Walker's concern was to point out the change in the African's perception of drinking; what they had done with abandon before the arrival of Christianity they now did in secret, knowing it was wrong.[3] In his view this was a good change. At the same time, Tucker was not completely blind to the perceived faults of African Christians, he was sometimes disappointed with their decisions and sometimes even wrote reprimands. An unhinged idealism could not account entirely for Tucker's decisions and actions.

Was Tucker carried along with the zeal of imperial domination which was so infectious in this age, or was it a true Christian egalitarian idealism, with the sense of brotherhood of all humankind and the call to raise others from impoverishment that formed Tucker's deepest orientation? The paradigm of "tectonic plates" proposed by Jeffrey Cox, Professor of History at the University of Iowa, offers a supportable alternative to both initial assumptions. Cox calls for a new master narrative apart from the narrative of western expansion with its binary categories of aggression and response. While explaining the previous approaches to the study of missionaries, Cox calls for an expanded concept of partnership, also articulated by Lamin Sanneh, Professor of World Christianity at Yale, and uses the metaphor of tectonic plates. His theory recognizes the frequent imperial involvement

---

1. Tucker accounts 1890–91, CMSA, F/Y/A6/2/60. And missionary allowances CMSA, GA/AM/12/1909.
2. Walker to Baylis, September 19, 1896, CMSA, G3/A5/O/403.
3. Tucker to Baylis, January 1, 1897, CMSA, G3/A5/O/1.

and approach of the pioneer missionaries but at the same time acknowledges the detailed references in missionary primary sources which point to a joint endeavor with indigenous people. Extensive reading and re-reading of Tucker's communications and related material confirms Cox's views which explain quite closely the dynamic found in Tucker's records. There is a constant rubbing of egalitarian ideals and imperial tendencies, like massive tectonic plates pushing against each other. This is a constant theme found in his letters and drawings. Both great forces were present but neither alone was explanatory of Tucker's life work. And Tucker was not a singular character, his attitudes and approach represented many others in the East African project.

SUMMARIZING CONCLUSIONS

Looking closely at Tucker's artistic contributions, he possessed an idealistic desire through his talent and ability to bring to the attention of a wider audience the needs of the disadvantaged. By exhibiting the housing, dress and customs found in the African environment in a somewhat encyclopedic style, he highlighted and contrasted the African lifestyle with the lifestyle found among his readership, even while admiring Africa's assets. As his tenure lengthened and the colonial apparatus strengthened, he objected vigorously to any exploitation of African land and labor, expressing a desire to guard "native" interests. He was quite convinced of the superior abilities of Africans over Europeans in many aspects of the mission project and presented them in his art with dignity, place, identity and status, often as the center of attention. Reminding his European co-workers that the African church would one day be independent, that the European role was a temporary one of mentorship, he invited them through his compositions to walk into the Africans' world. Tucker's art displays his idealism which had significant egalitarian leanings.

Yet his artistic offerings could not escape the influence of empire. Consciously or unconsciously his sketches were used in the process of centralized planning back in the homeland. Beginning with the process of accumulation, Tucker's art helped to translate knowledge from the periphery to the center where they were combined with other information to produce agendas resulting in domination from afar, as in the decision of how and where to build the Mombasa church. Even his ethnographic art, while eliciting support, also helped to build momentum for a shift in power. Tucker could not escape his background. The watercolor technique was considered a superior English skill and his training, associations, and artistic occupation pulled him toward imperial attitudes as evidenced by the Christian name imposed on Kiongosi and the flag of power over the Mochi (now Moshi) mission. Throughout his career he felt it important to keep on good terms with the colonial administration. In his art, almost as an illustration of the foreign apparatus imposed on Africa, Tucker often used a European structure, such as a doorway or garden arch, to frame or fence the breathtaking African landscape. Although the mission was initially portrayed as small and precarious, it sometimes bore resemblance in Tucker's sketches to imperial soldiers of Christ on bivouac.

During his initial period in Africa Tucker found himself being confronted with situations in the coastal section of the mission that did not square with his sensibilities. First and foremost, of these issues was the style of contracting and recording African marriage unions. Once again we see a dichotomy in Tucker's approach to the problems; one which was partly egalitarian and partly imperial. On the one hand he envisioned Freretown, and the coastal mission in general, to be a community of equality; one which was building toward self-support with an educated membership gradually moving into leadership positions. In this process there was no hesitation to consult fully with indigenous followers, whom he believed to be wholly redeemable, bright, earnest and without reproach when converted.

On the other hand, Tucker was not just the bishop of the indigenous church he was also bishop in a hierarchical British church and as such he did not hesitate to impose standards in a very autocratic way. He also did not hesitate to appeal to the center of power in London to legislate what he felt was needed change, such as the reformation of the dormitory system in Freretown. Not only were standards imposed from afar but also practices were imposed. For example, Freretown kept a marriage register as any parish would in England, recording the unions of all people within the purview of the mission compound. However, problematically, some of these residents were not Christian, as parish residents would be in England. Regardless of this fact, the Freretown missionaries recorded all unions, subjugating the African style of contracting marriages to the English style. The Freretown mission village operated quite independently from the Sultan of Zanzibar and the *Sharia* law and carried on a type of civil jurisdiction which included the settlement of disputes, crime, or divorces. Tucker accepted this arrangement and eventually accepted the IBEA court system as

Conclusion

well, as it gradually developed, rather than consult with the Sultan. In all these arrangements, his imperial side was evident.

Another issue which Tucker initially encountered on the coast was the presence and the practice of slavery. Coming from a Quaker background, Tucker held strong abolitionist views. In contrast, the British government in Mombasa and Zanzibar during Tucker's tenure leaned toward a deep respect for the indigenous culture, which included slavery as an institution, favoring a very gradual approach to changing this practice—sometimes slow enough to be standing still. Tucker's response to this situation was not only to protest and debate the administration but also to drag his feet in the forcible return of runaway slaves who took refuge at Freretown. In addition, he researched the statutes governing the policy of slavery and at an opportune moment, took the Karibu case in an effort to bring about an end to the institution of slavery in Mombasa and the coast. In the same vein, he advised the Ugandan chiefs to consider alternatives to slavery based on his understanding of the Christian scriptures. In his relationship with Mr. Jones, the African priest at Rabai who harbored runaways, he assigned responsibility and expected duty with no regard to nationality; part of his consistent commitment to rising African leadership together with a strong belief in their abilities. In all of these actions Tucker showed himself to have a clear egalitarian vision.

But once again Tucker was torn by an imperial counterweight. He labored under a strong sense of duty to serve under existing treaties and to obey the existing authorities, even if he perceived those authorities to be in error. Rather than disobey, his approach was to negotiate change while promising cooperation. While possessing strong beliefs in African abilities, he simultaneously referred to the students in the Freretown schools as "material," and generally placed them under European supervision.

In the power struggle between church and mission a similar tug-of-war took place; but in this particular area Tucker's imperial side seemed much stronger than his commitment to egalitarian approaches. The Bishop could be prickly; he was very conscious of his status and did not like to be challenged. Having a tendency to lead from the top, Tucker pressed the CMS for more executive authority similar to the style of a colonial governor. He not only sought to retain for himself the practice of instructing all missionaries and placing ordained personnel in the field, he also pressed to input nominations to the CMS Finance Committee, thus avoiding any dissenting voices in the local governing body. He seemed particularly aggravated by the tendency of the CMS to favor patterns of grassroots authority among the missionary decision-making apparatus, and to ignore his role. In particular, he complained of slights when CMS communicated directly with the Foreign Office, ignored his authority in instruction letters to the new recruits, placed ordained clergy without consultation, and communicated directly with the Secretary of the Mission regarding church affairs. Although a polite consultation was exchanged regarding the opening of new stations, Tucker always modified the initial assignment made by CMS headquarters of ordained personnel. Against constant resistance from Salisbury Square and from personnel in the field, Tucker consistently tried to retain a central role in all things.

It is therefore surprising that Tucker remained a member of the CMS and director of the mission for his entire tenure, given the commitment the society had to consensus decisions and especially by committees predominantly filled with laity. Tucker could be temperamental. Although many letters of resignation were offered, the fact that he remained is an illustration of the shadow side of his imperial tendencies. One could postulate that he enjoyed the high ranking personnel found among the members of the CMS Parent Committee, but Tucker also had a deep appreciation for precedent and written decisions made from higher levels. When he acknowledged that the Society had the right to constitute the local governing board of the mission in Africa without any input from the field, he may have had in mind the Ceylon controversy which produced a "ruling" by the Archbishop of Canterbury that bishops could not interfere with volunteer societies in their dioceses. After much friction in this area Tucker finally gave in to the constant resistance and turned over to the Finance Committee the assignment of ordained missionaries, concentrating his influence in the African church instead. In this case his egalitarian side was expressed reluctantly, but present none the less.

The relationship between mission and state is an area which also illustrates the half-way position held by Tucker. At the beginning of his tenure in Mombasa he maintained a cordial relationship with the Consul-General and the IBEA administrator, Col. Euan Smith and Sir Francis de Winton respectively, seeing both as potential instruments of peace. As Tucker was always concerned with the power and status of the mission, he found it necessary, especially in Uganda which was much further advanced in imperial patterns than the coast, to negotiate with the colonial administration in order to maintain a dominant place in the settlement of the country.

Conclusion

He was much in favor of a consolidation of imperial power in a uniform governmental system rather than a hodgepodge, crazy quilt pattern which had developed in East Africa. Chaos and messiness irritated him.

On the other hand, Tucker was committed to equality among the missions of various denominations and their adherents (as long as Anglicans were first among equals) and used his influence with the colonial powers to bring this about, such as the assigning of spheres of influence with Portal or the renegotiation of the Roman Catholic land assignments with Williams. If the administration attempted to curtail the free evangelization of the country Tucker was reluctant to go along. He was never one to refrain from the criticism of "high-handedness" or imperial tendencies on the part of colonial personalities. His assessment of this drift toward dominance became more vocal as time went on and the control of the administration became more developed. Tucker's tenure coincided with a massive transition of imperial dominance. Beginning with free-trade agreements which were basically mercantile, coastal related and interested in African business counterparts, they evolved into a direct occupation penetrating further inland with Africans as a labor force. As the influence of the colonial administration tightened, his advocacy for the Africans became stronger and more noticeable.

His commitment to egalitarian ideals is most noticeable in his interaction with the African followers of Christianity, but not without an imperial shadow. Diverse partnership arrangements were prevalent in Tucker's diocese with Africans being involved as equals in prayer, preaching, ordination, written material production, translation, work assignments, and evangelistic efforts. A partnership developed for the training and provision of priests, the mission providing the former and the indigenous church providing the latter. Tucker's egalitarian philosophy of the mission breathes through his letters; as in references to "brethren," or the insistence of African clergy reporting to the African church council, or the equal place given to African testimony. In addition, Tucker maintained a continuous crusade against financial dependence on the CMS—the African church should be self-supporting. Consultation with African leaders was pursued in decisions to open new stations, church policy matters and even the placement of European missionaries! Superior abilities were recognized in the areas of evangelism, teaching, start-ups, leading worship, pastoral care, and the design and building of worship space; African initiative was recognized in these areas and their opinion often prevailed in reports of injustice, malpractice by Europeans, African personnel assignments or the use of language materials. By the close of Tucker's time, African priests were already holding the office of district supervisor, as in the case of Nua Kikwabanga.

References outlining Tucker commitment to an egalitarian church vastly outweigh references to one characterized by European domination. But this opposite position existed none the less. Partnership was carried out but in many cases one partner remained senior and one junior in the relationship, as in the illustration Tucker used at Lambeth of using indigenous styles of administration but referring to Africans as "the child races." In keeping with the position of senior partner Europeans were in charge of most stations and most often Europeans organized, supervised and managed the work. Tucker clearly expressed his view that the Africans were not ready to govern themselves. Separate worship services were set up where a significant European population existed, such as in Mombasa and Tucker was in the habit of consulting the groups separately on issues of importance. Most often in the creation of the church in East Africa the Bishop used a gentle hand but not hands-off.

Tucker was not a consistent imperialist; neither was he completely an unrealistic egalitarian idealist. But at times he displayed elements of both perspectives as he walked the grinding rift between these opposing viewpoints. Byaruhanga recognizes this tension in his 1997 study of Tucker and postulates that Tucker occupied a third category which he does not name. But it is my belief that Tucker operated simultaneously as a member of both groups. Tucker's story is somewhat one of duel identities involved in a mutual interaction; but neither category—idealist or imperialist—can claim complete ownership. It is important to be fully aware of both perspectives in the memory of Tucker, and others like him, in a type of "joint recognition." He held great aspirations to raise-up an African church which was shared equally with European members, but he also possessed the power to impose practices and personnel from afar. Providing space for these differences does not mean one set of actions is replaced by the other. These differing sides of Tucker, and the other Victorian missionaries, need to be acknowledged and integrated in order for colonizers and colonized to get a full picture of the colonial situation and to hear one another's stories.

Conclusion

FURTHER CONCLUSIONS

Various impressions of missionaries are held in different circles of discourse and over different periods of time. The church in England at the time of Alfred Tucker felt that it had attached to itself "all the glamour of empire" through its missionaries and their work.[4]

If money and numbers are any indication of popular support it bears noting that just prior to Tucker's send off for East Africa there were fifty-eight national mission organizations in England with a total annual income of £1,316,798. Together these organizations supported in various ways 3,000 ordained men, 815 lay men, 2,430 lay women, 2,370 ordained "natives" and 26,800 followers.[5]

Some beyond the church looked favorably on the enterprise such as Stanley, the American journalist, who wrote to Livingstone's son-in-law: "These missionary societies certainly contrive to produce extraordinary men."[6] William Wordsworth called them "Christian knights on barbarous shores."[7] Churchill and Roosevelt had similar favorable comments. Churchill wrote after his visit to Uganda that the missionary enterprise had the "beneficial results ... of improving and elevating the population."[8] However Churchill also acknowledged that there were those who did not agree, especially among the "official classes" who were "inclined to view with anxiety or dislike missionary activity."[9] Sydney Smith, the founder of *The Review*, was prone to portray the missionaries as "perilously inept, blinded, zealous, or autocratic."[10]

Yet despite the mixed assessments, when news of Bishop Tucker's sudden and unexpected death reached Uganda in June of 1914, Miss Chadwick, CMS missionary in Uganda, wrote to her sister: "Bishop Tucker's sudden death heard by telegram last week has plunged the church here into mourning. I believe last Sunday the native preacher quite broke down and half the congregation were (sic) in tears."[11] Hearing the news, Apollo

---

4. Ford and Harrison, *A Hundred Years Ago*, 95.
5. Statistics, *Quarterly Review*, July 1886, 127.
6. Stanley to Bruce, CMS Annual Report, 1890, 57.
7. Comaroff, *Of Revelation*, 50.
8. Winston Churchill, CMS Annual Report, 1908, 64.
9. Ibid.
10. Comaroff, *Of Revelation*, 53.
11. Chadwick to Ethel Magowan, June 28, 1914, CMSA, Acc. 167, F3/23–41.

Kagwa fainted dead away.[12] There is no doubt that most of the missionaries held a large place in the communities they served, an insight unexplained and unattended to by Post-Colonial scholars.

The perception of the role of missionaries in general has evolved over time. Possibly it is a necessary evolution. It has also frequently been highjacked, leading to the problem of invisibility in academic circles where information has sometimes been selectively employed. Archives are often cherry-picked to prove assumptions and "complicity [is] often assumed rather than analyzed, interpreted, or explained."[13] Some of the reasons for this deficit have been explored already but one additional insight comes from Quentin Bell, an art historian, who offers a defense for his study of the sometimes discounted field of Victorian art:

> Why do I choose to examine it? The question contains an assumption that the historian must be an apologist. I am not an apologist ... I hope to bring to your notice some artist who have been almost forgotten and who I think deserve to be remembered, I shall also ask you to look at detestable painting which I shall not attempt to defend. I shall do this because the first duty of the historian in this field is to exhibit the evidence ... [even that] thought unworthy of examination. What would happen to a chronicle of the past if all regrettable persons and incidents were omitted? However much we may wish to do so we cannot omit Judas Iscariot from the story of the twelve apostles ... We cannot dismiss that which we do not like on the pretext that it has no importance.[14]

A study of a topic must be distinguished from a promotion of a topic. Regardless of voids in previous studies for whatever reason, whether it be misunderstanding, distraction, embarrassment or attention to a theme, a closer look at all of the various players in the Victorian East Africa project is required. Without increasing research into individual missionaries, the complicated place that they held, between egalitarian ideals and imperial presence will continue to be less than amplified. On the one hand they called for sweeping change and yet simultaneously held onto aspects of traditional religion and culture (such as the traditional name for God or the indigenous organizational structure). Old and tired categories continue to haunt us. Sanneh is correct when he writes that some pietistic evangelical

---

12. Johnston Notebooks, MUA, Book III.
13. Cox, *Imperial Fault Lines*, 10.
14. Bell, *Victorian Artists*, 1–3.

Conclusion

missionaries "eschewed having any truck with worldly arrangements, including indigenous cultures"[15] But not all. Tucker, who leaned pietistic and attended many Keswick gatherings, embraced many aspects of indigenous culture while at the same time believing that knowledge of the scriptures would transform some African cultural practices. One study of the history of the African church mistakenly states: "There was Mombasa with its Anglican cathedral and bishop since 1900."[16] Clearly revealing a lack of familiarity with sources; Mombasa had a bishop in the person of James Hannington, beginning in 1884! In light of these examples, this study agrees with Friesen as he observes, "With the increasing research on individual missionaries a more composite picture of early twentieth century missionary thought becomes more accurate and feasible."[17]

A fresh examination of initial encounters between North and South and a greater emphasis on archival sources will provide examples for wider venues of discussion. Although the missionary journals, letters, and reports do not give an "analytic account of the complex social forces of which they themselves are products" yet they are part of the "chain of collective consciousness" which is necessary to include for a greater breadth of discussion to be opened.[18] Unfamiliarity with the primary sources has produced a continuation of previous assumptions, frozen in the dynamics of collapsing colonial associations and the old binaries of aggression and response. To continue along similar lines is to ignore vast amounts of material or to squeeze existing records into outdated categories.

Records of the Edinburgh Missionary Conference of 1910 revealed surprising attitudes. "It is possible that contemporary scholars and historians have come to this material with anti-colonial biases . . . overstating and caricaturizing the position of missionaries at the 1910 Edinburgh Conference [who were] not radically abrasive or totally rejecting."[19] Re-examining the context of their quotations leads to a different interpretation: "The idea that missionaries at Edinburgh regarded African religion as demonic and to be uprooted is a judgment which is unwarranted from this evidence."[20] Byaruhanga, the Ugandan historian, agrees as he describes Tucker's position:

15. Sanneh, *Abolitionists Abroad*, 163.
16. Sundkler and Steed, *History of the Church in Africa*, 885.
17. Friesen, *Missionary Responses*, 17.
18. Comaroff, *Of Revelation*, 35.
19. Frisen, *Missionary Responses*, 5.
20. Ibid, 134.

> One of the most important arguments of the post-colonial revisionists against the European missionaries is that when the latter prepared the natives for greater responsibilities in their own church in Africa, the former wanted to remain in control. By pursuing passionately, energetically, and consistently the policy of majority representation and closer integration between CMS missionaries and the natives which was contained in the Native Anglican Constitution of the Church in Uganda, Bishop Tucker gives us a genuine reason for questioning the post-colonial revisionist assertion.[21]

With the work of scholars such as Cox, Peterson, Sanneh, and Byaruhanga who are recognizing the need for a shift in perspective, this writer is hopeful that the passing of a generation may not need to occur in order to bring about a change in assumptions. Brian Stanley's pessimistic prediction need not become reality; that "no amount of specialized historical monographs by academic historians is likely to affect substantially the received views of those unfamiliar with the world of historical scholarship."[22]

EPILOGUE

After twenty-one years in Africa, Tucker retired from his position as a diocesan bishop and returned to England. Close to his retirement and before leaving Africa, his letters began to reflect the striking changes that he had witnessed in East Africa. After a trip to Nassa he observed:

> In the old days such a journey [across the lake] involved at least a fortnight's voyaging in canoes. There was the long, weary daily paddle—six, eight, ten, or even twenty hours at a stretch . . . the blazing sun pouring its pitiless rays upon the bare backs of a score or more of poorly nourished and often weary paddlers . . . Now, however, all is changed. Instead of a frail canoe sewn together with fibre, and oftentimes leaking like a sieve, there is a magnificent steamer with saloon and cabins fitted with electric light and fans, bathrooms, and conveniences of every kind. Instead of hard tack and tough goat, eaten cold and washed down with a draught of water from the Lake, dipped as you pass along in your canoe, there is now the four-course dinner and the early morning and afternoon cup of tea . . . The old station of reed houses and grass

---

21. Byaruhanga, "Bishop Alfred Tucker," 278.
22. Stanley, *Bible and the Flag*, 12.

roofs of Emin Pasha's day has given place to one of brick houses with iron roofs and glazed windows ... Bukoba has become a busy place of trade.[23]

Similar changes had taken place eight years earlier along the land route of the caravan trails as well:

> We came up by train for one hundred miles. It was a wonderful experience to pass by all the places which I have tramped so often ... and to think how I have perspired over it, and slept on it, and how I have tramped it by night and day ... we asked the Station Master to telegraph on to the next station and asked them to have some boiling water ready for us. This he did, so that on arriving at Maungu not only did we have water but it was boiling. We made tea straight away and drank it in our saloon carriage as we were whirled across Taro at the rate of 20 miles per hour. What a strange contrast with three years ago.[24]

In addition, Tucker's letters to friends and colleagues describe the gradual coming into being of Colonial court systems, governors, contractors, district commissioners and sub-commissioners along with schools, hospitals, and administrative structure. An imperial world had gradually and incrementally imposed itself onto the East African milieu, but twining into it as one strand of the blended braid, an incorporation of the African setting and customs. Tucker's description of the investiture of Daudi to the Ugandan Kingship is an example. After a detailed account of the traditional ceremony which took place outside the palace gate while standing upon a drum, with gifts given of lion skin, leopard skin, bark cloth, bracelets, spears, shield, and symbolic gifts from courtesans, Tucker tells what followed: "When all this ceremony was over the men came forward whose office it is to carry the king. He got upon their shoulders and away they went with him to his house where he afterwards held a reception in the European fashion. Daudi is growing up to be a nice youth. He speaks English well and plays both football and golf."[25]

While the country was changing before his eyes, Alfred Tucker noticed a change in himself as well. His physical strength began to fade and his rheumatism and heart arrhythmia became more troublesome and noticeable, and at times incapacitating. He mused: "Indeed, I am wondering

23. Tucker, "A Visit to Nassa," *Intelligencer*, May 1906, 353.
24. Tucker to Mrs. Tucker, February 1898, CMSA, G3/A5/O/55.
25. Tucker to Carus-Wilson, August 13, 1910, BGCA, 135/1/3.

whether I ought to come out here again. I am certainly not so fit for these long and trying expeditions as I once was. I have now entered my 16th year of service out here and realize that I am not as fresh and vigorous as I was in 1890."[26] In addition his letters contain observations of changes in the missionaries which he found irritating; such as a lack of self-sacrifice, of simplicity in living.[27] He complained of missionaries who indulged in tobacco, built large houses, wore fancy dress, and drug large amounts of furniture to their assignments. Still five more years would pass before he finally acknowledged: "I fear that the heart trouble is not any better. Indeed, its intermittent action rather increases than diminishes. This and other things, tells me that the time has come for me to hand over this work into other and stronger hands."[28]

On receiving Tucker's letter of resignation, Archbishop Davidson was reluctant to lose a bishop with so much long experience in a specialized position and suggested an assistant.[29] Only at the private revelation to Davidson of Tucker's physical condition by his long-time correspondent Mrs. Ashley Carus-Wilson, did the Archbishop make plans to accept his resignation. Arranging, after much negotiation, for "the greatest missionary of our time, or perhaps of any time" to be admitted to the Sixth Canonry at Durham Cathedral in February 1912, the Archbishop referred to the assignment as: "Noblesse oblige."[30]

Reverse culture shock was not beyond his experience as the retired Bishop re-entered ministry in England. He writes almost whimsically: "We are here living in a 'band-box'... in the room in which I am writing I cannot see a single inch of sky, nothing but a blank wall!!! What a contrast to my study in Uganda where I look out upon the verdant vista, twenty miles of country."[31] Or his sarcastic and humorous observations:

> On Saturday last at the Chapter here there was a lengthened discussion on what do you think? How to touch the mass of the untouched! No! How to help preserve the missionary work of the Church? No! How to guide the great labour movement? No!

26. Ibid, May 10, 1905, BCGA, 135/1/2.

27. Tucker to Baylis, November 17, 1904, CMSA, G3/A7/O/233 and Tucker to Baylis, May 5, 1905, CMSA, G3/A7/O/121.

28. Tucker to Carus-Wilson, June 29, 1910, BGCA, 135/1/3.

29. Davidson to Fox, June 20, 1910, LPA, Davidson 168/14–15 and Davidson to Fox, November 3, 1910, LPA, Davidson 168/31.

30. Davidson to Bishop of Durham, July 17, 1911, LPA, Davidson 174/147–48.

31. Tucker to Carus-Wilson, October 14, 1910, BGCA, 135 / 1 /3.

Conclusion

> Nothing of the kind, but how, after the communion service was over, the vessels should be carried into the Chapter house for the ablutions ... It was asked for my opinion. Oh! I said, it is beyond me altogether. I cannot plunge down into such depths ... I asked myself whether it was for this I had come back from the Mission field.[32]

Yet Tucker threw himself into his work, thus fulfilling Davidson's prediction: "Tucker can never be an idle man. He will always do work to the limit of his tether."[33] He re-modelled his residence, attended Chapter meetings, took his share of preaching and services, attended Convocation, lectured at the College, took Confirmations, served on the Faith and Order Committee, in addition to taking speaking engagements all over the country[34]

Although the Dean of Durham Cathedral, Herbert Hensley Hensen, was not much impressed with Tucker's preaching style, which he called "obsolete, wandering, and ranting" with "the total absence of any didactic quality," there were elements of Tucker's ministry for which he expressed relief.[35] Hensen's diary records an occasional preaching compliment, an appreciation of Tucker's entertaining conversational abilities, but mostly he appreciated his Canon's attention to detail and his willingness to participate in the mundane duties, such as Convocation. Hensen writes: 'I shirked Convocation, where the agenda seemed rather trivial and released Tucker, who seems to enjoy the futile assembly."[36] He also appreciated Tucker's interest in the restoration of Cuthbert's grave and the baptismal font. But the area where the two colleagues found the most unity was in the unfolding of the very public debate regarding the "Kikuyu Controversy."[37]

At a concluding Anglican Communion service at a conference in Kenya, consecrated elements of bread and wine were distributed to non-Anglican attendees. When this news reached England a firestorm of public debate was ignited as to the nature of Christian unity, of Anglican sacraments, and prerequisites for the reception of Christian Communion. Tucker followed

---

32. Tucker to Carus-Wilson, December 24, 1912, BGCA.
33. Davidson to Bishop of Durham, July 17, 1911, LPA, Davidson 174/147–48.
34. Insurance/Loan Book and Chapter Acts Book, Durham Cathedral Records, L/EA. Tucker to Carus-Wilson, August 22, 1912, BGCA, 135 /1/3 and Hensen Diary, April 23, 1913, DCL.
35. Hansen, "Mission and Colonialism," April 13 & 27, 1913.
36. Ibid.
37. Griffiths, "Bishop Alfred Tucker," 257–60.

the proceedings closely and participated fully, finding an unexpected ally in Hensen. Tucker's interest in Christian unity was not surprising having been nurtured during his early years at Oxford by Canon Christopher, who himself was very interested in the subject. Not only did Christopher chair a committee of all denominations in Oxford (which sponsored the Moody/Sankey mission) he also taught that only as Christian unity was realized "would the full blessing of God be received on missionary work."[38] It was due to Tucker's interest and participation in these ecumenical issues which led to his appointment to the Faith and Order Committee, a precursor to the World Council of Churches.

Tucker was a frequent contributor to *The Times* regarding events in East Africa and his letters, according to an article in *The Record* "always excited attention."[39] Another avenue of valuable future research yet to be examined would involve an examination of this very public face of Tucker.

On the morning of June 15, 1914 Tucker visited his doctor in Walpole Street, who did not have the heart to tell him of his fragile condition. From there he rushed to the Royal Academy's summer exhibition where his painting "Monreale Cathedral, Sicily" was being hung. Moving quickly on to Westminster to participate in an afternoon meeting of the Faith and Order Committee, he collapsed on the lawn and was carried into the Deanery. He died two hours later as he had spent much of his professional life, without the presence of his wife or son, although they were near enough to be notified, a fact which caused them both much grief.[40]

In the various eulogies given for Bishop Alfred Robert Tucker there are many phrases which capture the duel characteristics found among Victorian missionaries. In keeping with imperial values he was described as great, courageous, strong-willed, stern, and able to formulate his own policy and carry it out. On the other hand, giving voice to the more egalitarian side of his ideals, are phrases such as affectionate, unselfish, loving—gentle as a woman with the weak.[41] But in keeping with the invisibility now enjoyed by those who first interacted with the peoples of East Africa there are also phrases that no longer apply. Such as: "widely known throughout

---

38. Reynolds, *Evangelicals*, 251.
39. "Sudden Death of Bishop Tucker," *The Record*, June 19, 1914, 605, col. 1.
40 Hathaway Tucker to Mrs. Carus-Wilson, June 1914, BGCA, 135 /1/1.
41. Ibid.

Conclusion

England and indeed in all parts of the Empire... the name of Alfred Tucker will forever occupy a conspicuous place."[42]

Jack Thompson, Senior Lecturer at the University of Edinburgh, calls for a process of "re-membering through remembering."[43] This involves going back and looking again at the history of encounters from multiple of perspectives, acknowledging the presence of each viewpoint. However painful this may be at times as past hurts and injustices are revisited, without such a process regional scholars write their histories separately without regard for integration with the whole.

But, while Europe may have forgotten his name, and his legacy waits in quiet, dusty archives, not all is forgotten. Whether driven by imperialism or egalitarianism or both at the same time, the work of Tucker continues on today. In 2013 Bishop Tucker Theological College in Mukono, Uganda marked its hundred-year anniversary. A number of celebrations were held. The notice advertising this Centenary celebration day also had these words to say:

> Tucker brought with him the vision of the "Native Anglican Church" as a self-governing indigenous church. Critical to the planting of such a church was education for its people, and so the Church under Tucker founded high schools for girls and boys and promoted theological training, which led to the founding of the work at Mukono in 1913.[44]

But, such an accolade and aging remembrance of one man, however glossed, is never the story of just one man; it is the story of a series of actors set on the complex imperial stage, African and European, government and church, rich and poor, helpful and unhelpful, authoritarian and egalitarian, slave and free, all caught in that great and complex struggle to grow and thrive. Perhaps that is also our same story today.

---

42. Ibid.

43. Thompson, *Remembering*, 127–43.

44. https://americananglican.org/current-news/100-years-old-ugandan-theological-college-celebrates-birthday/, June 23, 2016.

APPENDIX 1

Colonial Personalities
In Order of Appearance

Ernest Gedge (1862–1953)

Ludborough, Lincolnshire, England. Colonial Administrator. After serving as an assistant manager of a tea plantation in Assam, India he joined the Imperial British East Africa Company in 1889 assisting Sir Frederick Jackson with the pioneer caravan into Uganda and then Sir Frederick Lugard. During 1892 and 1893 he was special correspondent for the *Times*. In 1894 he returned to England and engaged in mining and prospecting in South Africa, Yukon, Rhodesia, and Kenya. Between 1898 and 1899 he visited Russia, East Africa, Asia and Mexico on similar business. After serving as a Special Constabulary during WWI he journeyed to the Far East and Australia regarding land speculation. *Rhodes House Library.*

Sir Gerald H. Portal (1858–1894)

Laverstoke, Hampshire, England. Eton. Diplomat. Entering the diplomatic service in 1879 he was sent to Rome in 1880. In 1882 he went to Cairo where he climbed the ranks to become charge d'affaires in 1888. In 1889 he became first the Acting Consul-General and then the Consul-General of Zanzibar in 1891. His duties expanded to include German East Africa in June of 1891 and British East Africa in 1892. He journeyed to Uganda in 1892 to assess whether the country should be retained or evacuated. Returning to England where he recommended retention, he died of fever January 25, 1894. He wrote two books, *My Mission to Abyssinia* and *The British Mission to Uganda*. Rhodes House Library.

Frederick Dealtry Lugard, Baron Lugard of Abinger (1858–1945)

Soldier, administrator and author. Sandhurst. Commissioned in 1878 he joined the second battalion of the Norfolk Regiment in India and in 1885 was dispatched to the Sudan and to Burma in 1886. After medical leave he signed up with the African Lakes Company where his defensive abilities came to the attention of Sir William Mackinnon of IBEA who sent him to Uganda in 1890 where for two years he maintained order. In 1894 he negotiated treaties in Nigeria and eventually became Commissioner for the Hinterland of Nigeria in 1897 and High Commissioner of Northern Nigeria in 1900. In 1907 he became Governor of Hong Kong where he was largely responsible for the creation of the University of Hong Kong in 1911. Returning to Nigeria as Governor in 1912 he was made Governor-General from 1914–1919 where he laid down the system of indirect rule which is associated with his name. After retirement he served in numerous high positions including the Privy Council and the League of Nations on various committees including education and African culture. *Rhodes House Library.*

Captain W. H. Williams

Employed by IBEA to act as Lugard's second in command. He arrived in Mengo January 1891. When Lugard left in April 1891 to fight in the western frontier, Williams was placed in charge of administration and security until December of the same year when Lugard returned. During this time Williams put pressure on the missions to curtail expansion. He was again placed in charge of Uganda in June 1892 when Lugard left for the coast and until the arrival of Gerald Portal in March 1893. At this time, he attempted to renegotiate Lugard's new treaty with Mwanga signed April 11, 1892 to give more power to the Catholics. *Tucker's letters.*

Colonial Personalities

Col. Sir Charles Bean Euan-Smith (1842–1910)

Colonial Administrator. Entered the Madras Army in 1859 as Chief Political Officer. Commander in Chief South Afghanistan 1879–1880 and in North Afghanistan May to August 1880. Military Attaché in Zanzibar in 1887 but by 1890 he was Consul-General until the arrival of Berkeley in 1891. He went on to become the Minister at Tangier from 1891–1893 and then the Resident at Bogota from 1898–1899. *The British Library.*

Sir Ernest James Lennox Berkeley (1857–1932)

Sandhurst. Colonial Administrator. After a brief career in the military he became Vice Consul for East Africa in 1885 and Consul for Zanzibar in 1891 while simultaneously IBEA Administrator, 1891 and 1892. He became Commissioner and Consul-General for Uganda from 1895–1899. He went on to become Consul-General for Tunis from 1899–1920 when he retired. He was a Fellow at the Royal Geographical Society and died October 24, 1932. *Cambridge University Library, England.*

Sir Harry Hamilton Johnston (1858–1927)

Explorer, Botanist, Colonial Administrator. Gaining African experience as a painter, natural history collector and journalist, he was in Tunis from 1879–1880, then traveled through Angola up the Congo River from 1882 - 1883. While on a botanical expedition to Kilimanjaro he obtained treaties which helped draw the frontiers between British and German territory. Joining the consular service in 1885, he spent three years in eastern Nigeria, then three years in Nyasaland and Northern Rhodesia obtaining treaties (1888–1891). He became Consul-General in Tunis for two years before becoming Special Commissioner and Commander in Chief in Uganda from 1899–1901. During his tenure there was a reduction in expenditure, increased revenue, a constitution, land settlement and completion of the railway. He died August 31, 1927 at Woodsetts House, Nottinghamshire. *Encyclopedia Britannica.*

Gen. Sir J. R. L. MacDonald

Soldier and engineer with the Royal Engineers. Before his arrival in East Africa he was engaged in making a survey along the Kabul River for a railway in Afghanistan. Arriving in Mombasa in January 1891 he began to carry out a survey for the railway leading inland to Lake Victoria, but he subsequently found himself obliged to try and assist Lugard to keep the peace in Uganda. In this he was to some extent successful having a small force of Sudanese and a maxim gun. He wrote, *Soldiering and Surveying in British East Africa, 1891–1894*. He went on to command a military escort for a treaty mission to Tibet sent by Lord Curzon and led by Younghusband in 1903–1904. A book about this expedition was also written; *Lhasa* by Perceval Landon. *Encyclopedia Britannica*.

Sir Arthur Hardinge, (1859–1933)

Diplomat and Statesman. The grandson of Henry Hardinge, 1st Viscount Hardinge, Governor-General of India, he entered the diplomatic service in 1880, becoming Commissioner of British East Africa from 1896 to 1901. He went on to become Ambassador in St. Petersburg from 1904 to 1906 and Permanent Under-Secretary at the Foreign Office from 1906 to 1910. He was appointed by Asquith as Viceroy of India in 1910. His tenure in India was a memorable one, overseeing the moving of the capital to New Delhi and surviving numerous assassination attempts. His admiration of Mohandas Gandhi and criticism of anti-Indian immigration policies helped him to achieve better relations with Indian nationalists and full-deployment of troops during WWI. In 1916 he returned to his former post in England as Permanent Under-Secretary at the Foreign Office and in 1920 he became Ambassador to France before his retirement in 1922. *University Library, Cambridge*.

Sir Charles Eliot (1862–1931)

Cheltenham. Diplomat, scholar, linguist. He served in diplomatic posts in Russia (1885), Morocco (1892), Turkey (1893), and Washington, D.C. (1899) before becoming Commissioner in East Equatorial Africa (1901–1904). He went on to become Vice-Chancellor of the University of Sheffield until 1912 when he was appointed the first Vice-Chancellor of the University of Hong Kong (1912–1918). He then became British Ambassador to Japan, (1919–1925). A formidable scholar of Buddhism he wrote *Japanese Buddhism* and *Hinduism and Buddhism: An Historical Sketch*. He died at sea in the Straits of Malacca. www.wikipedia.org.

Colonial Personalities

Sir James Hays Sadler (1851–1922)

Colonial Administrator. Before serving in East Africa, Hays Sadler was Commissioner and then Consul-General in Somaliland (1897–1901). Arriving in Uganda as Commissioner in 1902 he determined that the country was unlikely to be attractive for European settlers. He and Tucker established a very good working relationship due to his sympathy toward the mission. After three years he was appointed Commissioner and then Governor of Kenya (1905–1909). He went on to become Governor of the Windward Islands (1909–1914). www.winkipedia.org,

Sir Henry Hesketh Bell (1864–1952)

Privately educated in the Channel Islands, Paris and Brussels. Colonial administrator, author, scholar. Born in Chambery, France. Joining the diplomatic service in 1882 as a clerk in the Governor of Barbados' office he transferred to Grenada Inland Revenue (1883–1889) and became Supervisor of Customs in the Gold Coast (1890–1894) till he became Treasurer of the Bahamas. After five years he became the administrator of Dominica until 1906, when Bell left the West Indies to become Commissioner of Uganda, which became the post of Governor a year later. His administration was memorable for his development of the cotton industry and the near-eradication of sleeping sickness. He went on to become the Governor of Northern Nigeria in 1909 where he experienced a set-back. Inadvertently ignoring communication from the Secretary of State of the Colonies regarding mission expansion, he was demoted to the Governorship of the Leeward Islands, (1912–1916) a position of lesser rank. He then became Governor of Mauritius until his retirement to Cannes in 1924. During WWII he lived in the Bahamas but traveled frequently to London where he died on August 1, 1952. *Cambridge University Library, England.*

APPENDIX 2

Abolition Time Line—East Africa

2/23/1807	Britain abolishes the trade in slaves, illegal for British subjects to transport captive Africans for sale into slavery (Shillington, 233; Moorman, 321).
1808	The United States does the same.
1822	Moresby Treaty with Said to abolish overseas, slave trade; not fulfilled, used land route to continue (Liebowitz, 132).
1834	British abolish slavery in British Colonies (Shillington, p. 236); each colony gave effect separately.
1841	Joint treaty with allies to stop and board slave ships.
1845	British treaty with Said bin Sultan, anti-overseas slave trade.
1/1/1847	Treaty with Sultan of Muscat: Oman to prohibit slave trade from Africa; not enforced (Liebowitz, Appendix C).
1862,64,68	Additional proclamations from Sultan, against slave trade. British patrols (Liebowitz, 143 & 169).
1873	Frere and Kirk negotiate treaty with Bargash; slave trade illegal (Liebowitz, ix). Continues using land routes to Kilwa (180) and smuggling (181).
1874	Slavery abolished in Gold Coast

Abolition Time Line—East Africa

4/18/1876	Proclamation of Sultan; slave trade abolished on Coast, Zanzibar and Pemba. Trying to address slaving by land routes. (Beachey, 116). No way to enforce it.
1888	Sultan proclamation, illegal to hire out slaves.
10/1/1889	Sultan Khalifa declaration: Slaves brought in after 11/1/89 illegal. All children after 1/1/1890 born free. Ignored.
7/1890	Zanzibar declared a protectorate (Beachey, 117).
8/1/1890	Slave trade suppressed: Abolished from Suez to Madagascar including Mombasa, but holding slaves is legal. (FO 881/8098/#72, Cave to Landsdown, Report on Slavery); Joint Powers Act. Exchange, sale or purchase prohibited by Sultan for domestic slaves. Slaves can purchase freedom.
8/20/1890	Master must agree to free slave unless mistreated. Addendum to above.
6/3/1892	Tucker letter, says # of rescued slaves decreasing @ Freretown. But trade remains vigorous (Beachey, 230).
1893	Agreement: Slaves freed by HM Consulate-General are under his jurisdiction (concession from the Sultan) not of Sultan's.
1895 & 99	Registration and control of portage to prevent slaves.
4/1/1897	Abolish legal status of slavery in Zanzibar & Pemba (not Mombasa and Coast).
6/1897	Debate in Commons re: legal status of slavery in Mombasa & environs; return of fugitives illegal.
4/1898	Decree of 1876 reinforced, all imported slaves illegally held.
1900	All persons born in Mombasa & coast, born free, 47,000 freed in Zanzibar & Pemba (Liebowitz, 248) 53,000 remaining–12% emancipated since 1897 (Beachey, 255).
1902	Census of mainland–15,039 slaves (Beachey, 259).
1907	Legal status of slavery abolished in Mombasa & coast.

Bibliography

Anderson, Gerald H., ed. *Biographical Dictionary of Christian Missions.* Grand Rapids: Eerdmans, 1998.
Anderson, William B. *The Church in East Africa, 1840-1974.* Nairobi: Uzima, 1977.
Beachey, R. W. *The Slave Trade of Eastern Africa.* New York: Barnes & Noble, 1976.
Beidelman, T. O. *Colonial Evangelism: A Socio-Historical Study of an East African Mission at the Grassroots.* Bloomington: Indiana University Press, 1982.
Bell, Quentin. *Victorian Artists.* London: Academy Editions, 1975.
Bonk, Jon. "All Things to All Persons—The Missionary as a Racist Imperialist, 1860-1918." *Missiology* 8 (1980) 285-306.
Chatterjee Partha. *Nationalist Thought and the Colonial World: A Derivative Discourse* London: Zed, 1986.
Christensen, Torben, and William R. Hutchinson, eds. *Missionary Ideologies in the Imperialist Era: 1880-1920.* Aarhus, Denmark: Aros, 1982.
Church Missionary Society. Annual Reports, 1889-1912.
———. *The Gleaner.*
———. *The Home Gazette.*
———. *The Intelligencer.* London: Church Missionary Society, 1890-1907.
———. *Mengo/Uganda* NOTES *1900-1912.* Church Missionary Society, London.
———. *Register of Missionaries and Native Clergy: 1804-1904*, Part 1, London.
———. The Review, 1907-1912.
Collister, Peter. *The Last Days of Slavery: England and the East African Slave Trade, 1870-1900.* Dar es Salaam: East African Literature Bureau, 1961.
Comaroff, Jean, and John Comaroff. *Of Revelation and Revolution: Christianity, Colonialism, and Consciousness in South Africa.* Vol. 1. Chicago: University of Chicago Press, 1991.
———. "Through the Looking Glass: Colonial Encounters of the First Kind." In *Journal of Historical Sociology* 1.1 (1988) 6-3.
Cook, J. H. "Tucker of Uganda." *C.M.S. Home Gazette* (1929) 167.
Cox, Jeffrey. *Imperial Fault Lines: Christianity and Colonial Power in India.* Stanford, CA: Stanford University Press, 2002.
Fast, Hildegarde H. "In At One Ear and Out At the Other: African Response to the Wesleyan Message in Xhosaland 1825-1835." *Journal of Religion in Africa* 23.2 (1993) 147-74.
Ford, Colin, and Brian Harrison. *A Hundred Years Ago: Britain in the 1880's in Words and Photographs.* Harmondsworth, UK: Allen Lane/Penguin, 1983.

Bibliography

Frisen, J. Stanley. *Missionary Responses to Tribal Religions at Edinburgh, 1910*. New York: Peter Lang, 1996.

Frykenberg, R. E. "India." In *A World History of Christianity*, edited by Adrian Hastings, 183. Grand Rapids: Eerdmans, 1999.

Graves, Algernon. *The Royal Academy of Arts Exhibitors, 1769–1904*. London: Henry Graves, 1905–1906.

Griffiths, T. F. L. "Bishop Alfred Tucker and the Establishment of a British Protectorate in Uganda, 1890–94." *Journal of Religion in Africa* 31 (2001) 92–114.

Hansen, Holger Bernt. *Mission, Church and State in a Colonial Setting: Uganda 1890–1925*. London: Heinemann, 1984.

———. "Mission and Colonialism in Uganda." In *Mission Ideologies in the Imperialistic Era*, edited by Christensen, Torben and Hutchinson. Aarhus, Denmark: Aros, 1982.

Hastings, Adrian. *The Church in Africa 1450–1950*. Oxford: Clarendon, 1994.

Heald, Suzette. *Manhood and Morality: Sex, Violence and Ritual in Gisu Society*. New York: Routledge, 1999.

International Bulletin of Missionary Research 27.1 (2003) 24.

Jeal, T., ed. *David Livingstone and the Victorian Encounter With Africa*. Great Britain: National Portrait Gallery, 1996.

Latour, Bruno. *Science in Action*. Cambridge: Harvard University Press, 1999.

Liebowitz, Daniel. *The Physician and the Slave Trade: John Kirk, the Livingstone Expeditions, and the Crusade Against Slavery in East Africa*. New York: W. H. Freeman, 1999.

Lugard, Captain F. D. *The Rise of Our East African Empire: Early Efforts in Nyasaland and Uganda*. Edinburgh: Blackwood and Sons, n.d.

Marshall, P. J., ed. *Cambridge Illustrated History of the British Empire*. Cambridge: Cambridge University Press, 1996.

McManners, John, ed. *The Oxford Illustrated History of Christianity*. Oxford: Oxford University Press, 1990.

Moorhouse, Geoffrey. *The Missionaries*. London: Eyre Methuen Ltd, 1973.

Moorman, John R. H. *A History of the Church in England*. Wilton, CT: Morehouse-Barlow, 1954.

Oliver, Roland. *The Missionary Factor in East Africa*. London: Longmans, Green, 1952.

Paz, D. G., ed. *Nineteenth-Century English Religious Traditions*. Westport, CT: Greenwood, 1995, ix.

Perham, Margery, and M. Bull, eds. *The Diaries of Lord Lugard, vols. 1–IV*. London: Faber, 1959.

Peterson, Derek, and Jean Allman. "New Directions in the History of Missions in Africa." In *The Journal of Religious History* 23, no. 1 (1999) 1–7.

Portal, Sir Gerald H. *The British Mission to Uganda in 1893*. London: Edward Arnold, 1894.

Register of Missionaries and Native Clergy: 1804–1904, Part 1. CMS.

Reynolds, J. S. *Canon Christopher of St. Aldate's Oxford*. Abingdon: Abby, 1967.

———. *The Evangelicals at Oxford*. Oxford: Marcham Manor, 1975.

Sanneh, Lamin. *Abolitionists Abroad: American Blacks and the Making of Modern West Africa*. Cambridge: Harvard University Press, 1999.

———. "The CMS and the African Transformation." In *The Church Mission Society and World Christianity*, edited by Kevin Ward and Brian Stanley. Grand Rapids: Eerdmans, 2000.

Bibliography

———. *Encountering the West, Christianity and the Global Cultural Process: The African Dimension.* London: Marshall Pickering, 1993.
———. *Translating the Message: The Missionary Impact on Culture.* Maryknoll, NY: Orbis, 1989. Eighth Printing, 1997.
Shepherd, Arthur P. *Tucker of Uganda: Artist and Apostle, 1849-1914.* London: Student Christian Movement, 1929.
Shillington, Kevin. *History of Africa.* New York: St. Martin, 1995.
Stanley, Brian. *The Bible and the Flag.* Leicester: Apollos, 1990.
Stanley, Brian. *The Church Mission Society and World Christianity, 1799-1900.* Grand Rapids: Eerdmans, 2000.
Stock, Eugene. *The History of the Church Missionary Society, Vol. 1.* London: CMS, 1899.
Strayer, R.W. *The Making of Mission Communities in East Africa: Anglicans and Africans in Colonial Kenya, 1875-1935.* New York: Heinemann, 1978.
Sundkler, Bengt, and Christopher Steed. *A History of the Church in Africa.* Cambridge: Cambridge University Press, 2000.
Symondson, Anthony, ed. *The Victorian Crisis of Faith.* London: SPCK, 1970.
Tobin, Beth Fowkes. *Picturing Imperial Power: Colonial Subjects in Eighteenth-Century British Painting.* London: Duke University Press, 1999.
Treuherz, Julian. *Victorian Painting.* New York: Hudson Hills, 1992.
Tucker, Alfred R. "A Charge on The Occasion of the Division of the Diocese of Eastern Equatorial Africa, 1897." Kenya National Archives. Nairobi, Kenya.
———. *Eighteen Years in Uganda and East Africa.* London: Edward Arnold, 1911.
———. *Toro: Visits to Ruwenzori "Mountains of the Moon."* London: CMS, 1899.
———. "Tucker From Mengo." *The Church Missionary Intelligencer,* Vol. XLIV, Vol. XVIII, New Series. CMS London, 1893.
Ustorf, Werner. *Bremen Missionaries in Togo and Ghana: 1847-1900.* Legon, Ghana: Legon, 2002.
———. "Missionasreligion und Saekulare Religion bei Jakob Spieth (1856-1914)." *Zeitschrift fuer Kirchengeschichte* 117.1 (2006) 63-84.
———. "What If The Light In You Is Darkness? An Inquiry into the Shadow Side Of the Missionary Self." In *Mission und Gewalt,* edited by Ulrich van der Heyden, vol. 6. Stuttgart: Franz Steiner, 1996.
Walker, R. H. "Alfred Robert Tucker." *Church Missionary Society Review* (1914) 489-92.
Walls, A. F. *The Missionary Movement in Christian History.* Maryknoll, NY: Orbis, 1996.
———. "Missionary Vocation and the Ministry: The First Generation." In *New Testament Christianity for Africa and the World,* edited by Mark Glasswell and Edward W. Foxhole-Luke. London: SPCK, 1974.
Ward, Kevin, and Brian Stanley. *The Church Mission Society and World Christianity, 1799-1999.* Grand Rapids: Eerdmans, 2000.
Wilcox, Scott, and Christopher Newall. *Victorian Landscape Watercolours.* New York: Hudson Hills, 1992.
Williams, C. P. "Not Quite Gentlemen: an Examination of 'Middling Class' Protestant Missionaries from Britain, c. 1850-1900." *Journal of Ecclesiastical History* 31.3 (1980) 301-15.
Wilson, A. N. *The Victorians.* London: Hutchinson, 2002.
Yates, T. E. *Venn and Victorian Bishops Abroad.* London: SPCK, 1978.

Bibliography

Archive Material

Anglican Church of Kenya Archives, Nairobi, Kenya
Billy Graham Center Archives, Wheaton, Illinois, USA.
Bishop Hannington Theological College, Mombasa, Kenya
Church Missionary Society Archives, University of Birmingham (CMSA)
Churchill Archives Center, Cambridge
Durham Cathedral Library, Durham
Durham County Record Office, Durham
Durham University Library, Durham
Kenya National Archives, Nairobi, Kenya
Lambeth Palace Library
Makerere University Archives, Kampala, Uganda
Mombasa Memorial Cathedral, Mombasa, Kenya
Public Records Office, Kew, England
Rhodes House, Oxford
Uganda Christian University Archives

Unpublished Manuscripts and Theses

Byaruhanga, Christopher. "Bishop Alfred Robert Tucker, 1849–1914: His Role and Significance in the Creation of a Native Anglican Church in Uganda." PhD diss., General Theological Seminary, 1997.
Cope, T. "The Missionary Traveller in East Africa Prior to 1914" Seminar paper, Nairobi Kenya, 1992.
De Kiewiet, Marie. "History of the Imperial British East Africa Company." PhD diss., University of London, 1955.
Griffiths, T. F. I. "Bishop A. R. Tucker of Uganda and the Implementation of An Evangelical Tradition of Mission." PhD diss., University of Leeds, 1998.
Peiris, P. J. T. "The Echoes of a Faded Memory: A Contribution to a History of the Tamil Coolie Mission." PhD diss., Birmingham University, 2001.
Rhodes, M. I. "The Anglican Church in Egypt 1936—1956 and its Relationship with British Imperialism." PhD diss., Birmingham University 2005.

www.ingramcontent.com/pod-product-compliance
Lightning Source LLC
Chambersburg PA
CBHW070256230426
43664CB00014B/2548